RENEGOTIATING FAMILY RELATIONSHIPS

RENEGOTIATING FAMILY RELATIONSHIPS

Divorce, Child Custody, and Mediation

SECOND EDITION

ROBERT E. EMERY

THE GUILFORD PRESS
New York London

©2012 The Guilford Press
A Division of Guilford Publications, Inc.
72 Spring Street, New York, NY 10012
www.guilford.com

Printed in the United States of America

This book is printed on acid-free paper.

Last digit is print number: 9 8 7 6 5 4 3 2 1

The author has checked with sources believed to be reliable in his efforts to provide
information that is complete and generally in accord with the standards of practice
that are accepted at the time of publication. However, in view of the possibility of
human error or changes in behavioral, mental health, or medical sciences, neither the
author, nor the editor and publisher, nor any other party who has been involved in the
preparation or publication of this work warrants that the information contained herein
is in every respect accurate or complete, and they are not responsible for any errors
or omissions or the results obtained from the use of such information. Readers are
encouraged to confirm the information contained in this book with other sources.

Library of Congress Cataloging-in-Publication Data

Emery, Robert E.
  Renegotiating family relationships : divorce, child custody, and mediation / by Robert E.
Emery. — 2nd ed.
     p. cm.
  Includes bibliographical references and index.
  ISBN 978-1-60918-981-5 (hbk. : alk. paper)
  1. Divorce mediation—United States. 2. Custody of children—United States. 3.
Divorced parents—Counseling of—United States. I. Title.
  HQ834.E48 2012
  306.89—dc23
                                                                    2011030417

*To every parent who has put aside
his or her own hurt and anger
for the sake of his or her children*

And to every child whose parents haven't

ABOUT THE AUTHOR

Robert E. Emery, PhD, is Professor of Psychology and Director of the Center for Children, Families, and the Law at the University of Virginia. His research focuses on family relationships and children's mental health, with interests including parental conflict, divorce, mediation, child custody, family violence, genetically informed studies of family life, and associated legal and policy issues. He has authored over 150 scientific publications. His other books on divorce include *Marriage, Divorce, and Children's Adjustment, Second Edition* (1999), and *The Truth about Children and Divorce: Dealing with the Emotions So You and Your Children Can Thrive* (2006). He also is coauthor, with Thomas F. Oltmanns, of *Abnormal Psychology, Seventh Edition* (2012). Dr. Emery maintains a private practice as a clinical psychologist and mediator and is the father of five children.

PREFACE

Mediators work in what amounts to an emergency room for family relationships. Some parents use the ER for routine, even preventative, care. More are in crisis.

A wife discovers that her husband of 15 years is having an affair—with her best friend. Furious, hurt, and emotionally devastated, she is faced with the prospect of losing her home, finding a (better) job, dividing and potentially damaging her children, and "moving on" into a hopeless future, alone.

A husband returns from a business trip to find his wife, children, and furniture gone. Desperate to preserve his family, he instead is told he must give up half of the time with his children (probably much more), divide up everything he owns, and pay support for years to a woman who, he believes, abandoned him.

Parents in circumstances like these walk into a mediator's or a lawyer's office, ostensibly seeking guidance about the legal aspects of their divided family. Yet, of course, no one checks their emotions at the door.

A divorce (meaning the breakup of a family, married or not) commonly begins as a crisis, the eruption of the worst thing that has or probably ever will happen in a person's life. Most children, and parents, are resilient, even in the face of divorce. Most children and parents bounce back from all of the upheaval, uncertainty, and pain. Yet, the bounce hurts—more than you can imagine until you are there yourself.

How parents manage the immediate aftermath of a broken marriage, and how well professionals help them to do so, is partly a matter of crisis management. It also is a crucial choice point. The choice is between perhaps destroying already devastated relationships or, hopefully, beginning to repair and redefine them. In this sense, resilience is a choice for adults and especially a parent's choice for children. How parents manage their relationships with their children, and their relationship with each other, is critical to their children's well-being in divorce. That is the reason why this book focuses mostly on parents even though my concern is mostly with children.

This book is the story of what I have learned from my many efforts to help families in the "mediation emergency room." I have learned much from my research on mediation, children and divorce, and on related topics such as young adults' painful feelings about their parents' divorce or the process of grieving relationship resolution. I have learned just as much from my clinical work with so many families in crisis, for example, about the primal power (and nature) of emotion, the process of grieving a potentially revocable loss (it is both more subtle and more intense and volatile than normal grief), and the complexity of relationships in family systems. In this book, I weave together the lessons I have learned from both research and practice. That is the best way I know to tell my story. I hope empirically-minded readers will test my hypotheses and clinical suggestions in hard-data studies in the future. I hope that practice-oriented readers will be persuaded by my research and be able to apply my theories and suggestions right now.

This book is an outgrowth of my research and applied experiences with mediation, but, as the title suggests, *Renegotiating Family Relationships* is not just about mediation. The book is also about the emotional process of coming apart, about family relationship dynamics in divorce, about divorce and custody law, and about how to help parents resolve all kinds of disputes in a manner that protects their children. I never viewed mediation as a panacea. I fully embrace the efforts of collaborative lawyers, judges, more traditional lawyers, parenting coordinators, family therapists, and other professionals working to help make a devastating process less devastating. Different professionals need to work together, not in opposition to one another, if we truly want to embrace that elusive goal of promoting children's best interests in divorce.

While outlining what this book is, I should also note what it is not. This book is not an attempt to review every empirical study, legal issue, or controversy, or every professional role, variation in divorce experience, or intervention technique. In focusing on my own work, I leave much to you, the reader, to translate into your own profession, context, and methods. I think it will be an easy translation.

Of course, "my" work is not "all about me." I have had the pleasure and benefit of working with and learning from a great many students and colleagues. Joanne Jackson helped to establish and run the mediation service I created in order to study mediation. We also spent many hours in the trenches together as co-mediators. Judge Ralph Zehler allowed me to randomly assign real court cases, and he firmly supported both the mediation service and the mediation research. Graduate students Susan Peterman, Melissa Wyer, Sheila Matthews, Danny Shaw, Jeff Haugaard, and Nick Smith all were deeply involved in the initial study and the first 18-month follow-up. A few years later, graduate student Katherine Kitzmann worked creatively with data analysis, as did Peter Dillon, who also conducted a pilot study that, thankfully, got me started with the 12-year follow-up. Graduate students Lisa Laumann-Billings, Dave Sbarra, and Mary Waldron all were central contributors not only to the 12-year follow-up but also to ideas that still get me excited: psychological pain (Lisa), grieving relationship loss (Dave), and genetically informed family research (Mary). Most recently, Hyun Joo Shim followed me back from Seoul, South Korea, to become a graduate student who is deeply involved in new analyses of the mediation data and broadening my cultural perspectives. Graduate student Jennifer Simpson read and carefully critiqued the entire manuscript for style and clarity, as did Connie Beck, who offered numerous helpful, substantive suggestions. Bailey Ocker and Erin Horn cheerfully completed a great deal of practical, academic, and conceptual legwork that was essential in helping me pull this book together. I also am grateful to Jim Nageotte for his editorial support, whether dealing with "big-picture" issues or line editing. Jane Keislar also deserves praise for all of her editorial and administrative efforts.

Over the years, Mavis Hetherington has been an influential, supportive, and fun colleague in the Department of Psychology. The same description applies to Elizabeth Scott, formerly in the School of Law at the University of Virginia. The William T. Grant Foundation funded all of the mediation research described here. The Grant Foundation also supported an amazing consortium of divorce researchers of which I was fortunate to be a member. I would mention names, but the list is too long and too good to believe. The same is true of the list of experts, and friends, from across the United States and many other countries who have influenced, altered, and broadened my thinking. I am also grateful for financial support over the years from the James McKeen Cattell Fund, the Center for Advanced Studies at the University of Virginia, the Harry Frank Guggenheim Foundation, and the National Institute for Child Health and Human Development.

My wife, Kimberly Emery, has been a wonderful intellectual companion and life partner for an amazing 20 years. Recently, she has even become an occasional co-mediator. Kimberly read and critiqued the entire manuscript with her incisive skill and brutal honesty. Kimberly and our children Julia, Bobby, Lucy, and John are the answers to my "What is the meaning of life?" questions, as is my oldest child, Maggie. Maggie and Jean Emery also deserve special acknowledgment here.

Finally, I would like to thank all of the families with whom I have worked over the years, particularly those who consented to participate in my studies. I have learned much from you and feel privileged to have been allowed to share in your own painful struggles.

CONTENTS

1

CONFLICTING PERSPECTIVES

His and Her Divorce

Discourage litigation. Persuade neighbors to compromise whenever you can. Point out that the nominal winner is often the real loser in fees, expenses, and waste of time.

—ABRAHAM LINCOLN

Child custody disputes present problems from a variety of perspectives. Although most disputes are settled out of court, high divorce rates and conflicts between unmarried parents make custody contests one of the most frequent sources of litigation in the United States.[1] Thus, custody disputes are expensive from the perspective of the public interest. The current standard for determining custody according to children's "best interests" is a vague principle which, from the perspective of judges,

---

[1] I use "divorce" as a shorthand term for divorce, marital separation, the breakup of cohabiting relationships, and the end of serious romantic relationships between parents who are not living together. Emotional reactions to dissolution and dispute are more similar than different across these relationship types. Currently, the law differs according to marital status, for example, unmarried couples generally incur no alimony obligation. However, the law is evolving. Common law marriage is being reinvented in countries such as New Zealand. Future couples who cohabit in marriage-like relationships increasingly are likely to incur the same legal responsibilities as married partners, including financial ones (Lind, 2008).

makes custody disputes almost impossible to decide. Custody disputes also are troublesome from the perspective of many lawyers, who find the cases emotional, demanding, and unrewarding. Fears about losing your children, legal expenses, public embarrassment, and the divisiveness of a court battle are some of the many problems with custody disputes from the perspective of parents. Finally, from the perspective of children, a custody dispute epitomizes perhaps the worst thing about divorce: Getting caught, or put, in the middle of a war between your parents.

A DIFFERENT WAY TO DIVORCE?

What can professionals, parents, and society do to make divorce and custody decisions less devastating for children? Can we help to contain and control inherent emotional, interpersonal, and legal conflict? Can we protect children from being torn apart by their parents' disputes, and by the emotional chaos of divorce?

Together with a growing number of professionals and parents who have witnessed, or experienced, custody disputes at their worst, I believe we can do much to contain the turmoil of ending a marriage, of dividing a family. We can help parents to negotiate the terms of their divorce without exacerbating their pain and anger. Few divorces may be "happy" or "good," but parents and professionals can work to ensure that divorce is not as bad as it might be, especially for children.

I believe that we can effectively guide parents toward a more child-friendly divorce, but this is more than a belief. My research shows that a more cooperative approach to negotiating custody can benefit parents and children not only in the short term but even more so in the long run. As I summarize later in this chapter, and detail in Chapter 9, parents in my studies were assigned at random to either mediate or litigate their custody disputes. We followed these families over time and found that, 12 years later, an average of only 6 hours of mediation *caused* nonresidential parents to remain significantly and substantially more involved in their children's lives, to be better parents, and to be better coparents (Emery, Laumann-Billings, Waldron, Sbarra, & Dillon, 2001). One purpose of this book is to serve as a treatment manual for this evidence-based intervention.

Alternative Dispute Resolution

Divorce mediation is a form of alternative dispute resolution (ADR) in which a neutral, expert third party helps parents to negotiate custody and perhaps financial arrangements as cooperatively as possible. The mediator meets together, and often separately, with both parents to help them to identify, discuss, and hopefully resolve their differences. Legally, the goal of mediation is to negotiate a settlement that forms the basis of a binding, legal agreement. Psychologically and emotionally, the goal is to help partners to preserve their parental relationship even as their marriage is coming apart.

Mediation is a focus of this book, but the research, psychological, and legal issues outlined here are relevant far beyond the mediation context. Innovative professionals have developed many new forms of ADR for divorce and custody matters in recent years, and the list of alternatives continues to grow (see Figure 9.6. p. 220). Most share common goals: helping parents to negotiate more cooperatively, to make their own decisions about what is best for their own children, to contain conflict, and to truly protect children's best interests. Collaborative lawyers, for example, work to negotiate a fair and principled out-of-court settlement, refusing to represent their clients in court if negotiations break down (Tesler & Thompson, 2007). Divorce educators, parenting coordinators, child advocates, custody evaluators who use their feedback to encourage settlement, cooperative lawyers, and others involved in divorce ADR use different means toward the common end of making divorce less difficult, particularly for children (see Chapter 6).

My "emotionally informed" approach to mediation, which I describe in detail in Chapters 7 and 8, also shares elements in common with family therapy, particularly the structural approach (Minuchin, 1974). A major conceptual and practical focus is redefining the boundaries of family relationships which invariably change as a result of divorce. Relationships do not end with a divorce; they are transformed, dramatically. Divorcing parents must develop new family roles and responsibilities not only in relation to their children but also with each other. In the context of negotiating a separation agreement, mediation can help parents to *renegotiate* rather than end their relationship.

Mediators do not try to promote reconciliation or attempt to resolve all of a family's emotional conflicts. A mediator's "license" to address emotional issues is limited according to the overriding objective of negotiating a separation agreement. Nevertheless, the concepts and techniques described here are relevant to family therapy and other interventions where a professional holds an unrestricted license for dealing with emotions. In fact, mediation can feel something like family therapy on "fast forward." Family relationships change rapidly, even if some of the changes are superficial by family therapy standards. Thus, a second goal of this book is to outline concepts and techniques that can be used by therapists and by legal professionals who work with divorcing parents in therapy, ADR, and other contexts.

An Emotionally *Unnatural* Divorce

Even while encouraging a more child-friendly parting, professionals working with divorce and custody disputes must recognize parents' emotional struggles. Divorcing partners commonly are confused, perhaps overwhelmed, with emotions including hurt, pain, anger, fear, sadness, jealousy, and grief. In advocating for a less divisive divorce, we ask parents to do something emotionally *un*natural. Doing so can take tremendous effort. It is *natural* to be hurt and angry—and to want to hurt back—when "happily ever after" becomes "I'll see you in court." When can you be angry if not when you discover that your spouse is having an affair, or just doesn't love you any more? When can you be devastated, or out of control, if not when the mother or father of your children has found someone new who, they claim, is better than you as a lover, a friend, and perhaps as a parent?

In the middle of the emotional turmoil of divorce, mediators, collaborative lawyers, and other professionals concerned about the impact on children ask parents to contain their own, powerful emotions; to communicate with each other in a structured, businesslike fashion; to cooperate in rearing their children; and ultimately to retain control over their lives by making their own decisions about their children's best interests. We urge parents to love their children more than they may hate their ex (Emery, 2006). If professionals want parents to divorce differently, we first need to understand their emotional devastation. Thus, this book's third and perhaps most important goal is to detail the intense and complicated emotional and interpersonal dynamics of divorce from the perspective of parents, children, and the family system.

Real People

ADR professionals work to help parents settle custody disputes in a simpler, less emotional, and more rational manner. Yet for many former partners, the parting is far from simple, unemotional, and rational. It is an emotionally charged morass, the height of irrationality. Divorce is very common today, but statistics obscure the extreme upheaval divorce often causes real people and real families.

I am a psychological scientist first and foremost; thus this book is evidence based. The various conceptualizations, interventions, and policies discussed here are backed by, or at least consistent with, state-of-the-art research from several disciplines, including psychology, sociology, law, and economics. However, I also am a practitioner, an active mediator, and a family and individual therapist. As a practitioner, I recognize that the complexity, emotionality, and irrationality of divorce can get lost in empirical research, which necessarily focuses on simpler, quantifiable, and understandable aspects of the process. I therefore include case material throughout this book in order to enrich, enliven, and hopefully enlighten. In fact, much of this first chapter is devoted to case studies that illustrate central dilemmas in divorce and child custody disputes. These emotional quagmires explain how and why custody disputes create so many problems for parents, children, courts, and society. The cases also introduce key topics that I address more systematically in subsequent chapters.

LOVE IS BLIND

Discovery, that is, uncovering of the facts of a case, is one goal of legal intervention in divorce and custody disputes. However, there are many impediments to uncovering the truth in custody disputes. One of the most important is that family members have conflicting perspectives on divorce and family life.

There is much wisdom in the truism "love is blind." Love makes people see what they want to see, and believe what they hope is true. In a divorce, the blinders of love are ripped off. When former partners ask themselves, "What went wrong?" they often surprise themselves with complaints that they had only vaguely recognized in their marriage. When divorcing parents present the "facts" of their case to their attorneys, perspectives that already were in conflict can become dramatically polarized. The following case studies illustrate some of this conflict of perspective.

The Case of Sheila

Sheila hoped that her separation would give her a new start at the age of 31. She married right after finishing college, a decision that seemed impulsive and blind in retrospect. Her sweet college boyfriend soon became a distant and cold husband. They had been lovers and best friends, but once they got married, their relationship changed. They became housemates who had sex on occasion. Sheila's life grew increasingly empty, lonely, and meaningless. When she got pregnant, she hoped that a baby would revitalize her marriage. But much to her disappointment, her husband showed almost no interest in the infant. Sheila drew new energy from her little girl, but when Sheila stopped working to stay home with her baby, financial pressures and her husband's frustrations mounted. At his insistence, she ended up returning to work long before she was ready.

Sheila resented giving up her daughter to day care, and she was doubly disappointed when her husband showed no interest in their second child, a boy. She was determined to spend a few years at home now that she had two children, but money and her "laziness" became the topics of constant fighting. Sheila stuck by her decision not to work for 2 years, but as much as she loved being a mother, her marriage was in shambles. When she returned to work, it was with a purpose in mind. She would build up her income to the point where she and her two children could live on their own. She knew she had married the wrong man. She was frightened of divorce for herself and for her children, but the fighting and unhappiness were far worse. Sheila was convinced that staying married "for the children's sake" was an excuse for making the safe, easy, and wrong decisions that she had made her whole life. She had no real husband, and her children had no real father.

It took Sheila several years to prepare for her move and to muster the courage to tell her husband that she was leaving him. When she finally confronted him, she was unsure of what to expect, but she knew it would be bad. He yelled, he screamed, he threatened. He refused to leave their home and said he would do nothing to support Sheila, or the children, if she left. Sheila was prepared for this. She had already rented a furnished apartment, had money saved in a secret bank account, and had spoken with a lawyer who assured her that her husband would have to pay support for the children, and perhaps support her financially as well.

After she moved out of the house, the fighting stopped for a while, but the begging started. Her husband was sorry. He loved her. He loved the children. Life was worthless without them. He pleaded with her to come back. But Sheila had not made an impulsive decision this time. There was no going back.

And then it happened. Sheila and her husband had been separated for about 8 weeks. They had no legal agreement, but had settled into something of a pattern where the children would spend each Saturday night and Sunday morning with their father. But instead of getting the children back one Sunday afternoon, Sheila got a call from her husband. He said that he had filed for sole custody of the children. He might settle for joint custody, but he planned on keeping the children at least until the following Saturday no matter what. He would return them on that day, but only if Sheila signed a joint custody agreement that allowed the children to be swapped between them each week. If she refused to sign the agreement, he would not bring them back. When Sheila screamed into the phone to return her children immediately, he hung up on her.

The Case of John

Like Sheila, John had two young children who were the subject of a custody dispute. But his circumstances were very different otherwise.

John was very much a family man. He worked hard and his job was all right, but work was a means to an end for John. That end was his family. As soon as he left work, John headed for home, eager to see his wife and especially his children. John knew that his marriage was going through a rough patch, but he also knew in his heart that everything would work out. At least he thought he knew that.

John had gotten married and had children at a young age, but he knew that family life could be demanding. He expected that there would be hard times. Certain things bothered him, of course. His wife had been sexy and kind of wild when they were dating, but sex became infrequent and dull early in the marriage. Sex just about disappeared after his first child was born. John believed that it was wrong for him to complain about sex, so he just kept quiet and kept trying. His sexual advances were rebuffed far more often than not, and that left John feeling rejected too. Still, he kept trying. Besides, there was more to life than sex. He enjoyed his family, and loved playing with his children, especially his little boy, who was beginning to share John's interest in sports.

John was much more worried about money than about his family life. His wife worked some, even after the children were born, but from John's point of view, her working hurt as much as it helped. John felt that earning a good income was his responsibility. He had set a goal of having a nice house and a secure income by the age of 30, so the pressure would be off of everyone, especially him. Unfortunately, the economy worked against John. He was making ends meet, but he secretly felt like a failure. He sometimes saw his dreams as just that, dreams. He struggled to come up with new plans that would relieve the financial pressures, but nothing worked.

Still, John was far from giving up on his job, and he never considered giving up on his family. Then he got the shock of a lifetime. One day, out of the clear blue sky, his wife said that she was leaving him. John was shocked. Things had been rough at times, but nowhere near divorce. He begged, he pleaded, he promised anything, but his words fell on deaf ears. Within a few days, his wife and children moved out.

John was too stunned to do anything more than protest pathetically, but his objections had no effect. His wife had every move planned. Unlike him, she was not devastated. She seemed happy. She had a place to go, and money coming in from some mysterious source. John tried to pull himself together and figure out was happening. Then he hit upon the explanation. His wife must be having an affair. He felt like an idiot. Why else would she do something like this? She had planned it all too perfectly.

John's anger at being used energized him into action. Within a few weeks after the separation, he got himself a lawyer and a plan. His wife could leave if that was what she wanted, but she was not going to take his children. He asked his lawyer to file for sole custody of the children. When his lawyer warned "possession is nine-tenths of the law," John came up with another tactic on his own. He would not return the children after their next visit. He would keep them at least until he had a written agreement that protected his relationship with his children. After all, he was their father, and his wife had walked out on him with no cause. He had rights, and so did his kids.

HIS AND HER DIVORCE

As you may have guessed, John and Sheila were married to each other.

Sheila and John shared a marriage for 10 years, yet they experienced and remembered their time together as if they led separate lives. As they faced their separation and their custody dispute began, some differences in their stories may have been deliberate distortions. There is strong motivation to portray yourself as a saint and your former spouse as a sinner, because of the high stakes involved and because extreme positions can be a strategic advantage.

Still, many differences between Sheila and John surely resulted from legitimately different experiences, perceptions, and memories. His "family time" on Sunday afternoons may have been "football time" to her. His sexual initiations may have seemed like unrelenting and unfeeling demands to her. To him, reaching out in the face of constant rejection perhaps showed his stoic desire to get close to his wife. He may have viewed his preoccupation with work as fulfilling his responsibility to his family. She may have seen him as being married to the job.

In her book *The Future of Marriage*, sociologist Jesse Bernard (1972) wrote that couples do not have one marriage, but two: "his" and "hers." Each member of the couple experiences their union so differently that functionally there are two marriages. Nowhere is this provocative idea more evident than during divorce. As with Sheila and John, separated or divorced parents often have wildly different views about each other, their family roles, their marriage, and the reasons for its demise. "His" and "her" marriage results from differing experiences and perceptions. "His" and "her" divorce is a complete rewriting of those two versions of history. The revisions tell a new story, one that is consistent with the unhappy ending. Of course, each rewrite is also based on two very different views of how and why the marriage ended, and each rewrite serves two different purposes, his and hers.

Perhaps John was a cold and angry man who was as insensitive to his children as he had been to his wife. Or perhaps Sheila was a bored and self-centered woman who was unprepared for the realities of family life and captivated by fantasies of an affair. It is tempting to conclude that the truth lies somewhere in between the two extremes, and it often does. But perhaps there is no "truth." Even if some of John's and Sheila's actions can be established as legal facts, what a court determines to be true is unlikely to change John's or Sheila's perceptions of reality.

Even if they agreed about what happened to their relationship, for example, John and Sheila probably would disagree about why. Sheila might see her leaving as justified by John's long history of cold and calculated manipulation, a power game frighteningly evident in his refusal to return her children. John might view his actions as justified by Sheila's selfish disregard of his relationship with his children during their marriage and following the separation. Whatever the specifics, they both are likely to blame each other for past and present transgressions. Why? In addition to strategic advantages, the blame game is fueled by powerful emotional motivations. Here is one: anger is an easier and less painful (if less honest) emotion than the "real" feelings it often masks, including guilt, pain, fear, grief, or unrequited love (see Chapters 2 and 3).

His and Her Grief

The case of Sheila and John illustrates yet another dilemma in divorce and custody disputes: Conflicting experiences of grief. Sheila and John experienced a very different type of loss when they separated. Metaphorically and emotionally, Sheila lost her marriage to a chronic, terminal illness. She knew for years that her marriage was dying, and this knowledge allowed her to prepare for its end—emotionally and practically. The actual separation undoubtedly was painful for her, but as with the death of a loved one following a long and trying illness, her pain undoubtedly was tinged with a degree of relief.

In contrast to Sheila, the metaphor for John's loss is a train wreck. John knew something terrible had happened. His marriage was in the emergency room, in critical condition. But John could cling to the hope of a miraculous recovery. Miracles sometimes happen. And as bad as the outlook might be, no one could truthfully tell John there was no hope. John's fantasies of reconciliation were fueled by his contacts with Sheila, especially her guilt-ridden attempts to be friendly. To John, these were signs of life in their marriage. What was final to her was far from final to him.

Even as he begins to accept the end of his marriage, John's grief is likely to be much more erratic and intense than Sheila's. Sheila anticipated the separation, and grieved for years beforehand. She also prepared practically for her new, single life, and looks forward to it with some hope. Perhaps he was blind, but John's loss still was unanticipated.

He had little time to prepare for the separation, and he was forced to adjust to something that he did not want. The emotional roller coaster of intense and unpredictable grief is far from over for John, even after he begins to realize that his marriage really might be "dead."

John and Sheila's different places in their grief are yet another source of conflict between them. If he does not read her friendliness as a sign of hope, Sheila's apparent absence of distress may make John wonder if she ever loved him—or if she is involved with someone else. While John is hurt by Sheila's lack of emotion, Sheila is likely to be frustrated by John's emotional devastation. She may wonder where his feelings were when they were together, or grow angry over his self-pity and foot-dragging. Neither understands why the other does not feel the same way that they feel.

His and Her Acceptance of the End of the Marriage

John and Sheila illustrate another common "his" and "her" dilemma. They differ in their acceptance of the end of their marriage. Like most divorces (Braver, Shapiro, & Goodman, 2006), their decision to separate was not mutual. And as with conflict about their past, John and Sheila's opposing desires for the future of their marriage greatly complicate their separation negotiations. They not only disagree about *what* custody arrangement they want, but they also differ about *whether* they want an agreement. Sheila's push for a settlement collides with John's hope for reconciliation.

John is likely to resist reaching settlement, or he may insist on terms that are clearly unacceptable to Sheila, for a very simple reason: He does not want an agreement, because he does not want a separation. To him, agreeing to a settlement means accepting the separation, and John does not want to accept the end of his marriage. He certainly does not want to hasten or facilitate its end by agreeing to some custody arrangement for which he is unprepared emotionally or practically. As a result, John is likely to become angry and uncooperative with professionals who try to help him reach an agreement, whether those professionals are therapists, mediators, judges, or even his own attorney. Anyone who pushes for a settlement is on Sheila's side, trying to kill his marriage. (A client in John's position recently called me "Dr. Kevorkian," referring to the proponent of assisted suicide. For someone in John's shoes, the analogy is apt.)

In contrast to John, Sheila is ready to "do business" in their divorce negotiations. She contemplated the end of her marriage for a long time, and she has thought a lot, perhaps unrealistically, about what she wants. Sheila may see some of John's obstacles for exactly what they are: A refusal to accept the end of their marriage. But whether to end the marriage is not a question that she wants to reopen. Even if she harbors some ambivalence, Sheila wants to conquer her uncertainty, not explore it. She certainly doesn't want to share her doubts with John. Doing so would only fuel his hopes—and his obstinacy. Sheila does not want to understand John's hurt and pain. She has been down that road before, repeatedly. She has felt the guilt often and long enough. Sheila wants to get this over with, and the sooner, the better. Unlike John, she therefore is likely to see professionals who push for a resolution as being reasonable and helpful. To Sheila, mediation is surgery not suicide. Mediation is a painful but necessary step toward making her life better.

For a great many couples, disputes over custody ultimately reflect conflict between "his" and "her" version of history, being in different "places" in dealing with grief, and opposing wishes for the marriage, in accepting of its end. Couples fight over their children, and they have legitimate concerns about the children. But when they fight about their children, they also often are fighting about whether or not to end their marriage.

Contesting Divorce by Contesting Custody: Some Research

Evidence from my research, as well from other studies (Bickerdike & Littlefield, 2000), supports the perhaps provocative but central assertion that many custody disputes turn, at least in part (sometimes completely) on differences in the former partners' acceptance of the end of their marriage. In my studies, one month after settling their custody disputes in mediation or in court, in over 60% of the families at least one partner indicated that he or she felt that the couple should have tried to stay together longer. Both partners agreed that they were glad that they finally made the break in only about one-quarter of all cases. Remarkably and sadly, in a handful of cases *both* partners indicated that they were only going ahead with the divorce because it was what their spouse wanted (Emery, 1994).

Men were much less accepting of the end of their marriage than women in this sample of parents contesting custody. Over 40% of the men, versus less than 10% of the women, reported that they were going ahead with the divorce only because this was what their spouses wanted. Over half of the men agreed that they found themselves wondering what their spouses were doing; only about 15% of women did so (Emery, 1994).

This gap is not merely a reflection of gender differences in who initiates divorce. Available evidence does indicate that women initiate perhaps two-thirds of divorces (Braver et al., 2006). But the wide discrepancy in my sample appears to reflect another gender difference. Men who do not want their marriage to end contest custody. Women who do not want their marriage to end probably are more likely to fight about money.

What would explain this gender difference? First, the partner who does not want to divorce becomes intransigent about reaching a separation agreement. Consciously or unconsciously, they hope to prevent or at least delay the end of the marriage. But, second, the tactic only works if this partner objects about something of great value to the estranged spouse. Otherwise, the spouse who wants to divorce simply would concede in order to move the negotiations forward. Third, because many men and women still adopt traditional breadwinner and caretaker roles in marriage, the delaying tactic is more likely to "work" for men who are uncompromising about custody and for women who refuse to reach a financial settlement. (Of course, the opposite pattern can occur when couples have nontraditional marital roles.)

When a husband does not want a divorce, disputing custody is likely to be a more effective means of blocking an agreement than disputing the finances. Why? Because of her greater investment in childrearing in a traditional marriage, a wife and mother is unlikely to make substantial concessions about custody even when she is eager to end her marriage. In contrast, she may be willing to compromise on finances, because she views economic hardship as an inevitable consequence of her decision to leave. Thus, when we examine a custody dispute sample, as in my studies, we find that more men than women do not want their marriage to end.

The opposite pattern is likely when a wife does not want a divorce. A traditional husband who wants a divorce may feel like a hypocrite contesting custody when his wife assumed the primary responsibility for childrearing. If so, he is likely to make concessions about that potential dispute. But women who do not want their marriage to end may find that they can successfully delay a divorce, albeit temporarily, by insisting on an extreme financial settlement, a threat to the breadwinner role.

Consistent with this reasoning about men (we only studied custody disputes, not financial disputes), a reanalysis of my mediation data found that husbands reported *more* coparenting conflict when wives were *more* accepting of the end of the marriage than they were (Sbarra & Emery, 2008). A creative Australian study also found that differences in the partners' acceptance of the end of the marriage predicted parents' failure to reach agreement in mediation. This effect held even after controlling for the couple's level of anger. Furthermore, differences in acceptance also predicted less problem solving in actual mediation sessions (Bickerdike & Littlefield, 2000).

In summary, many divorcing partners object to the terms of a separation agreement, in part, because they object to a divorce. They contest the end of their marriage by contesting a settlement. Thus, mediators and other divorce professionals must always consider the possibility that a dispute over custody also reflects a dispute over the future of the partners' relationship.

His and Her Children

Sheila and John have conflicting memories about their past. They have conflicting feelings of grief. They have conflicting desires about separating. Given this, it is not surprising that they would be in conflict about the terms of their separation and its future fairness for themselves and their children. In fact, John and Sheila are likely to have different views on how the children are coping with the divorce. Sheila is likely to see the children as she sees herself: They accept the separation and are doing relatively well. John also is likely to see the children as he sees himself: They hate the separation and are emotionally devastated.

Each parent projects his or her own feelings onto the children. If no problems are apparent, John may argue that the children are hiding their feelings, protecting their mother, and defending against their terrible pain. Sheila may counter that the children's lack of reaction proves that they are doing fine. In fact, she may see them as *happier* now that they are no longer exposed to the daily tension, fighting, and unhappiness of the marriage. If the children are having obvious difficulties, John may see reconciliation as the solution, even if only for the sake of the children. To Sheila, the children's problems are proof of their need for stability. The children need a clear and stable custody arrangement—now.

Some of the parents' conflicting interpretations of their children's feelings and needs certainly reflect legitimate differences. Even impartial mental health professionals have difficulty discerning how children feel and what they want following their parents' marital separation. Still, intentionally or unintentionally, parents also are likely to project their own feelings onto their children, leading to a self-serving and somewhat inaccurate view of the children's needs. Once again, parents' differing emotions and projections mean that custody disputes often involve much more than questions about what is best for children.

The Children's Perspective

Perhaps the central dilemma in divorce is that children have a third perspective, one that often conflicts with the views of *either* parent. The children's needs are supposed to be paramount, yet they frequently are forgotten, or manipulated, as a result of their parents' emotional turmoil. Too often, concerns about the children's needs mask an attempt to resist the end of the relationship, to gain the upper hand in negotiations, to punish the other parent, or to satisfy one or both parents' own emotional needs. Too often, parents expect the children to side with them against their father or mother, rather than recognizing that the children's perspective differs from their own.

Some children do side with one parent or the other in a separation or divorce. In other families, loyalties are so deeply divided that different children end up allying with a different parent. However, from the children's perspective, the biggest problem typically is not choosing the right side but having to choose at all.

This is especially true in acrimonious divorces. Study after study shows that parental conflict predicts maladjustment among children whose parents have separated or divorced (Emery, 1999). A particular problem is when children feel caught in the middle between their parents (Buchanan, Maccoby, & Dornbusch, 1991). Most children do not want to be forced to take sides with one parent against the other. And as fervently as they may wish for reconciliation, children's foremost desire in divorce often is for their parents to stop fighting.

Conflicting Perspectives and Legal Justice

Thus, there really are three conflicting perspectives on divorce: His, hers, and the children's. As is illustrated by the case of John and Sheila, it can be extremely difficult to determine which perspective is true—or right. Perhaps Sheila was emotionally abused, and she needs a strong advocate who will help her to fend off her misplaced guilt and stand up to John at last. Perhaps John was used and manipulated, and he needs a strong advocate who will help him to put aside his hopes for reconciliation and protect his rights as a father. Perhaps the children need their own advocate to represent their rights (whatever they may be) in this family dispute. Or perhaps one or both parents' hurt, pain, and anger is being played out in one of the few available forums: A legal dispute about the children.

A natural inclination when confronted with conflicting facts is to dig further to uncover the "real" truth. Our legal system and our sense of justice presume that, if only we dig deeply enough, we will discover one true and right side.[2] You are either guilty or innocent. In the pursuit of the truth, we revel in righteous indignation. Someone is lying. If we keep

---

[2] A new legal theory, called "law and emotion," holds the promise of better accommodating human emotion in the law. The law-and-emotion perspective holds that legal disputes and dispute resolution are fueled and biased by emotion, and the law should recognize and perhaps accommodate emotional influences. The law-and-emotion perspective is particularly relevant to family law. See the 2009 special issue of the *Virginia Journal of Social Policy and the Law.*

digging, keep confronting, and tear through the fabric of lies, we will uncover the deception, perhaps in a dramatic courtroom confession.

But perhaps there is no "truth" in many divorces. Perhaps much of each parent's version of the truth reflects his and her perspective on their marriage, their parenting, and their divorce. Perhaps there is no ultimate right and no ultimate wrong in many divorce and custody disputes.

We might discover that Sheila was having an affair, for example, but we also might discover that John had been verbally abusive. Does the verbal abuse justify the affair, or does Sheila's infidelity justify John's denigration? Does either "fact" bear directly on the best custody arrangement for their two children? From the children's perspective, does the conflict that is inherent in settling a custody dispute create more problems than it resolves? These are some of the substantive and procedural questions that confound legal intervention in divorce and custody disputes.

Advocacy, fact finding, and legal protection may be necessary, irrespective of the divisiveness of a legal battle, when one side clearly is the victim and the other is the perpetrator. Our legal system can ensure due process and protect the weaker party. This may be needed, especially in custody disputes that involve victimization in the form of serious family violence or dramatically unequal bargaining power (Johnston et al., 2005). Yet the same advocacy, fact finding, and legal protections may only polarize parents in other cases, cases where there is no ultimate truth but only conflicting emotions, wants, and perceptions. In these cases, adversarial maneuvering can turn conflicting perspectives into a family feud, a feud that ultimately is destructive to children, whose perspective on divorce is considered last in this chapter as it often is in custody disputes.

More Than Legal Conflict

Whatever one's view on traditional legal intervention or ADR, the difficulty of determining the accuracy of his, hers, and the children's perspective on divorce leads us to three essential observations. First, much of the interpersonal and legal conflict that occurs in separation and divorce is caused by conflicts of perspective. Many disputes, including some formal, legal contests over child custody, involve conflicts over differing desires for the future of the marriage, differing experiences of grief, and differing projections onto the children.

Second, different family members have conflicting perspectives on their family, relationships, and the divorce, in part because of their different roles in the family and in the separation. Conflicting perspectives can be expected to be found between the partner who wanted the marriage to end and the partner who wants it to continue, between mothers and fathers, and between parents and children. Conflicting perspectives also can be expected to be found between different professionals who represent one of the parents, the children, or the entire family in a custody dispute.

A third observation is that all of the adults involved in divorce and custody disputes can benefit from recognizing the child's perspective. The perspective of one or the other parent is the one traditionally taken by family and friends and by the attorneys who represent each parent. One partner typically *is* seen to be the injured party. One party *is* expected to win custody. Divorce often *is* viewed as the beginning of a family feud. From the perspective of children, however, past wrongs often are much less important than current conflicts, conflicts that disrupt their daily lives. Particularly because it has become so common, we need to find a way to make divorce less divisive for children, legally, socially, and psychologically.

MEDIATION VERSUS LITIGATION: 12 YEARS LATER

So far, I have offered a clinical and conceptual overview of several key themes in divorce, child custody, and mediation, introducing topics that we consider in much more detail in subsequent chapters. The interested reader, or the skeptic, might want to know something about the evidence base for these observations, an issue that I also address at length in later chapters.

I developed a method of custody mediation based on the principles outlined in this chapter. Over the course of many years, a number of graduate students and I conducted randomized trials of this "emotionally informed" approach to mediation. We compared emotionally informed mediation with adversary settlement (usually litigation) among two samples of high-conflict families who had petitioned a Virginia court for a contested custody hearing. Parents were assigned (literally) at the flip of a coin to either try to resolve their disputes in mediation or to continue with the legal proceedings. Moreover, successive graduate students assessed these families over the course of 12 years after they had resolved their disputes in mediation, in court, or in whatever way they could.

Did emotionally informed mediation make a difference? Let me first offer an important disclaimer. Even when mediation is successful, parents are not happy. And why should they be? They just got divorced. Still, like many ADR professionals, I have always hoped that parents' (and mediators') efforts to put their children first at an extremely difficult time would pay off over time, as feelings and families begin to heal. I believed that, like the book title says, good mediation really could help many families not only to negotiate agreements, but also to renegotiate their relationships. The research findings turned this hope into certain knowledge about what good mediation can do. Unlike what is typically found for social and psychological intervention, the benefits of mediation grew larger, not smaller, over time.

Twelve years after an average of only about 6 hours of mediation, nonresidential parents who mediated were much more likely to remain involved in their children's lives (Emery et al., 2001). For example, 30% of nonresidential parents who mediated (the coin came up heads) saw their children weekly *12 years later* compared to 9% of parents who continued with adversary settlement (the coin came up tails).

Of course, children move around, as do parents, over the course of 12 years. This makes it more difficult for many parents and children to maintain direct contact, so we also asked about telephone contact—and found even larger differences. Fully 54% of nonresidential parents who mediated spoke to their children on the phone weekly 12 years later, compared to 13% of nonresidential parents who continued with their contested legal dispute (Emery et al., 2001).

Of critical importance, nonresidential parents who mediated also were better parents, at least according to the ratings of a potentially tough critic: the residential parents (their exes). Twelve years later, residential parents who, at random, mediated instead of litigated rated the nonresidential parent as significantly better in terms of discipline, religious/moral training, participating in significant events in children's lives, and discussing problems with them. In fact, residential parents who had mediated rated the other parent as significantly better on every dimension of parenting we assessed (Emery et al., 2001).

Also of critical importance, we found *less* coparenting conflict between parents who mediated, despite their increased opportunities for dispute. (They had more chances to fight, because both parents remained far more involved in their children's lives in the mediation group) (Sbarra & Emery, 2008).

As discussed in Chapter 9, several other findings from this study are important to note, as are various methodological details, particularly cautions about whether the results generalize to other mediation programs (especially if the mediation is of dubious quality). Still, the research provides strong empirical support for an intervention based on the concepts outlined in this chapter, perhaps especially the view that custody disputes are about *parents'* emotional issues, not just children's needs. The insights and techniques behind these broad ideas, which I elaborate on throughout this book, are critical to emotionally informed mediation. I hope and believe they can be of value not only to mediators, but also to a range of professionals who work with divorcing and divorced parents.

CHAPTER OVERVIEW

This chapter offered only a broad introduction to my conceptualization of the emotional and relationship dynamics of divorce and dispute resolution. The next four chapters delve into the psychological details. Chapter 2 suggests ways of understanding the chaos of emotions surrounding the time of divorce, particularly parents' anger and the emotions beneath the anger, including their hurt, pain, fear, longing, and guilt. Chapter 3 focuses on my conceptual model of grief in divorce (or for grieving any potentially revocable loss). Grief is probably the central emotional process in divorce, and the experience of grief differs in essential ways for the partner who leaves and the one who is left behind. Chapter 4 outlines my family systems conceptualization of divorce as renegotiating family relationships, and discusses how former partners who remain parents can successfully begin to redefine their relationship boundaries. Chapter 5 extends this view into the renegotiation of parent–child relationships and the triangular relationship between the child and both parents.

In Chapter 6, I review the complex and often vague guidelines that comprise the substance of divorce and child custody law. Chapter 7 introduces details of my "emotionally informed" model of mediation, focusing on setting the stage for mediation by developing clear policies and procedures, and on how to conduct the first, structured session (which is divided into five distinct phases). Chapter 8 describes how emotionally informed mediation works in the later sessions. The chapter uses case studies to illustrate key themes and techniques (e.g., focusing on issues not emotions, experimenting with parenting plans), and it also reviews the details involved in writing up a parenting plan. Chapter 9 provides the evidence base for my approach to mediation. This chapter summarizes evidence from about a dozen scientific papers my graduate students and I published on the families we randomly assigned either to mediate or to litigate their child custody disputes and assessed repeatedly over 12 years. To broaden the evidence base, the findings of other, key mediation studies also are discussed in this chapter.

2

BEYOND ANGER

Pain, Longing, Fear, Guilt, and Grief

Anger is a symptom, a way of cloaking and expressing feelings too awful to experience directly—hurt, bitterness, grief, and, most of all, fear.

—JOAN RIVERS

Mediators, collaborative lawyers, family therapists, and many other professionals ask divorcing parents to do something emotionally *unnatural*. We ask them to control their understandable anger so that they can negotiate a parenting plan (and perhaps a financial agreement) that works for their children, and for them. To promote effective parenting and coparenting, we ask parting parents to look beyond the heat of the moment, beyond their own pain, toward their children's future. This is an ambitious goal for professionals. It's a much harder one for parents, who must find a way to manage their legitimate anger—and the not-so-obvious emotions that lie behind and beyond their anger.

The first step for professionals working toward this emotionally unnatural goal is recognizing parents' anger or, perhaps, their rage. ADR is not about a "happy" divorce. ADR professionals must expect and accept their clients' anger, and come prepared with strategies for managing conflict. The professional's second step is to acknowledge and legitimize our clients' intense feelings, a recognition which, perhaps paradoxically, can help them to do what we ask: contain their anger during dispute resolution and around their children. The third step is to look beyond the anger. Recognizing the deeper emotions that fuel anger can help professionals to empathize with angry clients. The awareness also offers us, and them, insights into anger, insights that lead to new, critically important strategies for dealing with it.

This chapter offers a conceptual introduction into some emotions behind anger in divorce. Later chapters address the various steps involved in helping divorcing parents' to understand and manage their anger from a more practical, "how to do" perspective. But before delving deeper into what lies beyond anger, we need to acknowledge that people have many good reasons for being angry in divorce. When can you be angry if not when your husband or wife, your life partner, wants out? When can you be angry if not when your husband or wife tells you they love, or have been sleeping with, someone else? When can you be angry if not when all the plans you had been making, and working toward, are thrown up in the air? When can you be angry if not when you have to move out of your home, divide up your stuff, and spend what little free cash you have, or don't have, on lawyers, mediators, and therapists? When can you be angry if not when your relationship with your children is threatened, when your time with them is going to be limited, perhaps greatly? When can you be angry if not when your partner's lover thinks he or she is going to parent *your* children, maybe in *your* house, together with *your* husband or wife?

There are many obvious reasons to be angry in divorce. But there also are many hidden, emotional motivations behind divorcing partners' intense anger. In this sense, much of their anger is irrational—that is, the anger is fueled by emotion not reason. Even the anger that leads to legal actions often is driven by emotional impulses instead of (just) rational and reasonable concerns about the children, finances, and so on. This chapter is about looking beyond anger in ADR, in therapy, in the law, and inside oneself.

EMOTIONAL PAIN

In this chapter, we will explore the specific emotional motivations beyond anger in terms of evolution and the brain. While this chapter presents my own, unique taxonomy of motivations behind anger, a classification that is based in large part on my clinical work, the concepts outlined here also are rooted in emerging evolutionary psychology and neuroscience. In fact, I believe that affective neuroscience (Panksepp, 1998) offers a rich, new model of emotion that is consistent with biology and full of clinical implications. I have tried to be faithful to the emerging principles of affective neuroscience in this chapter, however, let us first consider emotions behind anger in commonsense terms.

Anger and Pain

Much of the anger felt and expressed in divorce, particularly in the raw days, weeks, and months before or after a separation, is a reaction to pain. This assertion may make sense intuitively, or it may not. Many people do not appear to recognize the hurt that, I am convinced, fuels much fury in divorce disputes.

Consider this analogy. Responding to pain with anger is a familiar reaction, one that we observe in ourselves all the time. You hit your thumb with a hammer and bang the tool down in a rage, even as you watch the blood blister growing under your nail. You wake up in the middle of the night to use the bathroom, stub your toe, and find yourself yelling at a bureau, perhaps kicking it a second time. Or consider this: you get "dumped" in your intense, teenage love affair, and call your girlfriend or boyfriend a string of vile names, trying desperately to hurt them back.

In each example, you act angry. You *are* angry. But what you *really* feel, at a deeper level, is hurt.

Recognizing Pain Behind Anger

Consider another example, one of my prototypical mediation cases. A couple in their early 30s, with two children (12 and 14 years old), sits down in my office. They have been referred by the court for mediation in an attempt to resolve their bitter and contentious custody dispute. The mother is a pleasant, outgoing receptionist. After years of unhappiness, she says she finally decided to leave her troubled marriage. She is in tears, not about her decision to divorce, but about her lost relationship with her 12-year-old son. She blames his father for turning their son against her.

The father is a well-muscled and tattooed factory worker. He's dressed in a sleeveless T-shirt and is wearing a ball cap, backwards. And he's furious. He calls his wife a "whore," and says her son thinks she is one too. That's why the boy refuses to spend weekends with her, he claims. "You can leave me," he growls, "but if that's what you want, you're going to lose your son too."

I try to get the husband to control himself, gently asking him not to interrupt, to lower his voice.[1] After 10 or 15 minutes of trying to talk through a storm of rising intensity, I call a time-out, telling the parents

---

[1] For reasons that I elaborate on in Chapter 7, I do not try to squash anger at the beginning of mediation. Many couples seem to need to fight, one last time, before engaging in the process. I often wait for them to turn to me in frustration over their failed efforts before really trying to intervene.

I want to caucus briefly with each of them alone. I ask the mother if she minds stepping out first, making the excuse that she's the one nearest to the door. What I really want to do is to speak with the father by himself.

The young woman jumps at the chance for a break. After she closes the door, I turn to her ex and say, not so brilliantly, "You seem angry." He agrees, but before he can launch deeper into his tirade, I interrupt and continue with a knowing look, "But I think something else is going on." He pauses, stares at me for maybe 5 long seconds, and then bursts into tears. "What am I going to do?" he blurts out. "I love her so much. She *can't* leave me. We've been together since we were 14. I had a scholarship to play college football. I could have gotten an education. But instead, I took a job at the frigging factory, so we could get married. We did, the weekend after we graduated from high school. She was pregnant a couple of months later. She's the mother of my children. She's my life. What am I supposed to do?"

This well-muscled young man was acting very angry. But how he *really* felt, at a deeper and more honest level, was hurt.

Addressing the Hurt Behind Anger

How might different mediators respond to anger of such intensity? A rational approach is one option, asking the father to lower his voice, control his anger, and focus on the children's best interests. An equally rational approach might be to end mediation. Perhaps this man was inappropriately angry. We might consider him to be verbally abusive. His intimidation might create an unmanageable power imbalance.

These are important considerations. Mediators sometimes have to end their negotiation efforts, or use forceful methods to maintain the integrity of the process, for example, using "shuttle diplomacy"—that is, never having both parents in the room at the same time and only meeting with each of them separately. However, my first and primary approach in cases like this, and cases like this are remarkably common (see Chapter 1), is to look beyond the anger. Especially early in mediation, I look for the emotional motivations that fuel intense, irrational anger. Much like when we stub a toe and yell at the furniture, many people act angry in mediation (or in lawyer's offices or in therapy) when they *actually* feel hurt.

Recognizing, and admitting to, the pain behind anger can help clients to better understand themselves. It also can help mediators and other divorce professionals to better understand and assist their clients. In particular, the emotional insight suggests alternative, potentially effective intervention strategies and techniques (Chapters 7 and 8).

When the young man was furious, my emotional impulse was to get him out of my office. I wanted him gone—to protect his estranged wife, and, honestly, to protect myself. His fury elicited little empathy. I didn't much care for or about him. Frankly, I would have loved to chew him out, or better yet, let some judge do that job for me. But when he burst into tears a few minutes later, I could easily empathize with his pain, express my sorrow over his loss, and suggest that he had, in fact, lost a great deal. From this position of understanding, I also could gently suggest that he needed to grieve. (I discuss grief at length in Chapter 3.) Such insights never really occurred to him, or if they did, he had not admitted the deeper feelings to other people or perhaps not to himself. And while I could agree that he *should* be hurt, angry, and sad over losing his marriage, over losing the love of his life, I could also point out—in a way he could now understand better—that we also needed to consider his children, *their* pain, and what they needed. Refocusing him on his deeper, more honest emotions in our 20-minute caucus was not the end of mediation. But it was, and often can be, a beginning.

ANGER IS NOT ANGER IS NOT ANGER

One way to summarize the basic and essential point that I want to make is this: Anger is not anger is not anger. "Anger is not anger is not anger" means that, contrary to many views of anger (and of emotions in general), anger has different meanings in different contexts. I am *not* suggesting that we must parse the intensity or method of expressing anger, for example, by contrasting loud, angry outbursts with the silent treatment, although such considerations are important for some purposes.[2] Instead, I am suggesting that anger has several different motivations, and different goals, both in the environment in which it is expressed and in evolutionary terms.

Offensive Anger

Aggression is the motivation for anger that we seem to recognize most readily both intuitively and in psychological science. Such "offensive

---

[2] For example, different expressions of parental anger and conflict cause children to react with greater or lesser emotional upset (Cummings & Davies, 2010).

anger" (my term) is an attack, an attempt to dominate. Images of offensive anger include husbands who batter, pumped-up football players, perhaps aggressive trial lawyers, or maybe hunters.[3]

Psychological (and intuitive) understandings of anger commonly focus on the dominance function of, and motivation behind, anger. The dominance analysis explains why a boss is allowed to be angry with a subordinate, a teacher with a student, an abuser with the abused, but not vice versa. Anger in these examples is a method of control, even if it's only a mild warning, about what the dominant figure *could* do.

Defensive Anger

A different but related motivation and function of anger is defense. "Defensive anger" (also my term) is an attempt to protect oneself or one's territory. Self-protection, not dominance, is the motivation behind the anger displayed by a cat cornered by a dog, or an abused woman cornered by an abusive man. The righteous indignation we feel when fighting for a cause that is just, or a right that has been trampled upon, also is an expression of defensive anger. Defensive anger feels necessary, justified, and "right."[4]

Rational versus Emotional Anger

Offensive and defensive anger clearly are different from each other. As I have noted briefly, moreover, each type of anger can and, for other purposes, should be parsed further. For our present purpose, however, we will ignore these complexities, and lump both offensive and defensive anger together and call them "rational anger" (again, my term). "Rational anger" fits people's general intuitions about anger. Rational anger is about winning, defeating, dominating—or self-protection. Rational anger "makes sense."

---

[3] The hunter example suggests that the motivations behind "offensive anger" also can and should be parsed further. For example, the motivation behind intraspecies anger (dominance) needs to be distinguished from the motivation for interspecies anger (food, survival) (Panksepp, 1998). Same-sex intraspecies dominance competition also should be distinguished from male–female dominance. For example, "mate guarding," observed in primates, dolphins, and other animals, serves the evolutionary function of ensuring that the dominating male is the one to inseminate the female (de Waal & Tyack, 2003). I do not delve into these important distinctions in this text beyond this footnote.

[4] The anger expressed by my muscled mediation client was defensive, not offensive, and therefore justified in his eyes. He may have appeared to be on the attack, and in the eyes of his former wife, he was. But inside himself, his anger was an emotional defense, a response to the inflicted pain of the lost love.

In contrast, we will call anger that is a response to pain—or to other emotions we consider shortly—"emotional anger" (my final new term). Emotional anger covers up deeper, more honest, and revealing emotions, for example, hurt feelings. The "covering up" of the underlying emotion serves a function both immediately and in evolutionary terms. Anger helps a wounded animal not to feel its pain, allowing the animal to fight back more effectively in its effort to ward off its attacker (therefore promoting survival, and, in turn, evolutionary selection of the response). Emotional anger in response to hurt feelings surely serves similar functions. Much as anger can numb physical pain, emotional anger numbs the pain of rejection. Feeling angry at your ex hurts less than feeling rejected by him or her.

The hurt party's expression of anger, as opposed to revealing their injury, also sends a warning signal that decreases the risk for further harm. Acting hurt shows your vulnerability to your attacker. Acting angry hides this vulnerability. This makes "covering up" an adaptive interpersonal (or interanimal) signal, as well as a salve for pain.

Again, this is true for both physical and emotional pain. The injured cat's bared teeth tell the predatory dog that further attack might be dangerous. The rejected lover's anger tells the rejecting partner to back off. If, instead of acting so angry, the rejected man in mediation told his wife that he wanted her back, he would have opened himself up to further rejection and more pain. (This is one reason why I talked to him alone, in caucus.) Interpersonally, his anger was much safer to express than hurt.

Anger that is overly intense and prolonged—anger that just doesn't make sense—is probably emotional anger. And recognizing emotional anger, and what fuels it, offers new insights into the irrationalities of overly intense and prolonged anger in divorce. Hurt, pain, and the primitive desire to hurt back explain the emotional logic behind economically irrational actions in divorce, for example, running up legal bills that exceed the value of a disputed property, or deliberately harming your own children in a desperate attempt to hurt your ex. Such anger makes sense only if we recognize that it veils motivations that have very little to do with professed goals of winning, self-protection, or protecting children's best interests. Emotional anger is driven by deeper, more honest, and more difficult feelings like the unbelievable pain of losing someone you love. Anger is not anger is not anger.

A Brief Detour: Pain and Anger in Behavioral and Brain Science

As noted, I developed most of my ideas about the different motivations behind anger from my clinical work. However, my observations and hypotheses also grew out of my long-standing interest in animal behavior and evolutionary psychology, an interest that began, but does not end, with attachment theory (discussed shortly). Jaak Panksepp's (1998) "affective neuroscience," an approach anchored in evolution and the brain, also has been particularly influential in both reinforcing and stimulating my ideas about the multiple functions of anger.

Social psychologists Geoff MacDonald and Mark Leary (2005), as well as Panksepp (2005), recently summarized the extensive behavioral and neuroscience literature on psychological pain. Their reviews concluded that new and growing evidence is consistent with the idea that people's rage in response to the pain of getting "dumped" is activated by the same emotional system involved in raging at a bureau over a stubbed toe (MacDonald & Leary, 2005; Panksepp, 2005). Social psychological and neuroscience research both support the idea that the linguistic similarity people draw between physical and emotional pain (e.g., hurt feelings) is more than an analogy (MacDonald & Leary, 2005). In fact, some types of social pain, particularly separation distress, appear to activate the same brain circuitry involved in certain types of physical pain (Panksepp, 2005). There is considerable empirical evidence, moreover, that humans and other animals react to physical and emotional pain with anger, often followed by aggression (MacDonald & Leary, 2005).

The anger provoked by physical pain—and hurt feelings—appears to be a part of an evolved threat-defense system, part of what I earlier termed "defensive anger." Humans can modify some emotional responses to pain as a result of learning and cognitive control (i.e., a degree of emotion regulation is possible). However, humans and other animals are "wired" to respond quickly to attack and physical pain with anger and counterattack (Berkowitz, 1993). Why? The response serves both immediate (warding off an attack) and ultimate evolutionary (survival) functions.

Responding to separation from a caregiver or social rejection with psychological pain may similarly serve both immediate and evolutionary functions. Specifically, psychological pain may promote social attachment by making separation painful. Maintaining proximity to protective caregivers or to a protective group, in turn, increases the likelihood of survival. How did the social pain response evolve? Evolutionary scientists speculate that evolution "used" existing (more primitive) brain circuits, designed to respond to physical pain, when "selecting" emotional pain as an adaptive response to separation, a response that increases inclusive fitness (MacDonald & Leary, 2005; Panksepp, 2005).

There are profound implications to be extracted from this new line of evolutionary reasoning about the intrapsychic, interpersonal, and evolutionary functions of emotions (or what I prefer to think of as systems of emotions). It is difficult to conceive how anger might increase reproductive fitness when we think of anger as a detached emotion, that is, not tied to broader motivations. In contrast, it is easy to see how anger might increase reproductive fitness if we view it as connected to sexual selection (e.g., dominance) or survival (e.g., self-protection). If we think in these terms, we must conclude that both rational anger and emotional anger are preserved in our genes.

This should mean, in turn, that these products of evolution are preserved in how the brain is "wired." The brain should contain circuitry that connects the different components of various motivational systems (e.g., separation distress, pain, and anger expression). Emerging research suggests that this, indeed, is the case (Panksepp, 1998, 2005). Anger does not exist in isolation in the brain, just as it does not exist in isolation in our behavior. Anger is not anger is not anger in behavior, in evolution, or in the brain.

Five Practical Implications for Professionals

Our brief detour into affective neuroscience offers fresh perspectives on emotional expression and its many meanings (even though many details of the theory still need to be fleshed out and tested empirically). Returning to a practical focus, I see at least five important implications of the idea that the same emotion can have different meanings in different contexts.

First, a given emotion is not really the same emotion when it is aroused in different motivational contexts—even though we may experience the emotion as the same, or a very similar, feeling. Once again, this means that anger is not anger is not anger. Rational anger (and its subtypes) is different from emotional anger (and its subtypes). For example, we may feel angry both when we are competing for dominance and when we are hurt emotionally. We may experience our anger very similarly in both cases, but the anger serves very different functions in the two situations. This means that our anger should or could convey different meanings in different contexts, both to other people and to ourselves. Of course, our anger often fools both us and other people. Until I pointed it out, for example, neither my muscled client nor his former wife identified his anger as a reflection of his pain over being rejected.

Second, understanding the motivational context gives professionals, and the person experiencing the feeling, the opportunity to understand emotions more deeply and more completely. We often are unable to identify the deeper meaning of our anger based on our affective experience alone. In fact, this is precisely the problem. While anger is not anger is not anger in terms of its immediate or evolutionary functions, anger generally *is* anger in terms of how we experience the emotion. We are mad, period. Because the phenomenological experience or interpersonal expression of anger can be misleading, angry people, and the professionals who work with them, need to analyze the *context* of anger to develop clues about its potential or "real" meaning.

Consider this: despite our immediate, "hard-wired" rage when we stub a toe and yell at a bureau, it is pretty easy to figure out that we are not *really* mad at the furniture. However, it is much more difficult to make accurate interpretations of the "real" meaning of our anger in more complex life circumstances, like a divorce. Still, in the context of a breakup, it is reasonable to hypothesize, and explore, whether some of our anger (or our clients' anger) might be a reaction to being emotionally hurt. Similarly, we can better understand irrational and impulsive attempts to "hurt back" in terms of the logic of emotion, that is, as a primitive, defensive reaction to being hurt.

Third, an important clue to the motivation behind the "same" felt emotion is its opposing emotion or emotions, that is, the (usually unexpressed) feelings that are activated together with the emotion that is consciously experienced. From the affective neuroscience perspective, emotions do not occur in isolation. A given emotion (e.g., anger) is a part of a constellation of feelings, a system involving one or more other emotions (e.g., pain). The different emotions prepare the animal (us) for alternative courses of action, depending on the environmental context. A wounded animal ignores its pain and fights back in anger, protecting itself. If the danger disappears, the animal licks its wounds, focusing on the hurt. Hurt "opposes" anger and vice versa.

As we will consider in detail shortly, different feelings oppose anger in different motivational contexts. Sometimes the emotional opposite of anger is pain; other times, it is love (or longing); sometimes sadness is the opposite of anger; sometimes it is fear; and other times, guilt (see Table 2.1).

TABLE 2.1. Emotional Motivations Beyond Anger

Evolved behavioral system	Goal of anger expression	Emotion(s) behind anger
Response to injury	Numbing; "hurting back"	Physical/emotional pain
Attachment	Reunion (love, proximity)	Love/longing
Freeze–flight–fight–fright	Responding to threats	Fear
Morality	Externalizing blame	Guilt
Grief	Ending old attachments, so new ones can be formed	Sadness, love

Fourth, suggesting to someone that he or she also may be experiencing an opposing emotion can help people to understand, and admit to, their range of emotions, as well as to the true source of their feelings, that is, the motivational context. When I suggested to the well-muscled father, "You seem angry," I was expressing accurate empathy, correctly reflecting his expressed feelings. (Identifying his anger was not difficult.) One of the exciting implications of the model outlined here is the guidance it offers to professionals about accurate *second-order* empathy, that is, the much more difficult task of correctly identifying *unstated* feelings that nevertheless are experienced, or could be experienced. "I think you also feel ... hurt, lonely, sad, frightened, or guilty." The process is akin to what happens when a soldier fights on despite a deep wound, but when someone calls attention to the injury after the battle is over, he faints. Attention shifts from the immediate, surface concern (anger) to the deeper, ignored problem (injury and pain).

Fifth, recognition of the complexity of their emotions and the motivational context can help clients to better control and contain difficult emotions by allowing them to focus on their "real" or underlying feelings. We can easily identify pain as the source of our anger in the case of a stubbed toe. When our feelings are hurt, however, it is not so easy to recognize, or admit to, the "real" source of our anger. Yet, identifying the feelings behind emotional anger aids understanding, and allows us to address the deeper, more honest pain. Dealing with the hurt still is more difficult than being angry, but it also is more honest, and ultimately, a more effective way to heal. In mediation, helping clients to recognize the pain behind their anger can help them to control their understandable anger, and to avoid impulsive actions that can hurt their children and the coparenting relationship. The insight also can encourage clients to seek help outside of mediation, for example, accepting a mediator's suggestion to find an understanding therapist.

ANGER AS REUNION BEHAVIOR: LOVE AND LONGING

Anger can cover up underlying hurt and pain. Anger also can mask other feelings (see Table 2.1). In this section, we consider anger as a form of reunion behavior, an expression of love and longing.

Attachment Theory

We need to outline a few basic tenets of attachment theory in order to lay the groundwork for understanding anger as reunion behavior, that is, as a veiled effort to reconnect with lost love. As with pain, this perspective on anger also is rooted in evolution and neuroscience. In his famous trilogy on attachment, separation, and loss, British psychiatrist John Bowlby (1969, 1973, 1980) outlined the basic premises of attachment theory, a set of propositions anchored initially in Bowlby's clinical observations and in ethology, the naturalistic study of animal behavior. Today, attachment theory and its clinical implications have spawned and are supported by thousands of research studies (Cassidy & Shaver, 2008).

Perhaps the most basic premise of attachment theory is that infants are born to love their caregivers. Loving, or more accurately, forming attachments, is a primary motivation in attachment theory.[5] Like a duckling swimming after its mother, or a colt trailing a mare, proximity seeking is the function of infant–caregiver love. The infant develops a selective bond with its caregiver, that is, an attachment. When close to the caregiver, the infant feels secure. When separated, the infant experiences anxiety. The anxiety motivates the infant to find its lost attachment figure, to reunite.

Evolution "selected" the attachment system and its motivating emotions, because the feelings keep infants physically close to their caregivers. Ducklings, colts, and human toddlers all are more likely to survive if they maintain proximity to protective caregivers. As a result, the circuitry underlying attachment motivations has been "wired" in our brains (Panksepp, 2005).

Separation, Anger, and Reunion Behavior

How is anger involved in the regulation of attachments? Consider what happens when a toddler is separated from, and loses sight of, its attachment figure. At first, the toddler becomes anxious and searches for the "missing" parent. If the toddler discovers the attachment figure, he moves closer, reduces anxiety, and perhaps seeks a reassuring hug.

But what happens if the toddler cannot reduce his anxiety by reestablishing proximity? In Bowlby's (1973) term, he "protests," perhaps bursting into angry tears and screaming, "Mommy! Mommy!" The function and goal of the toddler's anger is reunion. In the language of attachment theory, his anger is a form of reunion behavior. (Despair follows anger when such protests fail to bring about a reunion, as we consider in an extended discussion of grief in Chapter 3.)

In divorce, some expressions of anger apparently serve the same function as the toddler's protests. Some anger in divorce, sometimes a

[5] Harry Harlow's (1959) classic studies of rhesus monkeys demonstrated this.

great deal of anger, is reunion behavior. For example, we can view some of my muscled mediation client's angry threats this way. Consider his threat, "You can leave me, but if that's what you want, you're going to lose your son too." From an attachment perspective, the underlying (and unarticulated) meaning of this outburst was: "I'll make it so difficult for you to leave that you'll stay with me."

As introduced in Chapter 1, a great many custody disputes are not so much disputes about custody but about ending the marriage. In one-sided divorces, we can view much of the anger and actions of the partner who is left, perhaps including legal filings, as a form of reunion behavior.

Love and Hate Are Not Far Apart

How does viewing (some) anger as reunion behavior help us understand conflict in divorce? One basic and essential implication concerns a criticism I have long offered about Harry Stack Sullivan's claim that the opposite of love is hate (Emery, 1992, 1994). In the attachment system, love (attachment) and hate (angry protest) both serve the same function, namely, promoting proximity. From this attachment perspective, the opposite of love is not hate. The opposite of love is indifference. Indifference means that no attachment exists, or if there was an attachment, detachment is complete.

We have all heard, or said, "I don't love you! I HATE you!" What is the difference between love and hate in such a proclamation? Not much. Love and hate are not far apart. Let me offer one more example, one apart from divorce. My children have often told me, especially when they were 10 or 11 years old, how much they "hate" members of the opposite sex. They would relate stories of spending recess after recess "chasing" or "torturing" children of the opposite sex—because they hated them so much. I think something else was going on. The fourth grader's "hate" of the opposite sex really reflects the beginnings of budding, if misunderstood, interest.

The Opposite of Love Is Indifference

What are some applications of this central idea? A basic perspective is that couples who are constantly fighting with each other are *enmeshed,* not disengaged (Minuchin, 1974). Distant couples interact rarely and unemotionally. Enmeshed couples interact frequently, too frequently, and with too much emotional intensity. Enmeshed couples expend a great deal of emotional energy, positive or negative, on their relationship.

These observations about love, hate, and enmeshment are the foundation for my strategy of encouraging divorcing parents to work toward developing a more distant, business-like relationship, as opposed to either continuing their angry conflicts or trying to "be friends." Psychologically, the goal is to establish interpersonal distance, and give each partner time to separate, to detach, to grieve. In mediation, I rarely mention these psychological goals. (I might in therapy.) Instead, I simply note that a business-like relationship is more workable, and that, as parents, the divorcing partners do still have a job to do: To raise the children.

Still, in individual caucuses with mediation clients, I may directly suggest, briefly, that the opposite of love is indifference, not hate. I might hint that the client may need to "let go" of much of their anger over various injustices, past and present. Letting go is not about forgiving or forgetting or giving in. Instead, letting go of intense feelings, bad and good, is a part of grief, part of detachment, part of moving from love/hate to indifference. As I wrote in my book for divorcing parents (Emery, 2006), the goal is not to get furious when your ex calls. The goal is to not recognize his voice, and say, in all honesty, "Who is this?"

ANGER AND FEAR

Sometimes what lies behind anger is pain, sometimes it is love, and sometimes it is fear. As with psychological pain and attachment, let us begin our consideration of the relationship between anger and fear with some commonsense observations of animal, and human, behavior.

Fight or Flight

When surprised by a barking dog, a cat immediately arches its back. Its fur stands on end. It hisses. Physiologically and behaviorally, the cat is prepared for either of two options, lashing out with a claw or dashing to a nearby tree and a desperate climb to safety. This is an example of the familiar, long-recognized, and much-studied "fight-or-flight" response (Cannon, 1935). As the descriptive name suggests, in fight or flight the emotion that lies behind anger is fear.

Like pain and attachment, the connection between fear and anger is rooted in evolution and the brain. Fight or flight is an evolved, self-protective reaction to threat. Because it increases the chances of survival, the fight-or-flight response is adaptive in the short run and over the long course of evolution.

Fight or flight is an adaptive response to *physical* threats. However, neither running away nor an angry counterattack is an adaptive reaction to most *psychological* threats, for example, a demanding boss. Unfortunately, our bodies apparently do not know the difference. In fact, one explanation for why psychological stress causes physical illness is that threat prepares the body for fight or flight, but neither action is an appropriate response to an emotional stressor. Because we cannot act in the way our bodies are prepared to act, we are left "revved up" with physiological arousal that can damage bodily systems (Oltmanns & Emery, 2010).

Freeze–Flight–Fight–Fright

Before considering the anger–fear connection in divorce, we should note that fight or flight is now recognized to be an oversimplification of animals' possible responses to threat. Contemporary scientists call this more elaborate set of options "freeze–flight–fight–fright" (Bracha, Ralston, Matsukawa, Williams, & Bracha, 2004).

An animal's first response to threat is to freeze. Picture a deer caught in the beam of a car's headlights. Flight is the second option. The deer bolts if the car moves too close. Fight is the third option. Even a deer will fight back if it's trapped. Fright (tonic immobility or "playing dead") is the last option, one that is observed only under conditions of imminent death or, in humans, extreme trauma, for example, rape. The four options are ordered hierarchically, so that freezing is the first option, flight the second, and so on (Bracha et al., 2004).

This more nuanced ordering of freeze–flight–fight–fright can help us to more completely understand reactions to real and perceived threat in divorce. Freezing is an initial and common response, for example, refusing to talk about your marital problems, refusing to move out, or refusing to negotiate. Flight typically is not an option, however, because too much would be lost by running away. Therefore, people can quickly jump to fight, that is, anger. Like a cornered animal, they may feel trapped and under attack due to divorce. And while it is not exactly tonic immobility, some people seemingly get to the point of playing dead, completely giving up and letting their ex take whatever they want.

Real and Emotional Threats

Of course, there are many reasons to feel threatened in divorce. And some threats are very real, as is the fear they create. The appropriate response in such circumstances may not be to freeze, but perhaps instead to respond with a combination of flight (e.g., obtaining a protective order) and fight (e.g., retaining a strong legal advocate).

Other threats, however, are vague and psychological, for example, fear of the unknown, of an uncharted future of parenting, making money, and exploring new relationships alone. Many people become understandably angry at their estranged partners for throwing their life into such a state of uncertainty and upheaval. Others desperately try to hang on to a bad marriage when the alternative is facing an uncertain, frightening future.

Addressing Fear Behind Anger

In circumstances like this, facing the underlying fear is likely to be more productive than covering it up with anger. Facing fear is the only way to overcome it. Addressing fear, and its causes, can lead to productive solutions. Staying stuck on anger is, well, staying stuck.

In mediation, a common circumstance where anger covers up fear occurs when people threaten to scuttle a detailed agreement in the eleventh hour. One parent cannot possibly bend the agreed-upon schedule, so the children can see the other parent on their birthday. Or both partners now insist that they each must have a painting they bought at a yard sale and formerly stored in the basement.

Such conflicts make little sense rationally. What is *really* going on emotionally? One or both partners are afraid they are about to make a big mistake—about the agreement, about getting a divorce, about whatever. (Real estate agents often encounter a similar problem at house closings.) The stakes are high, and making a final move is frightening. This can cause clients to act angry when how they *really* feel is afraid.

For divorce professionals, the implications are straightforward: Look for fear that may lie behind anger. Helping our clients to recognize their fears and anxieties not only can help to "unhinge" them from conflict, but it can help them to identify issues that they need to address so that they can move on with their lives. In fact, when the crisis is over, when the future is not so threatening, many people say that one of the positive things to come out of divorce is the strength they found in themselves. They faced their fears and grew as a result.

The Professional's Response to Anger

The divorce professional's *own* response to anger is another area in which it is important to recognize the anger–fear connection. Even professionals are "wired" to react with freeze–flight–fight–fright when divorcing couples rage at one another. Therefore, mediators, and other professionals who work with divorcing parents together in the same room, need to recognize and learn to manage our own responses to expressions of anger. As the conflict escalates, it is natural to become increasingly anxious or angry. What professionals need to learn to do, however, is what we ask our clients to do: Recognize the feelings but do not act on them. We need to learn to use our insights into our feelings to help to control our actions.

Understanding the Children's Position

There is one valuable way in which we can use our uncomfortable emotional responses to parents' tension, bickering, or exploding in our offices. We can use our own reactions to the conflict as feedback to parents about how their children are likely to be feeling. Like a mediator, the children sit in the middle of their parents, and being in the middle can be a very uncomfortable place. When I am upset by parents' uncontrolled disputes, or their more subtle competition for my attention or loyalty, I often share my discomfort as a concrete reminder of their children's position. Parents may overlook their children's distress, but they cannot deny my self-disclosure in this context.

ANGER AND GUILT

Guilt is a fourth emotion that can be covered up by anger. In divorce, hidden guilt often lies behind the "blame game" that many couples play with earnest. Each partner tries to hold the other responsible for the divorce (or for all of the problems in their marriage) while absolving themselves of guilt. "We're getting divorced because you had an affair!" "I only had an affair because you rejected me—we haven't had sex in years!" "I rejected you? You never *talked* to me, and you wanted to have *sex*?" "Talk? You *refused* to talk to me. All you wanted to do was to be with your friends!" And so on. ...

Such vehement, iterative debates make it clear that being angry, or being a victim, is far less of an emotional burden than being guilty, or being responsible for so much pain. Guilt is a heavy load. Divorce can be devastating personally, to your ex, your children, extended families, friends, and the broader community. Being responsible for misery is tough. Being the hurt party is not easy, but it does absolve guilt, at least superficially.

Yet, many divorcing partners seem to need their anger because, in their hearts, their self-absolution is incomplete. They are wracked with inner guilt, some of which may be realistic. There usually is plenty of blame to go around, because, as we discussed in Chapter 1, there are at least two sides to every story of "his" and "her" divorce. So one reason why anger can be so intense in the blame game is that guilt lies not too far beyond the anger of blaming your partner.

A Strategic Advantage

The blame game may involve added layers of complexity. For one, the consequences are not just limited to an individual's feelings or the couple's relationship. Being the victim evokes sympathy from other people, too.

The blame game also can be a part of jockeying for position in settlement negotiations. Negotiating with a guilty or guilt-ridden opponent is a strategic advantage. Reminders of shameful behavior may be used to "encourage" the guilty party to capitulate. Or evidence of guilty behavior might be presented in an attempt to influence a judge or to formally assign guilt in a fault-based trial. (Many states retain fault grounds for divorce even in the era of no-fault divorce; see Chapter 6.) With or without the threat of such public revelations, the party who feels guiltier is at a strategic disadvantage. The emotionally guilty party may make concessions to assuage his or her guilt—or he or she may instead try to assuage the guilt by shifting blame, which, of course, takes us back to the anger–guilt blame game.

The Origins of Guilt

We discuss anger–guilt toward the end of this chapter, even though it typically arises early in divorce, because guilt is different from our previous topics of pain, love, and fear. Those three systems of emotional anger all are solidly based on animal models, as is grief, a topic we consider in detail in the next chapter. In contrast, guilt seems more cognitive, more human, more learned. We feel guilty when we fail to live up to imposed or internal standards of behavior. Developmental psychologists commonly view the internalization of parental and societal standards—developing a conscience, learning to experience guilt—as a key goal of childrearing (Mussen & Eisenberg, 2001).

Could guilt be more basic, something "wired" in our brains and in our genes like pain, attachment, and fear? Some fascinating, recent theory and research suggest that intellectual justifications actually may follow rather than guide morality. From this perspective, cognitive standards of behavior do not shape our morals; instead, moral reasoning justifies our intuitive judgments. Moral judgments may really be "gut feelings in the brain," as my colleague, Jonathan Haidt, has put it (Haidt, 2001). Perhaps this explains some of the vehemence of the anger–guilt blame game. Each partner is trying to convince not just each other, but themselves, that they did no wrong—even though their own gut feelings tell them that they did.

Embracing Responsibility

Whatever its origins, I have three recommendations for addressing the blame game and the anger–guilt dynamic. First, I encourage people to take responsibility for the decisions they make (Emery, 2006). A key example is to "own" your decision to leave a marriage. People have many good reasons for making this decision, but in the end, it is a decision—a choice—and choice implies responsibility.

Second, I urge divorcing partners not to try to convince each other, or their children, that their decisions are justified. Children do not need to hear details, justifications, arguments, or other efforts to win them over. Children need to be out of the middle, and the explanations parents give to children should embrace responsibility for decisions that have been made (and include a "PG" explanation of what happened, together with lots of emotional assurance). As for convincing an ex that you are right—and they are in the wrong, well, that's not going to happen. One of the benefits of a divorce is you no longer need to resolve these kinds of relationship issues, so my advice is to leave it be.

Third, as with hurt, longing, and fear, I urge former spouses to face their guilt. This is something that each parent must do on his or her own, perhaps with the help of a good friend or a therapist. An aware, guilty partner may want to make restitution, not out of anger, but out of a sense of fairness, of compensation. Both may find that, over time, they may want to apologize. Responsibility is not always a 50/50 proposition, but it is rarely 100/0 either. I urge parents to accept responsibility for their mistakes, embrace the guilt they do feel (and perhaps should), and stop trying to assign all the blame to their partner. The goal is partly to get beyond anger in the ongoing, coparenting relationship, and, more important, to get beyond anger in your own life.

SUMMARY

Former partners have many good reasons to be angry in divorce. Recognizing this basic fact is the first step for professionals who hope to help parents to control and contain their conflict and hostility. Mediators, collaborative lawyers, and other ADR professionals really do ask parents to do something that is emotionally unnatural. Before pursuing that laudable course, a second step for professionals is to acknowledge and legitimize the range and intensity of each parent's anger. Yet, while people have many good reasons to be angry in divorce, they also have many emotional reasons to be angry, too. Thus, the third, critical step is to look beyond the surface of anger to the hurt and pain, the loneliness and longing, the fear, the guilt, and as we will explore in the next chapter, the grief behind anger. Recognition of these deeper, more honest emotions can facilitate the process of reaching a settlement in a more cooperative manner. Recognizing these complex, more difficult feelings also can help each individual heal. And recognizing one's own pain, longing, fear, and guilt can help parents to better appreciate the depth and complexity of their children's feelings.

3

GRIEVING DIVORCE

The Leaver and the Left

Ever has it been that love knows not its own depth until the hour of separation.

—Kahlil Gibran

Grief is yet another emotion that can lie behind anger in divorce. Anger is a piece of the emotional puzzle of grief, a part of letting go. Just as anger can be an expression of pain, attachment, fear, or guilt, anger also can be a sign of underlying grief.

Grief encompasses a number of powerful, painful, and sometimes overwhelming emotions, including not only anger but also intense longing and sadness. Much conflict in the couple's relationship also can be traced to partners who are in different places in their grief. They misunderstand each other's emotions, or lack of emotion, and are left grieving alone, in their own way. Finally, how former partners manage their own grief, or ignore it, can affect how they adjust as individuals over time to a separation and to life beyond divorce.

Yet stunningly, grief often goes unrecognized or unacknowledged in a divorce. For reasons we explore, divorcing partners often fail to identify their own grief, or their children's. Attorneys and mental health professionals also frequently overlook the grief that is central to many emotional and interpersonal conflicts in divorce. In so doing, we miss a critical opportunity to help our clients put a label on their jumbled emotions, and to deal with their feelings directly—rather than enacting them in interpersonal or legal disputes.[1]

A TIME OF LOSS

Yet, divorce is a huge loss. Divorce involves the loss of a lover, a mate, a partner. Divorce is the loss of your role as a husband or wife. Divorce makes many parents fear they will lose their children; it almost certainly means lost time and experiences with them. Divorce also may feel like the loss of your children's childhood, a shattering of dreams of giving children a loving, carefree, and innocent upbringing. Divorce means losing part of your extended family, many friends, and other connections and roles in the community. Divorce may involve the loss of your home, of cherished possessions, of savings, and of financial plans. Divorce can create a loss of control, a loss of trust, and a loss of security. And at its core, divorce is the loss of your hopes and dreams. These multiple losses mean that divorce is a time of grief—even if that grief is unrecognized or unacknowledged.

Even Elephants Grieve

Grief is a common, familiar, and expected reaction to loss. Even elephants grieve (Archer, 2001; Moss, 2000). Like the other emotional processes we have considered, grief is rooted in our nature and in our brains. However, grief also is a far more complex, human experience. The unfolding of grief, especially in divorce, is prolonged. And our cognitive, interpersonal, religious, and cultural methods of coping with loss complicate grief, even as these aids help us to understand and come to terms with loss, to say goodbye, to let go, and, eventually, to move on.

Many rituals surrounding death and bereavement encourage and support grief. In divorce, grief is ignored. As noted, many divorcing parents do not even realize that they are grieving. Others may squelch their feelings to protect themselves or perhaps the children. Friends, relatives, and even helping professionals also typically focus instead on the estranged partners' more apparent anger. Grief is a normal, healthy response to loss, but in divorce, grieving is overlooked rather than encouraged.

---

[1] Even experts somehow overlook grief in divorce. Grief often goes unmentioned in books on divorce, whether written for professionals or for parents. A major research handbook on grief does not even mention grieving in relation to any loss other than death (Stroebe, Hansson, Schut, & Stroebe, 2008).

A Potentially Revocable Loss

There is one more obstacle to grieving divorce, the biggest: Nothing is ever final in divorce, especially divorce with children. The possibility of reconciliation remains for children—and especially for former partners. Hope, however faint, can live on even after the legal divorce is final, even after many years have passed, even after one partner has remarried. If a loss may not be a loss, is there anything to grieve? If a loss is uncertain, when does grief start? If hope is not dead, do we have to kill it? When? How? In contrast to bereavement following death, these uncertainties mean that grief in divorce (and other potentially revocable losses) is likely to be delayed, interrupted, repeated, prolonged, and unresolved.

Of course, different people grieve in different ways, even within the same family. A key contributor to these differences in divorce is whether the loss is seen as revocable. The partner who leaves (the leaver) mostly sees the loss of divorce as final; the partner who is left (the left) desperately hopes it is not. The leaver and the left thus grieve in different ways, and these differences can lead to misunderstanding, conflict, and insensitivity to the children. For example, left parents may project their own feelings of devastation on to their children; leavers instead project relief.

But children's grief is likely to differ from either parent's. Over time, in fact, children may have less to grieve than their parents do. If both parents stay involved in children's lives, keep them out of the middle, and do their job as parents, children can lose less in divorce than parents fear. Children still can have a childhood.

STAGE THEORIES OF GRIEF

Grief has been characterized in many ways, but the work of attachment theorist John Bowlby clearly is the leading contribution. Bowlby's (1979) model of grief proceeds in four stages: (1) numbing, (2) yearning and protest, (3) disorganization and despair, (4) reorganization and detachment. That is, children and adults initially are numbed by a loss; they next try to bring about reunion with angry protest; failing this, they fall into a state of depression and confusion; and finally the despair is resolved by becoming detached. The special bond with the former attachment figure is lost, and the bereaved individual moves on with life, alone.

Elisabeth Kübler-Ross (1969) outlined a similar and popular stage theory of bereavement. Kübler-Ross's familiar stages proceed from denial to anger to bargaining to depression to acceptance. With the exception of bargaining, the content and sequencing are very similar to Bowlby's.

Not surprisingly, these strongly articulated theories of grief have been challenged. One valid criticism is that there is no single, right way to grieve. It is not necessary, for example, for all bereaved individuals to express intense emotions in order to cleanse themselves through grief. In fact, some people apparently benefit from "suffering in silence" (Bonanno, 2004; Wortman & Silver, 1989; 2001). Another critique is that grief does not proceed in neat stages. Descriptions of grief in terms of stage theories can be helpful: They are easy to understand, convey a sense of organization and control, and imply that grief is time-limited. Real grief is not so tidy, however.

To be fair, neither Bowlby nor Kübler-Ross viewed their stages as fixed or unchanging. Still, their stages of grief often are interpreted literally (Bonanno, 2004; Wortman & Silver, 1989; 2001). Moreover, neither theorist emphasized the constant cycling that seems to characterize many people's grief, particularly in response to potentially revocable losses like divorce (Emery, 1994).

A CYCLICAL THEORY OF GRIEF

I developed a different theory of grief based on my case observations (Emery, 1994). (As discussed shortly, we have since tested aspects of the model empirically.) In contrast to Bowlby and Kübler-Ross, my model of grief highlights: (1) the central role of emotion, particularly feelings of love, anger, and sadness; (2) the constant cycling back and forth among these apparently conflicting emotions; (3) the integration of seemingly opposing feelings over time; and specifically in relation to divorce/relationship dissolution, (4) differences in the grief of the partner who leaves versus the partner who is left, as well as (5) the interpersonal consequences of the partners' conflicting experience and expression of grief.

Love, Anger, and Sadness

Figure 3.1 illustrates some key aspects of my cyclical theory of grief. The most prominent feature is the three different emotions that comprise the major affective components of grief: love, anger, and sadness. These emotion labels are intended to have broad meaning. "Love" retains all of its usual, elusive meanings, but also includes intense longing, vague hopes for reconciliation, guilt-ridden concern about the former partner, and related emotions that cause one person to want to move closer to the other. "Anger" refers to a variety of related feelings including frustration, resentment, fury, and rage. Anger typically is felt toward and motivates one partner to want to act against the other, although anger is not necessarily accompanied by conflict. "Sadness" refers to a constellation of

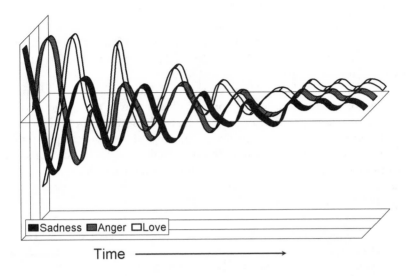

Time ——————————➤

FIGURE 3.1. Graphic representation of cyclical theory of grieving potentially revocable loss. Emotions swing between feelings of love, anger, and sadness. Note that emotions both diminish in intensity and come into phase over time.

associated feelings including loneliness, depression, and despair. Unlike anger, sadness is directed inward toward the self, rather than outward toward the other. Despite its inward focus, sadness still is an interpersonal signal. An expression of sadness says: "Help me."

The interpersonal motivations involved in love, anger, and sadness in grief are broadly akin to the well-known patterns of moving toward, against, and away from others as described by ego psychologist, Karen Horney (1939). The cycle of emotions also has obvious similarities with the theories of Bowlby and Kübler-Ross, which both include anger and sadness as stages of grief. A notable difference, however, is that my model includes swings back to loving/hopeful feelings not found in the other two theories, although Bowlby clearly assumes that love (attachment) is a precondition for grief.

Emotional Cycles

"Love" is absent from the theories of Kübler-Ross and Bowlby, because they were primarily concerned with irrevocable loss. There is no hope of corporeal reunion following death. Together with a few other theorists (e.g., Boss, 1999), I see grief as fundamentally different when it is a response to a potentially revocable loss. (Potentially revocable losses include but are not limited to divorce. Other examples include the grief, and renewed monthly hope, that can accompany efforts to get pregnant in the face of possible infertility, or the wild grief, and hope, surrounding a very serious, but uncertain, medical diagnosis.)

By definition, theories where grieving begins only after all hope is lost do not revisit the central "approach" emotion of love. The clear, if devastating, starting point of an irrevocable loss may make grief (seem to) proceed in one direction, in a series of stages. However, the possibility of revocable loss—of reunion in divorce—makes the limitations of stage theories clear when applied to that context. Feelings of love, anger, and sadness are revisited, over and over, as hope is repeatedly renewed—and repeatedly dashed.

This "emotional roller coaster," a term many people use to describe their experience, is central to my model of grief (see Figure 3.1). I recall, for example, a woman I saw in couple therapy. At one moment, she was professing her love for her husband—along with her commitment to work on her sarcasm and anger, a long-standing problem in her husband's eyes. When he interrupted to tell her gently, but firmly, that he was sorry but he wanted a divorce, his love had died, she immediately became enraged. She threatened him with devastating legal action. Yet, within a few minutes, she was in tears, wailing that she could not go on. Within minutes, her emotions swung from love to anger to sadness, all at full intensity. And this was only the beginning of a wild ride on the emotional roller coaster of grief.

"Stuck" on One Emotion

An important feature of such emotional swings, especially early in the process of grieving, is that people tend to feel, or focus on, only one emotion at any given point in time. When someone feels extreme anger, for example, he or she does not recognize the sadness or longing he or she also feels at some deeper level. Later, the hidden emotion surfaces—to the exclusion of the two other feelings.

In fact, some people get "stuck" on one feeling for a prolonged period of time. Either love, anger, or sadness dominates. The missing emotions may be felt, but the feelings are of lesser intensity and only last for a relatively brief time, at least in terms of the individual's conscious experience.

Thus, while we were concerned only with anger as a problematic "surface" emotion in Chapter 2, three problem styles characterize individual difficulties in grieving divorce. Some people get stuck on love; they seem to deny reality and endlessly hope for reconciliation. Others get stuck on anger, relentlessly pursuing punishment, vindication, or revenge.

Finally, many people get stuck on sadness, and become depressed, perhaps secretly blaming themselves for the failure of their marriage.

People may get stuck on one feeling for a number of reasons. Personality and mental health surely are important contributions. Someone prone to depression, for example, is surely more likely to get stuck on sadness. The other partner's behavior also can be a key influence. A partner who constantly fuels hope can encourage getting stuck on love; a selfish, hurtful partner encourages anger; a blaming, unfeeling partner may promote getting stuck on sadness. Importantly, time also is a key factor according to my model. As more time passes, most people eventually experience the full cycle of emotions (see Figure 3.1).

Time and Timing: The Leaver and the Left

Because time is key to the unfolding of grief, the left partner is more likely to be "stuck" near the time of the separation. The left partner may have only recently learned about the leaver's desire for a separation. Or even if he or she was aware of the intention, the left partner still may not have wanted or accepted the decision. This means the left partner's grief is likely to be fresh, raw, intense, and more likely to be dominated by one feeling.

Professionals need to recognize that the leaver also grieves. (It often is important for the left partner to recognize this too.) In many separations, however, the leaver began to grieve months or years earlier, when he or she first contemplated the possibility of ending the relationship. This means that leavers are likely to have cycled through feelings of love, anger, and sadness while still in their marriage, as they alternately pondered a separation, vowed to work on making things better, searched for alternatives, and eventually made concrete plans that may have included saving money, finding a new place to live, contacting a therapist and/ or lawyer, and perhaps starting a new relationship. The leaver, in other words, often has already moved through many of the cycles of grief by the time a couple separates. Leavers grieve, but their grief is less intense and less chaotic, because it began long ago.

Renewed, intense grief may await leavers, however, particularly if they failed to fully appreciate their losses (e.g., lost time with the children) or perhaps buried their grief in an affair. Affairs (or quick "rebound" relationships) can "cure" grief, but it is a cure akin to relieving a hangover with a shot of whiskey. Sooner or later, it seems, you have to deal with the pain. Moreover, the reality of a separation, and related practical and emotional complications, can quickly burst the fantasy of an affair. When this happens, leavers may find themselves facing real grief, perhaps for the first time.

Integrating Emotions

Despite the tendency to feel only one emotion at a time, the model as portrayed in Figure 3.1 is intended to suggest that people need to recognize and experience their "missing" or underlying emotions in order to progress through the cycles of grief. They need to look beyond their anger—or beyond their sadness or longing. Sooner or later, the hurt partner who is constantly holding out hope and waiting for the leaver to "come to her senses," needs to face reality, feel the anger that is a part of being hurt, and deal with his sadness over the loss. A partner who is stuck on anger, furious over the separation, eventually needs to let in their sadness and, still harder, feel the painful longing for their former spouse, their marriage, the feeling of family. When stuck on sadness, perhaps clinically depressed, a divorcing partner can move forward by admitting to reunion fantasies, and especially by recognizing and getting in touch with their anger, an energizing emotion that may help to counteract depression.

Yet, let me be clear on this last point. Getting in touch with your anger is not the same as acting on it. Divorced parents, and their individual therapists, need to take a systems perspective, to think beyond an individual parent's feelings (see Chapters 4 and 5). Expressing anger may temporarily help an adult to feel less depressed, or hurt, but parental anger and conflict create problems for children. Expressing anger also can hurt the left partner who needs to detach from the ex, not engage him or her.

Cutting across the Grain

The cycle of emotions suggests that, in addition to helping clients recognize their grief, professionals can help clients to experience their "missing" emotions. A therapist can draw out a depressed client's anger; a mediator can suggest, in caucus, that other emotions lie beneath the visible fury of a partner who has been left; a lawyer simply might recommend that a client "sleep on it," suggesting that he or she may have different feelings the next day about an aggressive, overly conciliatory, or passive plan of action.

I think of such strategies as cutting across the grain of expressed emotion. The goal is to help clients to identify, experience, and make better decisions based on their full range of feelings. Recognizing the anger behind depression, or the longing behind anger, does not mean that a client will act on the new emotion, or the old one. Rather, the goal is to help them to better understand their jumble of emotions, so they can make more rational decisions instead of emotionally impulsive ones. People cannot control all of their emotions intellectually, and trying to do so is a problem, not a solution. But divorcing parents can detach enough to make decisions that are not completely emotional. Ultimately, I ask them to do so for one reason: their children.

Time Heals

Two additional aspects of my model of grief also are illustrated in Figure 3.1. First, the intensity of emotions diminishes with time. Time does heal. The smaller, less overwhelming swings of emotion are a part of the healing process. Second, the apparently conflicting emotions eventually come into phase. That is, over time people increasingly recognize that they feel love, anger, *and* sadness. They begin to see that their feelings are not really in opposition (I either love him or I hate him), but are a part of a bigger process (grief). And even when one emotion comes to the forefront, there is a growing awareness of the other feelings, of the likelihood that the current emotion will not always predominate. For example, when a man is once again angered by his estranged wife's rejection, he is now more aware of the sadness and longing he also feels at some deeper level.[2] A single emotion no longer dominates in his grief.

Getting Over Grief

In fact, an important sign that people are getting over their grief is when they can recognize and experience all three emotions simultaneously. They are saddened by the loss of their marriage. They are angry about what has happened. Yet, they still have some good memories of a shared past, if only of the children produced by the couple's life together.

Time does heal. However, coping with grief is an emotionally intense task, one that is often prolonged[3] in divorce because of the potential impermanence of a separation, occasional sexual reuniting, or actual, if temporary, reconciliations. Even after a divorce is final, fantasies of reunion may live on. And while active grieving can end after a year or, more likely, two, I do not believe that the goal is ever to completely "get over" grief. Completely getting over grief means letting go of the

---

[2] He also should be more aware of the hurt that may provoke his anger more immediately. The different emotional processes we have discussed—for example, responding to pain, longing for reunion, and grief—are not mutually exclusive. They may be and often are activated simultaneously. I think of this as "emotional multitasking." Rejection causes immediate pain, for example, yet it also contributes to the broader process of grief.

[3] Many religious and cultural traditions suggest that active grief following the death of a loved one should come to an end after a year. The ambiguity of the loss means grief is likely to last longer in divorce.

good feelings, as well as the bad, and there are good feelings to preserve, if only those associated with having brought children into the world together.

Instead of "getting over it," my belief is that divorcing partners should work, over time, to diminish the intensity of their grief and the emotional swings associated it. The goal is for the feelings to grow small and manageable enough so that they have little effect on day-to-day relationships. Yet, grief may never disappear. Instead, grief can be revisited from time to time, as a way of preserving good feelings and remembering the lessons learned from bad ones.

STUDYING THE CYCLICAL MODEL OF GRIEF

The model of grief I have outlined is conceptually straightforward, if emotionally complex. However, like other emotional processes that unfold over time, vary from person to person, and differ from context to context, grief is challenging to study empirically.

Still, there is some empirical support for the model. My randomized trials of mediation and adversary settlement indicate that the model, which guided much of our approach to mediation (Emery, 1994; Emery, Shaw, & Jackson, 1987), produces many practical benefits, especially for parent–child relationships (see Chapter 9).

In the mediation studies, we also found that, 12 years later, feelings of longing were more intense, and conflict was less intense, among parents who mediated rather than litigated (Sbarra & Emery, 2005b, 2008; see Chapter 9). Parents who litigated got to indulge their anger. This may have eased the pain of longing, yet the "I never want to see you again!" approach to divorce came with a price. The litigation parents truly divorced their ex, and in the process, most of them also divorced their children: Nonresidential parent–child contact was infrequent (Emery et al., 2001).

In contrast, the mediation parents apparently did something emotionally unnatural. In negotiating a settlement, they focused more on their children than on their own anger. Even as the parents' intimate relationship came apart, they preserved their relationship as parents. Twelve years later, they reported less coparenting conflict even though they had many more opportunities to fight as a result of another important outcome: Following mediation, both parents remained far more involved in their children's lives than they did following litigation (Emery et al., 2001; see Chapter 9). The emotional cost, if it was a cost, was increased ambivalence about the end of the marriage. Or alternatively, maybe over the course of their children's childhoods, the mediation parents learned that their former spouse was a decent parent and maybe not such a jerk after all.

College Students' Grief over Relationship Loss

I also have been fortunate to supervise the dissertation of a former graduate student, David Sbarra, who designed a creative study to directly test my model of grief. The research supports some key aspects of the model—and illustrates some more general problems in studying grief as an emotional process (Stroebe et al., 2008).

Sbarra went to great lengths to conduct a rigorous study of grieving relationship dissolution. Ideally, such a study would enroll participants very soon after the breakup of their marriage, but we assumed that it would be impossible to recruit divorcing partners quickly enough. Instead, we did what academic psychologists often do as a substitute to studying "real people": We studied college students. Sbarra began the "Virginia Dating Study" and enlisted hundreds of undergraduate couples who had been dating for at least 4 months. But this was a sham study. The "dating study" really was designed to provide participants for Sbarra's real investigation of relationship dissolution. Students answered weekly e-mails about the status of their relationship, and, on learning that there had been or was about to be a breakup, Sbarra recruited people (both leavers and the left) into the real study of grieving relationship dissolution.

The dissolution study asked participants to complete a daily diary containing multiple item ratings of their ongoing feelings of love, anger, and sadness, as well as of autonomy/relief (Sbarra's unique, valuable idea). Moreover, to get an unbiased sample of emotions, Sbarra employed the experience sampling method. He gave participants a "beeper" and signaled them at random times between 10 A.M. and 10 P.M. They were told to complete the diary as soon as possible after hearing the beeper, which almost all participants did.

Sbarra's extensive data analysis combining all participants together supported some aspects of the model. For example, dynamic factor analysis strongly supported a three-factor solution of reported emotional experience—the factors were love, anger, and sadness. Furthermore, the dissolution sample reported more anger (anger *is* a part of grief) and more sadness, less love, and more variability in their emotions than did a comparison group of dating couples. Feelings of love and sadness also increased on days when the griever had contact with the former partner. And as time passed, the dissolution sample reported decreasing intensity and variability in their emotions. Finally, well-adjusted participants tended to experience all three emotions at once; poorly adjusted participants tended to experience love in the absence of other feelings. Alternatively, the combined analyses did not support other aspects of the model. In particular, the group data showed a monotonic decline in all emotions over time, rather than cycling across higher and lower intensities. The greatest declines in emotional intensity occurred in the first week after the breakup (Sbarra & Emery, 2005a; Sbarra, 2006; Sbarra & Ferrer, 2006).

Individual Patterns

Still, several patterns of emotional experience reported over 28 days by *individuals* look quite consistent with the theoretical model. One example can be seen in Figure 3.2, which shows the actual emotional swings reported by one grieving student next to the theoretical model from Figure 3.1. I offer no statistical evidence, but simply call attention to the general similarity between the theoretical model and the actual data reported by this one individual. Early on, feelings of love, anger, and sadness swing wildly and are out of phase. As grief proceeds, the emotions decrease in intensity and come into phase.

Figure 3.3 shows data from two more individuals. The first, "Stuck on Love," illustrates getting "stuck" on one emotion. This individual, who appears to be "keeping the candle burning," reported remarkably persistent feelings of love over the 28 days of completing the emotion

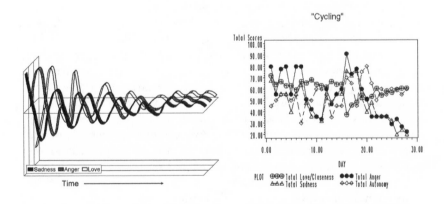

FIGURE 3.2. Theoretical model and one college student's actual report of feelings of love, anger, sadness, and relief/autonomy for 28 days following a breakup. Note the global similarity between the two figures, including wild mood swings and how emotions eventually come into phase.

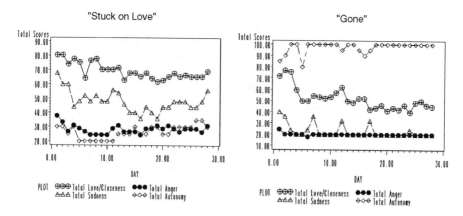

FIGURE 3.3. Very different patterns of grieving relationship loss for two college students. "Stuck on Love" (left) did not accept the relationship loss, but theoretically should cycle between love, anger, and sadness at some (unmeasured) future time. "Gone" (right) reported little negative emotion, but theoretically grieved at some (unmeasured) time in the past. Imagine a divorce involving "Gone" and "Stuck on Love." Such one-sided divorces are the source of many emotional and legal conflicts.

diary—along with some sadness and very little anger or feelings of autonomy.

The second graph, "Gone," illustrates how quickly grief can pass. This individual reported a little sadness following the breakup, together with some positive feelings toward the former dating partner. However, feelings of autonomy obviously dominated this person's experience of grief. In fact, "Gone" apparently "got over" his grief 3 days after the breakup.

Grieving Off the Chart

Was "Gone" really so cold and heartless? I presume not. According to my model, "Gone" actually began to grieve at some earlier point in time, off the chart to the left of the actual data. Much of "Gone"'s grieving was completed by the time he actually initiated the breakup. In a similar vein, my model predicts that "Stuck on Love" eventually would experience anger and sadness, in addition to loving feelings. But "Stuck on Love" would feel these new emotions only after accepting that the potentially revocable loss was, in fact, a loss. At some unmeasured future time, off the chart to the right of the actual data points, "Stuck on Love" should begin cycling through the emotions of grief as portrayed in my model.

We cannot know if these predictions are right, of course, but one thing is clear from the data: There are great individual differences in the experience of grief following a breakup. This leads us to an interesting thought experiment. Imagine a breakup in which "Gone" is divorcing "Stuck on Love." I predict fireworks. One-sided breakups are painful, volatile, and emotionally complicated, much more so than mutual partings. One of the most important complications in a one-sided divorce is that the two partners are in different "places" in their grief. This creates conflict about how one partner is, or is not, grieving and how the other partner thinks he or she should be feeling.

DIFFERENT CYCLES OF GRIEF
FOR THE LEAVER AND THE LEFT

As highlighted in Chapter 1, our thought experiment about "Stuck on Love" and "Gone" is the painful and complicated reality for many divorcing couples. Many custody disputes, often the most acrimonious ones, are not caused by the legal and practical complications of parenting apart. Instead, the emotions involved in a one-sided divorce are the source of the former partners' intense, irrational anger. The different ways in which the leaver and the left grieve is one, central dilemma in one-sided breakups.

Different Places in Grief

One key difference is that the leaver's grief is far less intense than the left partner's grief. Unlike what the left partner may claim, the leaver does have feelings. But emotion may seem absent, because the leaver's grieving began long ago, before the separation. The grief of the leaver is akin to bereavement following a long, chronic illness. When a loved one dies after a prolonged and trying illness, family members grieve, but they also feel a measure of relief. For them, and for the leaver, this leads to a lessening of the intensity of their emotions when the end finally comes.

The left partner, in contrast, has had little time, if any, to prepare for the loss. As a result, his emotions are wild, intense, and unpredictable. His grief is analogous to someone whose loved one has been in a train wreck. His marriage is in the emergency room, and in very serious condition, but still hanging on despite grim predictions. Any sign of hope, or of giving up, can provoke powerful, untamed surges of love, anger, or sadness. But because there is still hope, the left partner may not yet have begun to grieve, or perhaps may not yet have to admit or identify his emotions as grief.

Rejection versus Guilt

The leaver's and the left's grief also differ in their dominant emotional theme. In general, the leaver's grief is shaded with guilt, while rejection colors the grief of the partner who was left.

Guilt and rejection accelerate each partner's cycling through love, anger, and sadness. Consider what might happen, beneath the surface, during an exchange of the children. The left party approaches the exchange searching for signs of hope in a friendly interaction. Instead, the leaver is cold, distant, and distracted. Whether this is intentional, or just a bad day, the left party is hurt, perceiving the icy exchange as another rejection. Thus, her hope for reconciliation is transformed into anger. Anger fades into self-blame and sadness, however, as the intensity of the hurt subsides over time. Now, seeing the rejection for what it is, the left partner becomes depressed. Later, the leaver apologizes for having been preoccupied, explaining that it was just a bad day after all. To the left, this means that perhaps all hope is not lost. Her reconciliation fantasies are renewed—only to be dashed by more rejection and more pain, as the left's grief remains stuck in a relentless spin cycle (see Figure 3.4).

Guilt, not rejection, drives the leaver around his emotional roundabout. For example, guilt can turn anger into sadness if the leaver blames himself for being grumpy during the exchange. Perhaps this reminds him of bigger mistakes he has made. The heavy burden of guilt feeds the

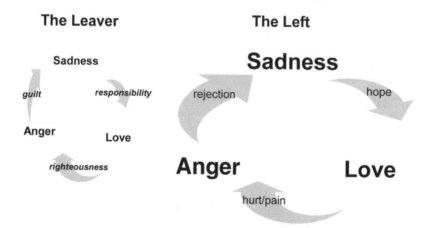

FIGURE 3.4. Different cycles of grief for the leaver and the left. Note the different intensities of grief (indicated by size) and differences in the feelings that lead to switches between love, anger, and sadness. The leaver's grief is tinged with guilt, while rejection colors the grief of the left.

leaver's growing sense of responsibility, converting sadness into a dutiful resolve to "do the right thing." Caring feelings are transformed back into anger, however, as the leaver has second thoughts about his second thoughts. He internally justifies his decision to leave, fueling a growing sense of righteousness. For a time, the leaver believes, again, that he is the one who was wronged—by the estranged spouse, or perhaps by life. Over time, however, the leaver's externalized blame is refocused inwardly, perhaps in response to seeing the suffering of the former spouse, the children, or maybe in response to a critical comment by a friend. Guilt again dominates, as the leaver's grief follows its own relentless, if less intense, cycle of love, anger, and sadness (see Figure 3.4).

Grief and Conflict

One unfortunate aspect of the leaver's and the left's different emotional triggers is that the two former partners rarely experience the same feelings at the same time. If they did, they might be able to reconcile or perhaps grieve together. Instead, their differences lead each partner to question the other's feelings, wondering why the other partner does not feel the same way that they feel. The left party sees the leaver as uncaring. The leaver sees the left as unable to cope.

There is one positive in this emotional morass. As each partner begins to accept the end of the marriage and resolve their active grief, conflict should diminish. Thus, addressing their own grief not only can help to move the former partners forward as individuals, but it also can help to diminish coparenting conflict.

Some couples give each other the time to grieve and devote emotional energy to grieving while they are still together. A separation is relatively uncomplicated for these couples, because their most intense emotions are resolved or at least under control. For one-sided or more impulsive divorces, however, the trick for professionals, and for the couple, is how to manage negotiating an agreement, relating to each other as parents, and coming to terms with the possibility that the loss might be permanent, while the partners are still in the middle of their grief.

EMOTION REGULATION, MEANING MAKING, AND A NEW IDENTITY CRISIS

Psychologists (and economists and philosophers) have long debated the respective roles of, and battles between, emotion and cognition, passion and rationality. The debates were answered for me in mediation. Emotion wins. Raw emotions are primal, powerful, irrational, confusing, and in the moment, often destructive and sometimes irresistible. Emotions are basic in evolution, in the brain, and in divorce.

Recognizing and Regulating Emotions

Emotion is more basic, but the cortex—cognition—also is critical. Within limits, we can regulate our emotions intellectually and in relationships. (Yet, another dilemma in divorce is that, for many people, the biggest aid in emotional regulation is your intimate partner [Coan, 2008]). Still, divorcing partners *can* act rationally despite their powerful, emotional impulses—and the loss of their emotional copilot. If people could not at least partially regulate their emotions, there would be little hope for mediation (or society).

As a first step toward emotion regulation, divorcing partners benefit from at least *recognizing* their emotions, for example, realizing that they are grieving or in pain. Recognition is a beginning. Recognition allows us to regain at least a small sense of control. And feeling in control, sometimes even in the illusion of control, eases coping with all kinds of stress, including loss (Sbarra & Emery, 2006). Emotions like grief are more tolerable, less overwhelming, when we know what we are feeling and why.

The Zen of Emotion

A second step toward emotion regulation is to learn, and to believe, that your feelings are normal. In divorce, it is *normal* to be hurt, angry, and to want to hurt back. Normalizing the affective experience can help people to accept their feelings, rather than resisting them. And recognition and acceptance are essential for embracing what I think of as the Zen of emotion. We gain control over our emotions by *not* fighting them. We gain control by recognizing, legitimizing, and experiencing our feelings.

Here's a simple, everyday example of this point, one that does not require a Zen master to comprehend. What statement puts you more at ease during a tense job interview? "Relax. There's nothing to be nervous about!" or "It's OK to be nervous." I vote for the latter. We can gain control over our emotions by accepting and not trying to completely control them. This is one reason why I emphasize that mediation asks parents to do something emotionally *unnatural*. It really is OK to be angry in mediation—and giving our clients permission to be angry can help calm their urgent need to express it.

A third step toward emotion regulation is to learn about the typical course of emotional adjustment. Again, there is a Zen quality to this process. We both gain control and accept our lack of control if we believe, for example, that our grief will proceed logically, in a series of orderly stages, or that it will be over in about a year (as many religious traditions suggest in the case of bereavement). My model of grieving divorce is a rough road map in comparison to stage theories, yet even the image of an emotional roller coaster, one where the ups and downs eventually even out, still offers some sense of predictability. And, I think, it also has the advantage of describing the experience more accurately.

Bare Beginnings

Of course, mediators and other divorce professionals most commonly work with clients in the immediate aftermath of a failed marriage, when emotions are raw and anger dominates grief, pain, longing, fear, and guilt. All anyone can reasonably expect of parting parents when we, and they, are negotiating a divorce settlement is the bare beginnings of emotion regulation. I count it as a success when, in this time of turmoil, divorcing parents identify their feelings, accept their inevitability and limited control, and make a sincere, ongoing effort to regulate their affect at least in the presence of each other and the children.

Dispute resolution clients are not with us long enough to see them through their grief. Yet, it still is worth asking: What emotional tasks lie ahead as the bumps even out, after hurdling through the worst ups and downs on the emotional roller coaster of divorce? Our clients may ask us precisely this question, or we may see them years later, perhaps when new disputes and issues arise, for example, in regard to remarriage and relocation.

Emotional Understanding

The main challenges ahead involve learning to live and parent apart—that is, to renegotiate family relationships, topics that form the focus of Chapters 4 and 5. For the divorced parent as an individual, however, perhaps the central task is attaining some degree of emotional understanding. Emotional understanding is a good term for this undertaking, because it connotes, as I intend it to, both an intellectual understanding of one's emotions and the formulation of emotion-laden beliefs about one's experiences. Emotion-laden beliefs are "hot cognitions," that is, emotionally charged views as opposed to emotion-free, purely intellectual "cold cognitions."

Figure 3.5 summarizes my conceptualization of the steps involved in achieving emotional understanding. The steps range from a dawning awareness that the divorce is, in fact, happening to a broad understanding

Disbelief   Dawning   Resignation   Acceptance   Meaning Making

FIGURE 3.5. Five steps involved in achieving an emotional understanding of loss. Vacillation occurs mainly between adjacent steps, thus the process can be thought of as proceeding in stages.

of the many losses involved in divorce (and perhaps some potential gains) to its ultimate meaning for your family and especially for yourself.

Unlike the cyclical model of emotional grief, I conceptualize the steps involved in achieving emotional understanding as being stage-like. The back and forth—and there is a lot of back and forth—generally is between adjacent steps. Achieving emotional understanding is not a roller coaster. It's a stairway, a "two steps forward, one step back" stairway.

Emotional understanding obviously is connected to the emotional cycle of grief, but I view the two as parallel processes. The emotional cycling is the *real* grief, the basic emotional reactions to loss that we share in common with other mammals. Emotional understanding is the separate, more intellectual process of observing, trying to control, and seeking to understand our emotional experiences. Emotional understanding is human. It uses our unique cortex to make sense of our experience.

Disbelief

Disbelief is the first, very shaky step toward achieving emotional understanding. Disbelief is similar to the stage of denial described by Bowlby (1979) and Kübler-Ross (1969). I prefer the term "disbelief," because denial connotes an active attempt to shut out reality. Disbelief is not effortful. Disbelief is a sense of unreality: "This is *not* happening!" Shock, numbing, and feelings of unreality comprise our immediate, limited understanding of a sudden loss or trauma.

Dawning

The second step in the model is dawning. Dawning is a beginning of allowing reality to enter consciousness. Dawning is, "This *might* be happening to me! Oh no. This *is* happening to me!" Still, dawning is as tentative as the term suggests. As we struggle to face reality, we frequently return from dawning back to "No! This is *not* happening."

Resignation

Resignation is a grudging acceptance of reality. "This happened and it's not fair." When resignation surfaces as a part of the blame game (see Chapter 2), it takes the form of "*You* did this to me!" Resignation is a battle of imagined alternatives to reality, a series of "if only … , then … " possibilities. Cognitive psychologists call these fantasies *upward counterfactual reasoning* (Fleming & Robinson, 2001). "If only I had married someone different, my life would be happy now." Upward counterfactual reasoning changes reality by changing the past. But because it is a fantasized attempt to change reality, upward counterfactual reasoning also is a coming to grips with reality.

Acceptance

Acceptance is "This has happened" with no italics and no exclamation point. Acceptance often involves *downward* counterfactual reasoning, imagining "it could have been worse" scenarios. "I'm glad I took the high road, because at least my kids are doing OK." Acceptance also includes an embrace of one's own contributions to a divorce, or at least one's failings or imperfections in a marriage. Responsibility in a failed marriage rarely is a 50/50 proposition, but it rarely is 100/0, either.

Like all the adjacent steps with two-headed arrows (see Figure 3.5), people battle back and forth between resignation and acceptance, between blame and accepting responsibility. And achieving emotional understanding can take a long time: years, perhaps many years. For example, one partner may not get to acceptance until their former spouse remarries. A remarriage may be the final symbol that the divorce really is irrevocable. The marriage is done. For some people, unfortunately, even a former spouse's remarriage is not the end. Some people never make it to acceptance.

Meaning Making

Meaning making, the highest level of emotional understanding, is the broader, sometimes spiritual process of coming to grips with pain, grief, and loss. Meaning making involves not only accepting the occurrence and the consequences of a very difficult life experience (divorce), but also finding meaning, even value, in having endured adversity. Meaning making is not simply "turning lemons into lemonade," that is, focusing on the good parts of a bad experience. Meaning making is broader and more abstract, and includes lessons learned both from growth and from pain.

Janoff-Bulman (1992) argues that the experience of grief or trauma threatens three fundamental assumptions we make: (1) the world is a benevolent place, (2) the world is meaningful, that is, the world "makes sense," and (3) the self is worthy. Meaning making involves finding new reasons to hold on to the first two assumptions. (We turn to the third shortly.) Meaning making may involve a sense of discovery ("I am stronger than I thought") or growth ("I no longer take life for granted") or some similarly abstract benefit of living through pain ("I found out who my real friends are," "I renewed my connection to God").

Finding meaning in loss is very much an individualized task, one that typically unfolds over years. Professionals, even therapists, are likely to be dismissed as glib if they suggest, when a client is in the throes of divorce, that that they need to find meaning in their struggles—or even acceptance of them. At the most, a professional might offer a very general suggestion about perspectives to come. "I'd like to talk to you in a few years to see if you feel the same way." Such statements suggest change, but leave the details for a distraught client to ponder, if they are even able to do that much.

Identity Conflict: "Who Am I—Now?"

What about Janoff-Bulman's (1992) third challenged assumption, that the self is worthy? Questioning your worth, your very identity, often becomes a focus of internal struggle during and in the aftermath of divorce. Identity is our sense of self, our life story, the cohesive, internal narrative we internally "write" about ourselves (Pasupathi, 2001). Erik Erikson's (1959) ideas about the adolescent identity crisis are relevant here. Our identity is the composite answer to the question, "Who am I?"

We do not have one identity, but multiple identities corresponding to our various life roles. This makes identity more fluid than fixed. Our identity changes throughout life as we abandon old roles and assume new ones. Divorce is a prime example, because it typically forces adults in midlife to redefine who they are, much like they once grappled with that question during the transition to adulthood. To paraphrase Erikson, the central question becomes, "Who am I ... now?"

The Label "Divorced"

One simple example of such identity conflict is incorporating the label "divorced" into your definition of self. I have had clients grapple for years with the "divorced" label. More personally, my own separation in 1989 went unmentioned in the 1994 edition of this book. Integrating the idea of being divorced is challenging, in part, because the descriptor is dissonant with the definitions of self we construct. Divorce is not a life experience that many people plan on becoming a part of their own lives, or their children's. "Graduate degree at 26," "Great job at 27," "Married at 29," "First child at 30" is the sort of social clock that many people set for themselves. "Divorced at 35" would be an unusual event to include in the planning.

Lost Roles, New Roles

More complex challenges to identity in divorce arise as a result of lost roles and the need to assume new roles, or revamp old ones, in family, social, and work life. Divorce means that you are no longer a husband or a wife, so who are you now? Singlehood, dating, and all that entails are difficult for many people to quickly embrace as a part of a new definition of self. And divorce brings about the loss of or changes in other, important role identities too: as an in-law, a member of certain social groups, perhaps as a homeowner, or feeling like an effective parent. Difficulties in performing new roles are particularly likely to challenge identity. Much of the difficulty in identifying oneself as a competent single parent, for example, comes from the very real struggles involved in competently parenting alone.

Many life roles are more informal than "wife," "mother," or "law firm partner," but informal roles also can be vital to our identity. We all identify ourselves, in part, based on assumed roles in our families or in other key relationships. We are called, and come to see ourselves, as "the smart one," "the pretty one," "the caring one," "the reliable one," and so on. Our sense of self may depend deeply on these social roles, and these too can be challenged by divorce. For example, how does someone with the lifelong role of being "the responsible one" integrate their decision to leave a marriage into a cohesive sense of self?

Another challenge to identity is uncertainty about how, or if, we are supposed to act differently following separation or divorce. A prime example is dating, which would seem to be a normal part of life after divorce. But dating is greatly complicated by considerations that may be emotional (e.g., anxiety), interpersonal (e.g., do you tell your ex you're dating?), practical (e.g., do you introduce your kids to your date?), or legal (e.g., many jurisdictions frown on overnight "guests"). Such complications can cause severe doubts about a role that many adults were glad to be "done" with when they got married.

And dating is hardly the only unclear role after divorce. Stepparenting is another prime example. Romantically involved lovers, cohabiting partners, and stepparents all need to figure out how they, or their new partners, are supposed to relate to the children, how they should relate to the ex(es), and perhaps how two sets of children should relate to each other.

Multiple Role Identities

The extent to which divorce creates identity conflict and necessitates a redefinition of self depends both on one's roles in the marriage and on the magnitude of change brought about by divorce. Divorce can cause more identity conflict when the transition entails more financial pressures, lost contact with the children, diminished social support, or similar upheavals. In addition, the more closely one's roles and role identities had been tied to a marriage, the more a divorce challenges one's sense of self. A woman who viewed her primary roles as being a wife, mother, and homemaker, for example, will go through considerable redefinition of self as a result of divorce. In contrast, a woman who has had other central role identities, for example, as a friend, daughter, and schoolteacher, will have more stability in her sense of self. The continuity in these identities can temper and modulate the changes that divorce necessitates. In fact, a composite identity—one that is based on several different roles, each of which is significant, but none of which is paramount—is probably an important protective factor through the chaos of most major life transitions.

SUMMARY

Grief is important to recognize not only because it lies beyond anger, but also because grief is central to many aspects of divorce. Grieving divorce is different from "normal" grief, because the loss is potentially revocable. This sets partners off into potentially wild cycles of love, anger, and sadness, an emotional roller coaster with no clear demarcations about when the bumps will smooth out. Another complication is that the leaver and the left typically are in different "places" in their grief. The leaver's loss is more tempered, akin to grief following the death of a loved one after a long, chronic illness. In contrast, the left's grief can be out of control, like the crazy, intense emotions of someone whose loved one is in the emergency room after a train wreck. While the emotions often are chaotic, parents and professionals can gain a degree of control by recognizing and legitimizing grief. In this way, parents can be helped to make less impulsive, more rational decisions that put children first, while allowing themselves the time to work through their loss, perhaps find meaning in it, and eventually integrate the painful experience into a new sense of self.

4

RENEGOTIATING RELATIONSHIPS I
Separating Marital and Parental Roles

Never cut what you can untie.
—Joseph Joubert

The legal task of negotiating a parenting plan[1] is inseparable from the psychological task of renegotiating family relationships. On the one hand, many parents struggle to resolve custody and other disputes, not so much because they disagree about the children, but because of their own issues. As we have explored, the leaver and the left bring opposing emotional agendas to settlement negotiations. Anger often covers up deeper feelings, so the parents' disputes are indirect. Many conflicts about the children in day-to-day parenting, mediation, legal negotiations, and even court battles really are enactments of the parents' old conflicts and ongoing emotional struggles.

On the other hand, a parenting plan is not only a legal settlement but also an important step toward redefining family relationships. A well-constructed parenting plan explicitly details when parents and children

---

[1] A "parenting plan" is a detailed agreement about legal and physical custody, schedule details (e.g., holidays), communication, and dispute resolution. Many jurisdictions have templates for creating individualized parenting plans (see Chapter 6).

will spend time together, and outlines basic rules of coparenting. Implicitly, the plan also limits the former partner's interaction to one domain: coparenting.

Because negotiating agreements and renegotiating relationships are intertwined, ADR professionals need to understand both sets of issues. Chapters 6, 7, and 8 discuss legal issues and dispute-resolution techniques. This chapter focuses on renegotiating the relationship between former partners who remain parents. Their overriding task and goal is to separate their relationship as parents, a relationship that is going to continue, from their relationship as husband and wife, which is coming to an end.

Chapter 5 outlines various goals and challenges in renegotiating parent–child relationships, as well as the triangle which includes each parent and their child(ren). Parent–child relationships and the parents' relationship are knotted tightly together in a marriage. In a divorce, one goal is to loosen that knot (see Figure 5.2).

RENEGOTIATING FAMILY RELATIONSHIPS: BASIC CONCEPTS

Parents must renegotiate their relationship in a divorce. Many estranged partners find this observation more than ironic, because at least one of them is trying to *end* the relationship. However, partners who are also parents can never fully divorce. When children are involved, former spouses inevitably must maintain a relationship in some form. Going forward, parents must determine practicalities such as how to exchange the children, how to share basic information about them, how to act when everyone is present at some event, and how to coparent—together, independently, or in opposition to each other.

Former partners can develop a cooperative, a distant, or an angry coparenting relationship (Ahrons, 1995; Emery, 2006; Hetherington & Kelly, 2002; Maccoby & Mnookin, 1992).[2] However, even an angry relationship is a relationship. In fact, intense conflict is a sign of an overly involved relationship, not an overly distant one. (I explain why shortly.) For the children's sake, former partners hopefully learn to cooperate or at least to respect each other's boundaries in a more distant coparenting relationship. To do so, they must let go of their

---

[2] These authors and others have developed useful typologies of divorced couples, often based on variations in parental conflict and cooperation. I do not delve far into these details here, although I have elsewhere (Emery, 2006), as my present focus is on normative developmental processes within families, not individual differences between families.

troubled relationship as spouses, while redefining and building on their relationship as parents.

The Divorced Family Is a Family

One reason why parents must renegotiate their relationship in divorce is because each parent and the children form the vertices of an enduring family triangle. Marriage and parenting are tied together in two-parent families (Cowan & Cowan, 1999; Emery & Tuer, 1993), and parent–parent and parent–child relationships remain connected in divorce. For example, extensive research shows that children are adversely affected by their parents' conflict (Cummings & Davies, 2010; Emery, 1982; Grych & Fincham, 1990). And children are a part of the family triangle even when conflict is absent, or for that matter, even when *contact* is nonexistent. The "other" parent is psychologically present even when physically absent, as indexed by the messages children carry back and forth, the questions parents ask, or simply by what is *not* discussed about one parent in the presence of the other.

In short, the divorced family is still a family, a family defined by shared relationships, not a shared residence. In fact, most children from divorced families list *both* parents as members of their family, even though their parents rarely include the former spouse in the list (Peterson & Zill, 1986). Whether they think of each other as family members or not, conceptually and practically, the feelings, thoughts, and actions of divorced family members cannot be understood apart from a family system that extends across households.

Boundaries in Relationships

Family systems theory, particularly the structural family therapy perspective (Minuchin, 1974; Minuchin, 1985), offers some valuable concepts for describing how relationships are renegotiated in divorce. The concept of boundaries is particularly useful. *Boundaries* are rules that define limits around relationships, often unstated rules. Interpersonal boundaries are akin to the boundaries that divide the territory of two nations. Interpersonal boundaries mark *psychological* territory, however, and they are more subtle, flexible, and complex than international boundaries.

The boundary of interpersonal space offers a concrete illustration of the construct. Unstated social rules dictate acceptable physical proximity in social interaction. In fact, subtly different rules about physical proximity apply to different relationships and across different cultures. As with other psychological boundaries, rules about interpersonal space are most apparent when they are violated. We are uncomfortable, perhaps frightened, when a stranger stands too close. Our psychological space, our territory, has been invaded.

More subtle rules govern family relationships. The boundary around a typical marital relationship, for example, is defined, in part, by topics that parents do not discuss in front of their children (e.g., sex, money, personal conflicts). Like acceptable physical proximity, family rules are not usually negotiated explicitly. Still, the rule becomes obvious when it is broken. For example, when one parent brings up an "adult" topic in front of the children, everyone recognizes that an invisible line has been crossed. Similarly, parents who ask teenagers embarrassing questions about dating are likely to provoke an angry defense of the adolescent's territory of autonomy. In many families, parents and children, even adult children, will not discuss topics like money, death, and inheritances. Doing so means "crossing a line you're not supposed to cross."

Divorce: Crumbled Boundaries

A huge problem in divorce is that the family's boundaries have crumbled and may be in dispute. No one knows where they stand in relation to each other. And different family members are likely to want different rules, different relationships. Typically, the central conflict is intense debate about distance, or closeness, in the relationship between the former partners.

Couples sometimes negotiate new boundaries directly, as might occur in couples or family therapy. Without good professional guidance, however, separating spouses rarely are so direct. Instead, they negotiate through their actions. For example, one partner telephones the other late at night to find out if they are home, or alone, or just to see if they are willing to talk, or argue, at an inconvenient hour. Unfortunately, many of these conflicts occur in the children's presence or over topics that concern the children, because the children tie the parents together. The children are an excuse for contact.

Like labor and management in a heated strike, moreover, estranged partners sometimes use increasingly strong words and dramatic actions to try to force through a change, or to keep things the same. This further disrupts family life for everyone, especially children. And as negotiations break down, parents may violate even old, well-established boundaries. A parent may end up "explaining" divorce to their children, for example, by sharing intimate details about their marriage, or perhaps by making inappropriate accusations about the other parent.[3]

---

[3] Elsewhere, I have outlined scripts about what parents might tell children of different ages about the reasons for a divorce. All are rated "G" or "PG" (Emery, 2006).

Building New Boundaries

Unclear boundaries are a major source of emotional distress and inter-personal conflict in divorce. Thus, an overriding goal of helping family members to renegotiate their relationships is helping them to build new, clear boundaries, particularly around the potentially volatile relationship between the former partners who remain parents.

The parents' schedule for spending time with their children is one of the most important, new boundaries. As with other rules, its significance is particularly obvious when it is violated. A father who fails to pick up his children as planned violates an essential rule of his relationship with his children. Similarly, a mother violates parent–child boundaries when she pops by for an unscheduled visit during her children's time with their father. Both actions also cross boundaries in the relationship between the former partners.

This last point is critical. A parenting plan explicitly defines boundaries in parent–child relationships. As noted earlier, moreover, a parenting plan also implicitly defines boundaries in the *parents'* relationship. The plan implies that the former partners will *not* be in contact, except, as needed, about the children. In mediation, I typically make this implicit rule explicit, but that is getting ahead of the story.

Love and Power

Nations define borders around geographical territory, but what makes up the psychological territory of family relationships? With its overriding emphasis on process over content, family systems theory offers few answers to this important question. Over 15 years ago, however, I began arguing that love and power are the two major substantive domains of family relationships (Emery, 1992). I stand by that position. Family members construct boundaries around psychological territories of love and power.

My emphasis on love and power as basic dimensions of relationships seemed unique when I first conceived this scheme. In fact, however, numerous psychologists and psychological specialties have highlighted these two relationship dimensions. Ethologists view dominance (power) and affiliation (love) as the basic dimensions of relationships among social animals (Sloman, Gardner, & Price, 1989). Ego psychologist Harry Stack Sullivan (1953), interpersonal theorist Timothy Leary (1957), and their followers (Benjamin, 2002; Plutchik & Conte, 1997; Wiggins, 1982) constructed a theory of personality around the two dimensions. A metaphorical interpretation of Freud's intrapsychic instincts, sex (love) and aggression (power), yields the same relationship domains (Cameron &

Rychlak, 1985). Finally, the dimensions of love and power form the foundation of the most widely accepted classification of parenting styles used by developmental psychologists (Baumrind, 1971; Maccoby & Martin, 1983; Parke & Buriel, 1998).

Love and Power Defined

I intend the terms *love* and *power* to have broad meaning (Emery, 1992). Love refers to emotional closeness in general. The dimension can be used to characterize businesslike relationships, which are low in emotional closeness, as well as intensely intimate relationships between lovers and spouses. I should note, however, that my definition of love differs from Sullivan's. Sullivanian theorists place love and hate at opposite poles of a continuum of intimacy. I place love and hate next to one another at one end of the continuum. Disinterest is the polar opposite of *both* of these intense feelings (see Figure 4.1). Thus, the key to my definition is emotional intensity, not emotional valence (Emery, 1992). Love and hate are both intense emotions. Disinterest is so low in intensity that it is, at most, mildly positive or mildly negative.

Power is supposed to flow from designated authority, but I define it in terms of actual social influence. A forceful parent holds much power in a family, but so might a coercive child. In the absence of conflict, interpersonal power is akin to the ethological concept of dominance: holding generally uncontested privileges that are not held by others. During conflicts, power is defined as having control over the outcome of disputes. In dyadic conflict, power usually is indexed by winning and losing, but a more powerful party occasionally may "let" a less powerful party win some battles (e.g., when a parent lets a toddler win a minor tantrum). In

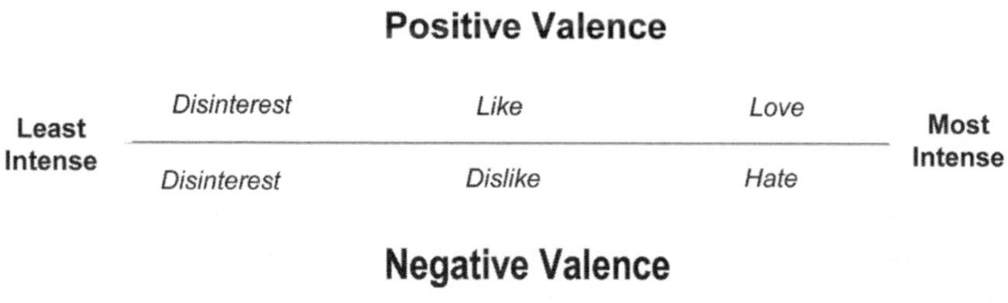

Positive Valence

	Disinterest	*Like*	*Love*
Least Intense			**Most Intense**
	Disinterest	*Dislike*	*Hate*

Negative Valence

FIGURE 4.1. A continuum of love (emotional closeness) in relationships. Love and hate together anchor one pole. Both emotions involve greater emotional intensity and indicate greater emotional investment. The opposite of both love and hate is disinterest.

triadic conflict, a third party who directs the dispute resolution process may be the most powerful (e.g., a judge, a mediator). Thus, for example, a child who mediates parental disputes is in a powerful (and developmentally inappropriate) position in the family (Emery, 1992).

Power Struggles and Love Struggles

Family members sometimes argue directly about love or power, but they more typically dispute specific issues. Parents and children argue more about bedtimes or curfews than about parental authority or adolescent autonomy. Former partners argue more about late-night telephone calls, or unfaithfulness, than about whether they still harbor feelings for one another.

Yet, any given argument is about more than what may be apparent on the surface. As family members resolve specific disputes, at a deeper level the resolution helps to define love and power boundaries (Emery, 1992). When parents enforce bedtimes, for example, they reinforce (or establish) their authority in addition to getting youngsters to sleep. Similarly, when a divorced partner refuses to speak to a former spouse except during a scheduled time, at one level they are simply avoiding annoying interruptions. At a deeper level, however, they are redefining the boundary of love in their relationship. The refusal indicates that their relationship now is more distant and formal, more businesslike.

The distinction between two levels of meaning, one on the surface and a second, deeper one, is analogous to two stags competing for dominance. At one level, the stags fight for the opportunity to mate with a given female. At a deeper level, however, the stags are competing for much more: dominance. Similarly, when divorced family members fight about some specific issue, the dispute and its potential resolution holds both a surface and a deep meaning. The deep meaning of conflict and its resolution always is a meta-communication about love and/or power boundaries. All family conflicts are either power struggles or love struggles at this deeper level of analysis (Emery, 1992).

Five Goals for Boundaries in Divorced Families

The discussion of boundaries and of love and power brings us to my fundamental thesis about the family dynamics of divorce. Divorce entails *the renegotiation of love and power boundaries in the system of family relationships*. In working with divorcing families, I have five broad goals for renegotiating family relationships:

- First, help (in therapy) or encourage (in ADR) parents to rebuild their own, individual boundaries of love and power by, respectively, working through grief and resolving renewed identity conflicts (Chapter 3).

- Second, establish clear, emotionally distant boundaries in the former partner's relationship, that is, develop a more "business-like" coparenting relationship (this chapter).

- Third, weaken the connection between parent–child and parent–parent relationships, making divorced family boundaries look like two overlapping circles, both of which include the children (this chapter, Chapter 5).

- Fourth, maintain, reestablish, or create clear boundaries of love and power (parental authority) in the relationships between children and each of their parents (Chapter 5).

- Fifth, renegotiate relationships with as little conflict and as quickly as possible, while being realistic about the "as possible" qualification (entire book).

Disentangling Marital and Parental Roles

Parents do not divorce their children, and because of this, they can never completely divorce each other. Children form a continuing tie between former spouses, who remain parents throughout their lives. Thus, former partners must disentangle their continuing role as parents from their past role as spouses.

Parents' first step toward separating their marital and parental roles is recognizing and beginning to address their grief, as we discussed in Chapter 3. In fact, parents' central task in defining new boundaries around themselves as individuals is achieving some resolution of grief and identity conflict. At the same time, the former partners also need to redefine the boundaries of love and power in their relationship.

RENEGOTIATING THE BOUNDARY
OF LOVE BETWEEN FORMER SPOUSES

The boundary of love between a husband and wife obviously changes in a divorce. What is less obvious is that the parents need to negotiate a *new* love boundary. Quick attempts to redefine the relationship may include cutting off all communication, trying to "be friends," provoking jealousy, or a sexual reuniting. But quick fixes are unlikely to become lasting solutions. In fact, the renegotiation of the parents' love boundary can take years to complete. Yet, for many families, redefining the boundary of love between former partners who remain parents is the key to renegotiating *all* family relationships.

The Leaver and the Left

As we have discussed, a basic reason why former partners struggle with renegotiating their relationship is because most divorces are one-sided (Braver et al., 2006). The leaver wants out of the marriage; the left wants it to continue. This means that each partner wants a very different love boundary.

The leaver wants the marriage to end, but he or she may still hope to "be friends." Why? The wish may be motivated by guilt, concerns about the children, or genuine caring for the former spouse. Or the leaver may want to be friendly so that the legal negotiations will proceed smoothly and quickly.

The problem, of course, is that the left partner is unlikely to want to be friends—or to quickly wrap up a legal settlement. In fact, he or she is apt to interpret the leaver's friendliness either as a sign of hope for reconciliation, or alternatively, as a glib rejection. "Love and hate are not far apart," and the left partner may (mistakenly) feel like she or he has only one emotional choice: We can be lovers or we can be enemies.

Pursuer and the Pursued

Neither the leaver nor the left wants the love boundary that the other wants, and this can lead to a prolonged and painful "dance," as the partners struggle to find a mutually acceptable emotional distance. The leaver might suggest having dinner together, for example, a gesture he sees as an attempt to keep communication open. But the left views dinner as a date, and hopes for a nightcap. When this secret hope is revealed, the leaver makes his "friendly" intention clear. As a result of this perceived rejection, the left partner angrily refuses the next invitation—or perhaps ends the "friendly" dinner by storming home. The leaver fears the loss of the desired friendship, and as a result, pushes for another dinner, or at least lunch.

In short, the interaction between former spouses is a "pursuer–pursued" relationship, a common and troubled pattern when love boundaries are poorly defined (Eldridge & Christensen, 2002; Emery, 1992). The pursuer chases and the pursued distances. When the pursuer gives up and moves away, however, the partners reverse roles. The pursued becomes the pursuer.

Conflicts frequently erupt as a result of ill-defined boundaries of love. The conflicts sometimes are direct and focus on topics like spending time together, attempting to reconcile, or dating others. For reasons we have discussed, however, the conflicts often are indirect. Not surprisingly, the children are a frequent focus. Why? The children are a continuing link between the partners, perhaps the only remaining tie. The children also are a "safe" topic of dispute, one that can arouse strong feelings but not involve much personal risk to the parents. The parents deny their real feelings of hurt, longing, grief, fear, or guilt (see Chapter 2). "I am only concerned about the children." Despite such disclaimers, of course, many conflicts that are superficially about the children really are all about the parents' ill-defined boundary of love.

Getting a Reaction

In trying to understand love struggles, we need to recognize that they are not about winning. Instead, the conflict really is all about getting an emotional reaction, positive or negative (Emery, 1992). For example, consider when a young woman breaks off a dating relationship, and her boyfriend screams, "You can't do this to me!" His anger conveys far more emotional involvement than a detached answer like, "OK. If that's what you want." Similarly, when a rejected, divorced woman storms out of the restaurant on her "date" with her ex, the magnitude of her anger reveals the depth of her feeling.

In a love struggle, emotional *intensity* is what conveys meaning, not emotional valence. The more intense the emotion, the more the other is still "hooked," even when the intense reaction is anger. Again, love and hate are not far apart. Thus, an important clue that a couple may be caught up in a love struggle is when their conflicts are emotionally intense, out of proportion to the topic at hand, ongoing, and resistant to even reasonable resolutions. One (or both) of them is not looking for a resolution. They are looking for a *reaction*.

Enmeshment

I see former spouses with high-conflict relationships as enmeshed, not disengaged (Minuchin, 1974). This observation is obvious to some people, but others insist that their anger is a sign of their *lack* of feeling for their former spouse, or at least that is what they profess. "I don't love him. I HATE him!" But the vehemence belies the denial. It's a case of, "Methinks thou doth protest too much."

The problem with contentious divorcing couples, therefore, is *not* that they need to be friendlier and communicate more frequently. Rather, the opposite is true. The partners need to disengage, to be less involved in each other's lives. They need to communicate less often and more formally. They need a boundary of love that is both more distant and more clearly defined.

Defining New Love Boundaries

This is precisely what I offer to enmeshed couples or couples in one-sided divorces. As mediation is moving into a second or third 2-hour session,[4] I might draw Figure 4.2 on a flip chart and tell this story. "Relationships are like a river. You begin with business-like relationships. They are polite, distant, formal, and structured. When we are lucky, a business-like relationship moves downstream and becomes a friendship, which is less structured, closer, relaxed, and rewarding in its own right. If we are very lucky, we plunge over a waterfall. That's when a friendship becomes a loving, intimate relationship."

"The problem is that relationships are like a river with a very strong current. You cannot swim upstream. When a loving relationship ends, you cannot be friends. You have to get out of the river and walk back to the beginning. You have to start all over, back to the beginning, and focus on developing a business-like relationship."

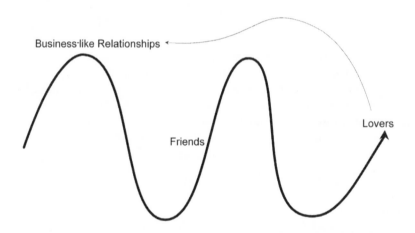

FIGURE 4.2. Diagram illustrating how relationships are like a river. People move from business-like relationships to friendships to loving relationships. But the river has a strong current. You cannot swim upstream. When a loving relationship ends, you need to get out of the water and walk back to the beginning. Divorcing parents have a job to do, not a relationship to resolve. A business-like relationship can help you to do your job, which is to raise your children as best you can.

---

[4] This is *not* something to do early in mediation. See Chapters 7 and 8.

"You two don't have a relationship to resolve. You have a job to do. Your job is raising your children. What you need to do is find a way to become partners in the business of parenting your kids."

I sometimes vary the river metaphor, but I never change the business one. Divorced parents *do* have a job to do. They can do that job far more effectively if they disengage, if they are more polite, distant, formal, and structured in how they relate to one another. Someday, perhaps, their relationship will move downstream and become friendlier, but that is not necessarily the goal.

A Solution for the Leaver and the Left

Becoming partners in the business of parenting not only puts needed distance between enmeshed, divorced parents, but it also offers a novel solution for the leaver and the left: It gives neither partner what they are looking for. The leaver wants to be friends; the left wants to be lovers. Neither is looking for a business-like relationship, so no one wins when we offer this third alternative.

I use the business metaphor far more often than not, but unless they are psychologically minded, I don't typically discuss the dynamics of boundaries and boundary conflicts directly with parents. Such information is too personal or too tangential for many parents involved in a custody dispute. And, as noted, a good parenting plan does much to reshape boundaries in the parents' relationship even without a direct conversation about the topic. A very specific parenting plan makes rules of parenting and coparenting clear, and thereby cuts down on the need for communication—and reduces opportunities for conflict. This is one reason I recommend that mediators and other dispute resolution professionals write carefully detailed parenting plans (see Chapter 6).

RENEGOTIATING POWER BOUNDARIES

Former partners who are parents also must renegotiate the power boundaries of their relationship. While this can be challenging, fortunately, power boundaries usually are less difficult to redefine than love boundaries. Power boundaries are thrown into flux in divorce, but power struggles usually do not involve the same degree of affective intensity as love struggles. Unlike love struggles, the goal of a power struggle is not to "get a reaction." The dispute at hand is truly important in a power struggle, and the outcome of the conflict does matter. Power boundaries are defined by who wins and who loses.

Power Boundaries in Marriage

In a marriage, power boundaries are determined, in part, by each partner's marital role. Power is rarely equal in all areas of a marriage, as most couples specialize in their duties. A "breadwinner" husband assumes more responsibility and authority for earning income and relating to the external world, for example, while a "caretaker" wife assumes more responsibility and authority for raising the children and managing family relationships.

Of course, many couples do not adopt these traditional gendered roles. In fact, marital roles today are far more ambiguous and therefore a source of potential—and actual—conflict. Power struggles probably are far more common in marriages today than they were in the past. There was little to dispute when society dictated appropriate marital roles.

Power struggles from earlier in the marriage can and do carry over into the renegotiation of relationships following separation and divorce. Many people view divorce as an opportunity to free themselves from roles that constrained them in a marriage; others are threatened by changes in their partner's assertiveness. Some former partners attempt to dominate long after a separation; others remain locked in a fight to gain the upper hand at last. In still other cases, what appears to be a power struggle really is a love struggle, as we discuss shortly.

Unsettled conflicts over power boundaries sometimes lead to prolonged disputes. However, the degree of control that former partners can exercise over one another is dramatically reduced by divorce. Moreover, the topics that define power boundaries following a separation are limited and relatively straightforward. Once a couple reaches a financial settlement, the only real power to share is their authority as parents. Thus, like conflicts over boundaries of love, power struggles also are likely to focus on the children. Fortunately, power struggles really are about what they are about—winning as opposed to "getting a reaction"; thus they typically are not nearly as intense, prolonged, or seemingly irrational as love struggles.

Power Boundaries and the Law

The law explicitly addresses many power issues in the relationship between divorcing spouses. There are legal guidelines for redefining financial power, including dividing marital property, alimony, and child support (see Chapter 6). Power boundaries concerning childrearing also are addressed in the law, at least generally. The major issues are commonly termed *legal custody* (parental decision making) and *physical custody* (a parenting plan).

Because of the legal issues, we limit our discussion of power boundaries here, returning to specifics in Chapter 6. It is worth noting now, however, that divorcing couples must negotiate their own, individualized roles for parenting and coparenting after divorce, much like today's couples negotiate individualized marital roles. Neither society nor the law clearly articulates default roles for men and women, or for mothers and fathers. Instead, custody law offers only a very general set of guidelines. The blurring of men's and women's family roles has many benefits—and creates more than a few complications, especially when it comes to renegotiating relationships in a divorce.

Not only is the law vague about basic, preferred custody arrangements, but it also is silent about how parents should make necessary, day-to-day decisions about childrearing. Judges are understandably reluctant to get involved even in relatively major parenting conflicts, such as deciding where children should go to school, or their religious upbringing. Judicial reticence increases exponentially when disputes arise about more minor parenting concerns, such as rules about appropriate bedtimes, dress, or snack foods.[5] Still, these all are important issues in day-to-day parenting, they can affect children's well-being, and they are ripe for conflict between parents who are angry, or who just aren't practiced in parenting across two households.

Changing Power Boundaries

I raise the day-to-day parenting issue now, though I do not detail specific strategies for addressing the problem until later, because anticipating areas of potential dispute is critical to negotiating new power boundaries. For example, I typically help parents to develop a structured, weekly method for communicating about routine parenting matters, such as a brief, weekly telephone call at a set time when the children are in bed. I also urge parents to cooperate as much as possible about more serious issues in day-to-day parenting, for example, discipline for serious transgressions, managing children's illnesses, and school and extracurricular activities. At the same time, I review topics where parents do *not* have shared authority or veto power, particularly the autonomous, day-to-day decisions each parent must be allowed to make while the children are with him or her.

---

[5] Actually, I would like to see the law take a much stronger "hands-off" position. Married parents get kicked out of court when they try to litigate disputes about education, medical care, or religion. I think divorced parents should be treated more like married parents. For a number of reasons, I want courts to tell divorced parents, "Work things out yourselves" (Emery & Emery, 2008; see Chapter 6).

In addition to specifics, there are some important generalities that people need to face about parenting apart. Perhaps the most basic is that all divorced parents need to accept the inevitability of lost control over their children's lives. This is not because parents become less effective disciplinarians (although they often do), but because they have less influence on each other's parenting. Some parents rarely communicate about their children; others talk about the children on a daily basis. At both extremes and in all cases in between, however, both parents lose some influence over each other's parenting. The coparenting power boundary invariably is defined more sharply than it was in marriage.

CONFUSING POWER STRUGGLES AND LOVE STRUGGLES

A basic problem with renegotiating any relationship is that power struggles and love struggles often get confused (Emery, 1992). For example, consider a wife who is upset that her husband never calls when he works late. She is concerned about what this means about his feelings for her. "Doesn't he care enough to call?" For her, a fight about this is a love struggle.

For the husband, however, power is the issue. He refuses to be controlled by his wife. Not calling his "mother" proves his independence. In short, while they both are fighting about the same issue on the surface, at a deeper level the wife is engaged in a love struggle, while the husband is involved in a power struggle.

In fact, the idea that power struggles and love struggles get confused is a major point of this chapter. On the surface, legal or parenting disputes about "the children" are about power, who "wins" more time and control with the children. At a deeper level, however, love often is the real issue. Conflicts about the children often are tests of, punishments for, or attempts to resist changes in the former spouses' boundary of love. "If you leave me, you'll lose your children." Prolonged, seemingly irrational custody disputes make sense from this perspective. In fact, the very irrationality of a former couple's conflict often is a sign that the dispute really is a love struggle.

The confusion between love struggles and power struggles brings us back to a basic theme of this chapter and this book: Former partners must separate their spousal and parental roles. The role of spouse ends in divorce but the parental role does not. Parents have to separate their shared concerns about their children from their own hurt, pain, grief, longing, guilt, and anger. As partners in a failed dream, divorced parents are entitled to their emotions. Yet, they must keep their feelings separate from their "job" of raising their children. Or as I often say to parents, "You need to find a way to love your children more than you may hate your ex."

SUMMARY

This chapter introduced the view of divorce as requiring the renegotiation of love and power boundaries in the system of family relationships. Divorce throws all of the old rules of family relationships into a state of uncertainty, perhaps chaos. In order to decrease conflict, and provide children with a healthy family environment, family members need to develop new rules for their new relationships as a family that no longer lives together. Ironically, the single most important relationship to renegotiate is the one that seems to be ending, the relationship between former partners who remain parents. Divorcing partners need to separate their marital and parental roles—roles that are bound together in marriage but that must be disentangled in divorce. Often the best way for parents to renegotiate their relationship is to establish more business-like rules for their new, coparenting partnership.

5

RENEGOTIATING RELATIONSHIPS II

Two-Parent Divorced Families

You need to love your kids more than you may hate your ex.
—MEDIATORS' ADVICE

Successfully renegotiating the relationship between former partners who remain parents typically is the key to resolving psychological and legal conflicts in divorce, and ultimately to children's well-being. Still, children face other challenges. Practical and emotional upheavals—for example, moving, changing schools, faltering family relationships—can upset children in the short term and may contribute to their psychological problems over the long run. During this time of turmoil, moreover, parents often are less available or less effective, as they struggle to regain their footing, not just for a few weeks or months but more typically for a year or two (Hetherington & Kelly, 2002; Wallerstein & Kelly, 1980). In a child's life, 1 or 2 years is a long time.

Parent–child relationships are stressed by divorce, and invariably change, even when consistency is a parent's utmost (and laudable) goal. Parenting on a schedule can seem disruptive, forced, or just plain wrong. As we will see, the only thing worse for children is *not* parenting on a schedule. We explore some of the unique challenges of residential parenting, nonresidential parenting, and joint physical custody in this chapter. In general, however, parenting alone tests each parent's resources. Patience and discipline both can be in short supply.

Even if parents successfully manage the tumult, the breakup of their family still is painful for children. Children experience multiple losses of their own in divorce. Even the best parents cannot protect them from the resulting pain and grief, and they should not try too hard to do so. Concerned parents might instead give children permission to feel however they feel.

Yet another challenge for children in divorce is learning how to balance relationships with both of their parents. Perhaps the most basic question is: How can children love two parents who do not love (and who may actively hate) each other?

All of this means that, like the former partners, parents and children also must renegotiate their relationships in divorce. Children in divorced families have two parents. The parents' task is to find ways to raise their children effectively alone and across two households. Helping parents to reach this goal is the ultimate objective of mediation, and of the law.

AUTHORITATIVE PARENTING

As with the former partners, parent–child relationships need to be renegotiated along the basic dimensions of love and power. In fact, the most widely used classification of parenting in developmental psychology is based on dichotomies of love and power (Baumrind, 1971; Maccoby & Martin, 1983; Steinberg, Dornbusch, & Brown, 1992; see Figure 5.1). *Authoritative parents* are warm and loving, and they are firm but fair in discipline. *Authoritarian parents* also are strict, but they are autocratic and offer their children little love, understanding, and support. *Indulgent parents* are the opposite. They give their children a lot of love, but little discipline. Finally, *neglectful parents* provide little affection or discipline. They are unconcerned about their children and have scant interest in parenting (see Figure 5.1).

Dozens of studies link these four parenting styles to children's mental health. Children of authoritative parents are generally independent, responsible, and self-confident, while children of indulgent parents are likely to be self-confident, but they also may be selfish and impulsive. The children of authoritarian parents tend to be less self-assured and socially competent than the children of indulgent parents, even though they are better behaved. Neglectful parenting is linked with extreme problems such as child abuse and juvenile delinquency (Lamborn, Mounts, & Steinberg, 1991; Maccoby & Martin, 1983). Although parenting hardly accounts for all of children's psychological difficulties and some parenting difficul-

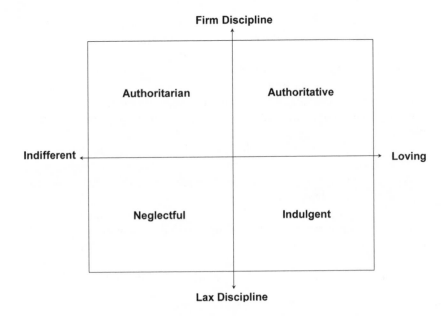

FIGURE 5.1. Four styles of parenting created by dichotomizing two dimensions of parental love and parental discipline (power). The preferred approach is authoritative parenting, a loving but firm style.

ties are a reaction to dealing with a troubled child, the numerous benefits of authoritative parenting are clear nevertheless.

Authoritative parenting is the goal, but for a number of reasons, parenting often suffers in divorce. Problems may result from the parents' preoccupation with their own emotions, continuing conflict in the coparenting relationship, or the challenges of parenting alone. Continued changes in the adults' life—a more challenging job, new relationships, perhaps relocation—also pose special challenges for parenting and for children.

Residential, Nonresidential, and Shared Parenting

The amount of time each parent spends with his or her children is an important and common influence on parenting in divorce (Hetherington & Kelly, 2002). Residential parents often are overburdened, overwrought, and overwhelmed with parenting alone. Finding the time and emotional energy to devote to children can be a challenge. Nonresidential parents, in contrast, are likely to feel cut off, isolated, and left out. They may try to cram weeks of fun into every other weekend, or whatever relatively brief amount of time they spend with their children. Parents with joint physical custody experience both of these problems to a lesser extent, but they face the added task of coordinating more integrated schedules and childrearing with their former partner.

As a result of their circumstances, nonresidential parents usually have more difficulty redefining boundaries of love with their children. Residential parents often face more problems with discipline. Families with joint physical custody can struggle most with balancing the parent–child–parent triangle. We consider these prototypic issues in this chapter, but note two important caveats. First, the issues that may best characterize one custody arrangement (e.g., balancing the triangle in shared parenting) also apply to other parents and parenting plans. Second, our present focus is conceptual not empirical. I review research on the potential risks and benefits of alternative parenting plans in Chapter 6.

PARENTAL LOVE:
REASSURANCE AND CONSISTENCY

A basic ideal of contemporary, Western family life is that children love their parents and feel loved by them. Children can question their parents' love, however, when they learn that their divorcing parents no longer love each other (or at least not in the same way). Some insecurity stems from realistic concerns such as spending less time with one or both of their parents. When children are with one or another parent, moreover, the attention, affection, and support they receive may be diminished as a result of the parents' own emotional preoccupations and practical concerns.

Other doubts about parental love stem from children's fears and fantasies. The limited cognitive capacities of preschoolers, for example, prevent them from understanding the reasons for and meaning of a divorce. As a result, they may openly or secretly fear that their parents will abandon them. Many school-age children also fear abandonment by their divorced parents (Kurdek & Berg, 1987), and even adolescents can harbor unrealistic fears—or more realistic ones. Divorced parents might be less willing or able to pay for college, for example, a circumstance that may feel like (and perhaps be) a form of emotional as well as financial abandonment.

Reassuring Children: Words and Deeds

Because reality and fantasy both can threaten children's security, parents are wise to reassure children of their unconditional love. The reassurance needs to be repeated, but it also should be developmentally appropriate. Preschoolers typically want to be told "I love you" several times a day; teenagers do not. Parents need to remember that the goal is to reassure their children, not themselves.

Parents also can, and hopefully will, reassure children that the other parent loves them too. With all of the uncertainty and conflict, children often need to hear that they are permitted to love and be loved by *both* of their divorced parents. A particularly important time for discussing this bedrock of affection is when divorcing parents sit their children down for "the talk"—the painful discussion about their plan to separate.

Ultimately, however, reassurance about the boundaries of parental love and affection stems from actions not words. Children need their divorced parents to be consistently available, offer support, and prove their love through their individual and joint deeds, as we discuss in the following sections.

Loving on a Schedule: Nonresidential Parents

Nonresidential parents often ask: How can I be a parent on a schedule? How can I show my children how much I love them when I only see them every other weekend? These are tough questions, and I do not have terribly satisfactory answers to them.

Nationally in the United States, about 70% of nonresidential parents are fathers, and their modal level of contact with their children is in the range between every other weekend and several times a year (Amato, Myers, & Emery, 2009). About 15% of divorced fathers are residential parents and another 15% of parents share joint physical custody (see Chapter 6). Nonresidential mothers maintain somewhat more frequent contact with their children, but it typically remains in the range of every other weekend to several times a year (Furstenberg, Peterson, Nord, & Zill, 1983). Finally, evidence shows that the frequency of nonresidential parent–child contact drops off sharply over time, particularly as a result of events like remarriage or relocation (Seltzer, 1991).

Those are the current data. In Chapter 6, we consider the evidence in more detail, including examining how primary residence, joint physical custody, and contact levels have changed over recent decades. In those chapters, we also consider some of the vigorous debates about what contact levels between children and both of their parents could be or should be, as well as alternative explanations about why contact levels are what they are.

I should reiterate now, however, that my primary explanation for the relatively low levels of nonresidential parent–child contact is straightforward—and far different from the typical "mothers' rights" and "fathers' rights" explanations. Divorcing parents break up the "emotionally natural" way. They tell their ex, "I never want to see you again!" Acting on that emotional impulse, one of them ends up seeing the children infrequently, too. My mediation research shows that, when parents find a different way to come apart, they both remain far more involved in their children's lives.

Children's Experience of Schedules

Whatever its cause, the drop off, low level, and declining frequency of contact with one of their parents can cause distress and grief for children. When separated from an attachment figure (and children have multiple attachment figures), children experience periods of protest and despair before accepting the loss (Bowlby, 1973, 1980), much as parents move through cycles of love, anger, and sadness. Also like their parents, ambivalence and uncertainty prolong children's grief.

This means that uncertain and inconsistent plans for seeing their nonresidential parent create practical and emotional ambiguities for children (Healy, Malley, & Stewart, 1990). If children know when and how they will see their parent(s), they can feel secure in that knowledge. When the boundaries of the relationship are uncertain, however, children are subject to the immediate disappointment of unmet hopes and plans, as well as to much deeper feelings of insecurity about their parent's love. As a sobering and concrete reminder of this possibility, Lisa Laumann-Billings and I (2000) found that 28% of young adults from divorced families (in two different samples) agreed with the statement, "I sometimes wonder if my father even loves me."[1]

Sticking to a schedule can be a particular problem for parents shortly after a separation. They may not have agreed to a parenting plan yet, or one or both parents may not like the schedule. These problems frequently surface near the very beginning of mediation. My response is that the parents need to agree to a schedule right away, and stick with it, even if the agreement is only temporary. Why? From a child's perspective, a schedule is loving. A schedule is reassuring. I appreciate the complaints of nonresidential parents who do not want to "parent by the clock." But the schedule is not about constraining the parent. The schedule is about children's need for reassurance, predictability, and consistency.

---

[1] Most fathers were nonresidential parents. Distressingly, 10% of young adults who grew up with their married parents also agreed that they sometimes wondered if their father even loved them.

Discouraging "Flexible" Visits

Once parents agree to a parenting plan, I encourage them to follow it religiously. Why? A host of problems can develop when a schedule is unclear or too flexible. To a nonresidential parent (or sometimes, a residential parent), unscheduled contact with their children may seem spontaneous and natural. From a child's perspective, however, this can create uncomfortable uncertainty—and uncomfortable, unsatisfying visits.

Equally problematic is contact that is scheduled, but is late or never occurs. An hour or two may seem like a short amount of time for a parent to be late, but it can be an eternity to a child. Young children, especially, perceive time differently than adults. (Recall how the few hours between the end of school and the beginning of dinner once seemed like forever.) When time moves slowly, it takes on added importance. This is especially true when a child has looked forward to a visit for a week or more. Thus, it is more than wise to follow a schedule strictly, at least until a pattern, a clear boundary of love, is reestablished. Some modifications can come later, but even then, parents should remember that what may seem flexible to them can feel chaotic to their children.

Unplanned or erratic contact also clearly violates a boundary in the new relationship between former spouses. Residential parents make plans for times when the children are to be with them—and for times when the children are supposed to be with the other parent. For many overburdened residential parents, time without children is not a chance to have some fun; it is an opportunity to complete chores. Again, clear, consistent schedules offer many benefits.

Quality and Quantity

From the perspective of children's emotional well-being, there is no single, ideal amount of time for nonresidential parents (or parents with shared parenting) to spend with their children. The quality of the nonresidential parent–child relationship, particularly authoritative parenting, is a far more potent predictor of children's psychological adjustment than the quantity of contact (Amato & Gilbreth, 1999).

Still, quantity does matter in ways that are not always so easy to observe. For example, young adults report fewer feelings of loss owing to divorce if they had weekly contact with their nonresident fathers during their childhood than if they saw their fathers one to three times per month (Laumann-Billings & Emery, 2000). This evidence and other considerations make me want to maximize children's contact with *both* of their parents, provided that the logistics are not too complicated and the parents have a fairly cooperative relationship (see Chapter 6). Note, however, that weekly contact is not necessarily equal time or even joint physical custody—it might be every other weekend plus dinner on the "off" Wednesday. A parenting plan is not about dividing the child 50/50, but about constructing a schedule that works for the children first and the parents second.

Preoccupied Residential Parents

The security of children of residential parents can also be tested in divorce. At a time when children need extra attention and reassurance, residential parents may be preoccupied with their own emotions, focused on finances or other practical matters, overwhelmed with the burden of parenting alone, and less confident in their abilities. A troubled coparenting relationship can exacerbate these concerns. For strategic or emotional reasons, parents may subvert rather than support each other's relationship with their children.

Residential parents also may simply have less time to spend with their children. They may need to spend more time at work, while the children spend more time in child care. New social activities such as dating also can take residential parents away from their children. Thus, children's relationships with both their residential and nonresidential parents can become more distant and erratic as a result of separation and divorce.

Parentification and Role Reversal

More distant parenting has been documented frequently in research (Hetherington & Kelly, 2002), but many clinicians have noted a very different kind of problem with the boundary of parent–child love (Emery, 2004; Wallerstein & Kelly, 1980), as have a few empirical studies (Peris, Goeke-Morey, Cummings, & Emery, 2008). Some parents become over-involved with or dependent upon their children following a marital separation. Often this leads to a reversal of roles, so that the child becomes the caretaker for the parent's emotional needs. A preadolescent child may be encouraged to sleep with a lonely parent, for example, or a teenager might be treated as a depressed parent's peer and confidant. In such circumstances, the problem is that the parent's emotional needs take priority over the child's.

Our concern is not children who take on increased practical responsibilities as a result of divorce. Chores can be unpleasant, but they generally are not psychologically harmful. However, assuming responsibility for a parent's psychological well-being is a *huge* emotional load. In the normal course of development, parents are stable sources of support for their children. In role reversal, however, the child becomes the parent's source of security. A "parentified" child may *look* resilient on the outside, but parentification is not resilience. Resilient children in divorce get to be "just kids." Parentified children are manipulated into being parents to their parents, a role reversal that may set them up for future depression and relationship problems (Emery, 2004; Peris & Emery, 2005; Peris et al., 2008).

DISRUPTIONS IN DISCIPLINE

As long as parents respond to the children's needs, not their own, they are not likely to love their children *too* much. And despite their struggles, most parents succeed in quickly establishing new boundaries of love with their children. Recall, however, that authoritative parents are loving *and* firm in discipline. Discipline often is a big problem for parents in divorce, at least for a time (Hetherington & Kelly, 2002).

The key to effective discipline is maintaining clear boundaries of parental authority while gradually expanding the boundaries of children's autonomy. Children get to make decisions within their "territory" of autonomy, whether that involves choices about food, clothes, or friends. The key discipline issues are boundary conflicts—for example, dating, driving, and curfews among adolescents (Emery, 1992).

Unfortunately, guilt, uncertainties about appropriate expectations, or preoccupation with having fun (or otherwise focusing mainly on loving/being loved by children) can make both divorced parents less effective disciplinarians at and well beyond the usual boundaries of parental authority. Perhaps one parent also may have relied on the other to discipline the children, or, when doing the disciplining, at least counted on the other as an ally. Yet, single parents do not have a partner to consult about appropriate discipline, or to enforce rules with them or for them. One parent may find, in fact, that the other is actively undermining their discipline efforts.

As parents struggle with rules, children often behave badly. Sometimes this is due to the distress of divorce. Other times children test the boundaries out of anger, or as a way of seeking attention. Children also may have more selfish motivations; they may just want to get their way. All children "test the limits," particularly during certain developmental stages like the "terrible twos" or early adolescence. Many of children's challenges in divorce are normal, too. The problem, instead, is the parents' discipline, or more accurately, their lack of discipline.

Residential Parents: Learning to Set Limits

Residential parents spend more time with their children, and for this reason if no other, they often encounter more difficulties with discipline. The cliché approach to discipline, "Just wait until your father gets home," conveys a bigger problem that many residential mothers face. Residential mothers (and fathers) sometimes must master an entirely new parenting role.

Other struggles also can make discipline difficult for residential parents. Emotional and practical burdens can lead to a decrease in monitoring of children's activities and misbehavior. Children also may be given increased independence from former family rules, perhaps together with increased responsibilities for helping around the house or caring for younger siblings. Growing up a little faster can have positive consequences, but not all children are capable of adequately exercising autonomy at a younger age.

Parental Guilt and Coercive Interactions

Many problems with discipline stem from parents' guilt and self-doubt. Because of their inner uncertainties, parents can mistakenly attribute children's misbehavior to the divorce or related causes, rather than to more normal influences. Rules that had been standard become a source of internal debate and perhaps an indulgence. Parents now may wonder if it is right to say "No" to bad behavior. They ask themselves if the child is disobeying because they are upset over the divorce. This is a reasonable question, but it generally is one that a parent should ask only *after* enforcing discipline.

Consider the common problem of coercive cycles in interactions between parents and difficult children (Patterson, 1982). In a coercive interaction, children are positively reinforced for misbehavior as parents give in to their escalating demands. Parents, in turn, are negatively reinforced as the child stops pushing once the parent caves in. Since both child and parent are rewarded, the pattern of demand and capitulation continues.

In divorce, a unique variation of this common problem occurs when a child learns to pull the guilt trigger. A mother might tell her son that it is time for bed, for example, but the boy pushes for another television show. After two or three ignored warnings, the 8-year-old shouts in anger or in tears, "Dad lets me stay up. I wish I was at his house!" Feeling guilty, or perhaps afraid that her son does not like being with her, the mother caves in, perhaps joining her son to watch another show, or two. As a result of such "successes," children quickly learn to "push the guilt button."

As parents slowly begin to recognize such coercive cycles, they may assume that a child is being malicious—or that the other parent is undermining them. Both problems are possible, but enforcing the bedtime rule still is the appropriate, immediate response. And because testing the limits is completely normal, I often take a few minutes in mediation to warn parents about how to respond. I encourage them to remain consistent, separately and together, in enforcing their usual rules. After all, a child's "job" is to get through life in the easiest way possible. A parent's responsibility is to ensure that the easiest path is the most adaptive one.

Thus, the appropriate focus of renegotiating boundaries of power in parent–child relationships often involves increasing parents' confidence, rather than questioning children's motivations. As with redefining other boundaries, clarity and consistency are the keys to reestablishing effective discipline in divorce. Specific rules are not so important. Bedtime can be 8:30, 9:00, or 9:30. What is essential is having a bedtime and consistently enforcing it.

Nonresidential Parents: Parenting Isn't Always "Fun"

Like residential parents, nonresidential parents also tend to discipline less often and less effectively. In fact, many nonresidential parents discipline their children very little or not at all. These "Disneyland dads" (or "merry-go-round moms") turn their limited time with their children into a trip to fantasyland. Everything is always fun, too much is never enough, and nothing is ever wrong.

Hectic, fulfilled weekends often are motivated by a parent's attempt to make up for lack of quantity time with intense "quality time." Nonresidential parents understandably want to make the most of their limited contact with their children. They may desperately want to have a normal relationship with their children—but fantasyland visits are *not* normal. Normal fathers and mothers do not entertain their children endlessly, and many nonresidential parents need to be reminded of this. A normal relationship includes "down time" and discipline. In mediation, I frequently offer this reality check to parents if things are going badly or to prevent problems from developing.

Not only can children benefit from a more normal relationship with the nonresidential parent, but the relationship between parents also should improve if they both take an active hand in discipline. Many residential parents feel like they do all of the work, while the nonresidential parent has all of the fun. Nonresidential parents who discipline appropriately, however, not only share the load with their coparent but they also achieve their goal of being more of a presence in their children's lives.

CHILDREN IN THE MIDDLE:
LOYALTIES AND ALLIANCES

Joint physical custody, in which children spend approximately equal amounts of time with each parent, is an important alternative to children living primarily with one parent and having limited contact with the other. As a rule, children are better adjusted when custody is shared (if the parents cooperate), but they can fare worse when parents are in conflict (see Chapter 6). Thus, successfully renegotiating relationships in the parent–child–parent triangle is key to joint physical custody (see Figure 5.2). Parental conflict and balancing relationships in the larger divorced family system also is central to children's well-being in more traditional custody arrangements (and in married families).

Parental conflict can create problems for many reasons. Fights are frightening and disruptive to children, and conflict and strong emotions can undermine each parent's family focus and effectiveness. And children "caught in the middle" of their parents' disputes (Buchanan et al., 1991) face dilemmas in balancing family loyalties and coping with following inconsistent rules.

The Parenting Alliance

A key to a well-functioning, married family is the parenting alliance, parents working together and ultimately "siding" with one another on matters concerning the children, even when they disagree. If they devote the time and emotional effort, as we have discussed, divorced parents can preserve their parenting alliance or develop a new one. In contrast, for-

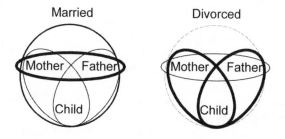

FIGURE 5.2. Schematic representation of ideal boundaries in married and divorced families. The boundary around the parents' marital relationship is strongest in marriage, while parent–child relationship boundaries become more important in divorce. Still, a parenting alliance is preserved in both family types.

mer spouses who fail to renegotiate their relationship put children in the middle of their conflict. The parent–child–parent triangle is unbalanced.

Love and Power in Triangles

Unbalanced parent–child–parent relationships can lead to problems balancing both love and power in the family system. I use the term *loyalty* to refer to love struggles in triadic interactions, while the term *alliance* describes triadic power struggles (Emery, 1992). When two family members side together against a third, they form an alliance. Two less powerful family allies sometimes can dominate a third who has more power than either alone. Siding together also demonstrates loyalty. Taking sides means, at least temporarily, "I like you more" (Emery, 1992).

Balancing alliances and loyalties can be at issue in many family triads, not just those involving two parents. A boy who complains about his mother "siding" with his younger brother, for example, is upset about both loyalties and alliances. Part of his concern is about losing a battle, but his complaint also reflects his fear that his mother may like his sibling more than she likes him. "*You're always on his side!*"

Divided Loyalties

Divorce creates an inherent loyalty conflict from a child's perspective. The parent–child–parent triangle appears unbalanced. Even when the parenting alliance is preserved, children confront the dilemma of loving two parents who no longer love each other. In this circumstance, loyalty to one parent can feel like disloyalty to the other.

When parents are in conflict, not only do children feel the pressure of divided loyalties, they also *are* often pressured to take sides. Children may not be allowed to talk about their time with the other parent, they may be quizzed about their activities, or they may be forbidden to bring their "stuff" back and forth between households. In these and dozens of other subtle and not-so-subtle ways, a child's relationship with one parent may become a test of loyalty.

Being caught in the middle is uncomfortable, and children's discomfort over divided loyalties can take a number of forms. Anxiety, anger, and sadness are some of the most common affective reactions that children report when exposed to conflict and anger not directed at them (Cummings & Davies, 2010). If two parents allow their children to have separate relationships with each of them, these emotions can dissipate over time. Children can maintain relationships with both of their parents without ongoing emotional tension.

For other children, however, loyalty dilemmas are a lasting and central aspect of being in the middle. Parents may share their scorn for a former spouse directly with their children. They may deride any real or perceived disloyalty on their children's part. Or they may strongly express their loneliness when their children are with the other parent, acting especially hurt if the children seem to have enjoyed their time with the other parent.

Mediators often feel many of the same pressures as children do. Conflict is unsettling even to trained experts. And parents can try to pull a mediator over to their side, even in little ways, for example, by closely monitoring how much attention the mediator pays to each of them. Like a mediator, of course, many children do *not* take sides. These children work constantly to avoid any appearance of favoritism.

Balancing Divided Loyalties

The best solution for avoiding or resolving divided loyalties is for parents to minimize or at least manage their conflict. If the former partners can work together as parents, children do not need to divide their affection. An alternative is to create strong boundaries around the parents' relationship. The parents keep children out of their "stuff," and parent–child relationships function independently.

When children remain caught in the middle, they have a handful of ways of coping with their predicament (Vuchinich, Emery, & Cassidy, 1988; see Figure 5.3). One possible solution is balancing. A child can attempt to maintain separate but approximately equal relationships with each parent. This is a workable resolution when the parents' relationship is disengaged, and each parent allows the children to have a relationship with the other. Balancing is anxiety provoking, however, when the parents compete over their children's affection.

When competition and conflict are uncontrolled, children may turn to other tactics. Resolving the parents' problems is one possibility, as some children do become mediators themselves. They act as go-betweens who try to solve their parents' problems. Mediators carry messages back and forth, sometimes distorting them in order to soften the blow. Like a professional mediator, children also may encourage their parents to "be nice" in one way or another.

A third strategy involves distracting the parents from their disputes. Children can distract their parents by being either "devils" or "angels." Devils distract parents with their misbehavior, and unite them in their shared anger or concern about their child. The devil child is a scapegoat who, like a common enemy in international politics, makes allies out of parents in conflict. Devil children are like Germany during World War II,

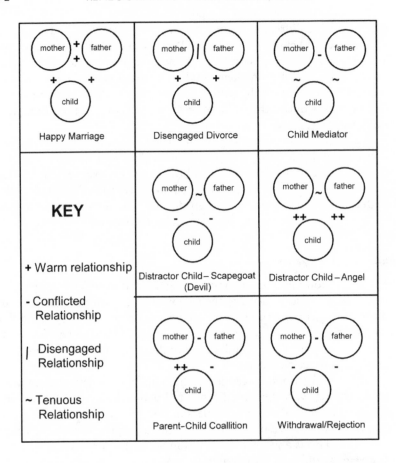

FIGURE 5.3. Possible triadic relationship patterns in divorced families. Note the similarity between a parent–child relationship in a happy marriage and in a disengaged divorce.

which turned the United States and the Soviet Union into allies (temporarily).

Angels, in contrast, redirect parental attention onto their achievements or other "good" behavior. Angels are a source of common pride and purpose. Undoubtedly, this is a more adaptive strategy for children than being a devil. Still, both "angels" and "devils" take on a burden of responsibility, as they work to distract their parents from their problems.

Yet another option for children is to pick sides. A child can form a coalition with one parent against the other. Children who use this strategy may incur the loss and potential wrath of one parent, but they gain the protection of the other parent in return. Taking sides makes sense if one parent abandons a child, but we generally do not want children to have to pick between two, reasonably decent parents.

The last and perhaps the most unfortunate resolution of a loyalty dilemma is to withdraw from *both* parents. Children might withdraw emotionally into themselves, or they may physically withdraw from their parents, perhaps spending their time with friends, in romantic relationships, or with "substitute" families. Attempts to escape from parental conflict explain some of the preoccupation with romantic relationships, running away from home, and early marriage that are infrequent but still more common among children from divorced, rather than married, families (Emery, Beam, & Rowen, in press).

Again, the key to a healthy resolution of loyalty conflicts is the parents' relationship. As we have noted, however, what is less stressful for children may be temporarily more difficult for the parents who cannot indulge their anger. One of the many ironies of divorce is that, even in the midst of their parting, parents need to find a way to work together for their children's sake.

Inconsistent Discipline

Whether married or divorced, parents are far more effective if they are allies in discipline. Parents who are a "united front" set clear and consistent rules, and as a result, they are more likely to enforce them successfully. Divorced parents often have difficulty working together, however. Their parenting alliance falters or fails. And when parents' discipline is in conflict, children are unlikely to respect either set of rules. In fact, children may learn to gain power over their parents by dividing and conquering.

Defining Boundaries of Authority between Parents

Some inconsistent discipline simply requires a clear definition of the boundaries of authority in parenting and coparenting. It may be unclear what rules will be the same or different in each parent's household, for example, or who has the authority to make what decisions. The parents may also have no plan for communicating as needed about the children. Divorced parents in these circumstances need an organizational chart of sorts, an outline for who is responsible for what decisions under which circumstances.

Some of these problems can be alleviated by clearly defining the meaning of joint or sole legal custody (parental decision making). Because of the strains of coparenting, I generally urge parents to limit their shared authority. Thus, I make it very clear that joint legal custody means sharing decisions only about major issues, specifically religious upbringing, education, and elective medical care. This is how legal custody typically is defined in the law, but it may not be how parents expect to share their authority. If so, the parents need to change their expectations. They need to respect and honor each other's authority to make day-to-day decisions in their own home. They need to minimize the need for communication and cooperation between them. And though it is difficult, they need to accept that divorce means a loss of some control over their children's lives.

Communication between Parents

Many day-to-day or week-to-week parenting issues cannot be addressed in advance, and some aspects of effective parenting do require coordination across households. A child may start taking prescription medication, for example, which needs to be continued over a weekend, or a special form of discipline (e.g., improved study habits) may need to be enforced in both homes. This means that divorced parents do need to communicate, or their united front will crumble. The children will quickly learn to play parents off against each other. When this happens, the problem is not a manipulative child. The problem is the parents. Parents have a responsibility to teach their children. Some lessons can only be taught when parents work together.

As with other aspects of coparenting, a business-like structure often is crucial to effective parental communication. For example, parents might plan a telephone call for a set night during each week. Parenting is the only legitimate topic for this 5–10 minute conversation, a rule designed to minimize conflicts about potentially difficult topics. For last-minute issues, an e-mail or telephone call or voice message may be needed. Again such messages should be restricted to topics that concern the children and are expected to be very brief. If as a parent you need to vent, do so in person. (Better yet, vent with a friend or a therapist.) E-mails and messages get read and played over and over, fueling fury and misunderstanding, and they often surface as damaging evidence in court hearings.

Deliberate Subversion

Unfortunately, some problems with inconsistent discipline are not simply a matter of unclear authority or the lack of structured communication. Some divorced parents deliberately subvert each other. Too often parents use children as conduits or spies in their power struggles. They ask children questions about the other parent's "close friends," or tell them to deliver messages about inappropriate topics such as a delayed child support payment. Their children become pawns in the battle between the parents.

Sometimes a parent's subversion is an attempt to win a child's loyalty. Other times it is a means of punishing a former partner. In still other circumstances, it simply is a means of demonstrating their power. As usual, in all of these cases the problem can be traced to the parents' relationship. This is why Chapters 2, 3, and 4 preceded this chapter. Before they can negotiate new boundaries in the triangle that still includes them both and their children, divorced parents must learn to renegotiate their relationship. If they fail to do so, they run the risk that pain, hurt, and anger over a failed marriage will destroy their relationships with their children.

OTHER PARENTING FIGURES

I focused on residential and nonresidential parents in this chapter, because the two biological parents are typically involved in custody disputes, and their relationship obviously is central to the emotional dynamics of divorce. Still, I recognize the importance of other parenting figures. In many single-parent families, extended family members, particularly grandparents, play a key role in rearing children. Cohabitation, remarriage, and stepparenting can also dramatically affect the life of children after divorce. Let us briefly consider a few major issues about extended family and new romantic relationships.

Extended Family

Extended family members can be an extremely important source of support in divorce. The maternal grandmother is particularly likely to play a key role, especially among African American and other ethnic family groups. Grandmothers and other relatives may offer routine childcare while the biological parent is working. They also may serve as consultants and allies in discipline, and provide a secondary source of security both for the parent and for the child. Of course, extended family also can provide essential financial and practical support to overburdened single parents. In fact, it is not uncommon, particularly among minority families, for the maternal grandmother to live with the single parent and the children together in a three-generational family and serve as a secondary parent, or perhaps as the primary one (Caputo, 2000; Wilson, 1989).

Children benefit from a close relationship with a grandparent who serves as a parenting figure, perhaps especially when children have a troubled relationship with the biological parent(s) (Goodman, 2007). Thus, grandparents who play a parental role in single-parent families assist both their children and their grandchildren. But there is a critical caveat to the benefits of giving. Becoming a "new" parent is not always such a good deal for the grandparent, whose psychological well-being, health, and economic status all can suffer as a result (Goodman, 2007; Lee, Ensminger, & Laveist, 2005).

Dating, Remarriage, and Stepparenting

Most divorced adults eventually want to start dating, get involved in new romantic relationships, and perhaps remarry. These interests are normal for the adult. The problem is that they don't seem normal to the children. Moreover, it is not easy to manage new romantic relationships around children. Divorced adults get to pick their new partners. For them, a remarriage may be a second chance at happiness. To the children, it's an "arranged marriage," maybe an arrangement they do not like.

Remarriage typically is yet another difficult transition for children, one that does not lead to improvements in their mental health (Hetherington & Kelly, 2002; Pryor, 2008). And the presence of children increases the already higher risk that a second marriage will end in divorce (Teachman, 2008), one indicator that children can stress their parents' new romantic relationships.

Dating, cohabitation, and remarriage also can make a former spouse jealous, or threaten a nonresident parent's relationship with his or her children. In fact, children's contact with nonresident parents often declines following either parent's remarriage (Amato et al., 2009). As a result of these changes, coparenting conflict may increase.

The interconnections between relationships, new and old, suggest a complex network of boundaries that need to be negotiated as a result of dating, cohabitation, and remarriage. The new partners need to negotiate boundaries in (1) their own relationship, (2) the relationship between the stepparent (or dating or cohabiting partner) and the children, (3) the biological parent–child–stepparent triad, (4) the relationship between the stepparent and the former spouse (i.e., between mothers and stepmothers or fathers and stepfathers), and (5) possible new relationships between stepsiblings (and *their* other parent) and perhaps (eventually) between half-siblings. Clearly, this involves a lot of negotiating, the complexity of which is beyond the scope of this chapter or this book (for resources, see Pryor, 2008).

Despite the complexities, I have three general suggestions about dating and forming new relationships after divorce. First, I urge parents to go slowly with dating, for their children's sake—and their own sake.

(After all, divorced adults are emotionally vulnerable, too.) Parents, especially the leaver, also should go slowly for their former partner's sake. (And as difficult as it can be, they should tell their former partner when they do start dating.) Going slowly means taking time to explore relationships before getting too serious. This includes waiting, probably for several months, before introducing or involving new romantic partners in children's lives. The wait should be long enough to make sure that, if the romantic partner is going to be involved with the children, the relationship is likely to last for some time.

Second, I urge dating, cohabiting partners and stepparents to go slowly in their new role with children. In particular, I encourage romantic partners to first try to become an "adult friend" with the children. That is, work first to establish a boundary of involvement/closeness/love with children, while following the biological parent's lead in enforcing discipline. Stepparents may assume more "parental" roles later, including the role of disciplinarian. Then again, they may not. Their primary role may remain that of adult friend, particularly if the children are older at the time of the remarriage (Hetherington & Clingempeel, 1992).

Third, I urge biological parents to expect to retain their role as "primary parent" in a stepfamily, and to expect to continue to have a business-like, coparenting relationship with the children's other parent. I similarly urge new romantic partners to respect the role of each biological parent, as well as their coparenting relationship. The biological parents remain their children's parents, even following a remarriage. While sometimes a stepparent becomes a substitute parent, this role is not automatic and generally not necessary, unless one of the parents has essentially abandoned the children.

Whom to Include in Mediation

I have a fourth rule about other parenting figures and mediation. It is not uncommon for a grandparent or stepparent to request to be a part of mediation or to show up for a scheduled appointment. However, my standing rule is to limit mediation to the two biological parents. I not only exclude grandparents and stepparents but children and lawyers, too.

My rationale for doing so, as I elaborate upon in later chapters, is that biological parents bear the responsibility of making decisions about their own children. Biological parents are also responsible for managing children's relationships with their side of the extended family. In fact, many disputes that arise with grandparents and stepparents result from the biological parent's failure to assume this responsibility. Yet, because I appreciate the roles played by other parenting figures, as well their potential contributions to creating or resolving custody disputes, I sometimes break my rule. As with any rule, however, it is easier to break an established rule than to try to establish a rule after the fact.

SUMMARY

A goal of parenting in divorce is to maintain authoritative parent–child relationships. Just as parents must renegotiate their own relationship, the boundaries of love and power in each parent–child relationship must be reaffirmed or redefined following a divorce. Residential, nonresidential, and joint custody parents all face difficulties maintaining the warmth and discipline that combine to form authoritative parenting. However, as a result of infrequent contact with their children, nonresidential parents typically have more problems establishing new boundaries of love. In contrast, residential parents struggle more with the discipline. Balancing the triadic relationship between the child and the two parents is perhaps the major task for parents with joint physical custody. Irrespective of the parenting arrangement, all families must redefine loyalties and alliances in the parent–child–parent triad as a result of separation and divorce. Even under the best of circumstances, children confront the loyalty dilemma of loving two parents who no longer love each other. Divorced parents also must find ways to maintain consistent discipline across two households, while keeping contact and communication between themselves to a minimum. Finally, many divorced parents eventually need to find ways to integrate new parenting figures into their children's lives, and into their children's other parent's life.

6

DIVORCE AND CUSTODY LAW

Perfect Problems,
Imperfect Solutions

In criminal court, you see bad people at their best. In family
court, you see good people at their worst.

—FAMILIAR LEGAL QUIP

Caught in an emotional morass, estranged parents turn to the legal
system for direction and protection. If he or she has not already consulted
a lawyer, perhaps long ago and repeatedly, the leaver may seek practical
answers to practical questions, for example, how to get divorced. Talking
to a different lawyer, perhaps for the first time, the left partner may still
be searching for ways to *prevent* a divorce.

No-fault divorce is a widespread legal concept, as we discuss in this
chapter, but fault often is an issue of contention as a marriage unravels. If
the worst is going to happen, the left partner may insist that other things
should stay the same: he or she should stay in the family home, along
with the children, and remain financially secure. Such an arrangement
may partially assuage fears about a suddenly uncertain future or possible
anger over a betrayal. After all, the left party did not want or precipitate
a divorce.

The leaver is likely to have a different perspective. In contrast to the left partner's diffuse fears and expectations, the leaver also is likely to have a different plan, one that is specific, detailed, and in the leaver's mind, far more fair and balanced, for example, "split everything 50/50," including time with the children. Eager and ready to "do business," the leaver's emotional detachment can vanish if the left demands too much.

LAW AND EMOTION

Emotions are the hard part of legal negotiations in divorce, but emotions have no place in the law, which strives to detach emotion from decision making.[1] And the traditional[2] legal system does not offer the clear direction and protection sought by many divorcing parents. Custody law theoretically is designed to preserve and protect children's "best interests," but two basic contradictions can thwart this laudable goal.

Adversary Procedures

The first problem is that the legal system treats parents as adversaries. This is not an aspersion. The American system of justice is called the "adversary system." As a part of a set of legal procedures designed to protect individual rights, attorneys are ethically obligated to "zealously represent" the interests of their clients, and only their clients. Unfortunately, a lawyer's zeal can fuel anger and conflict in divorce, as a growing sense of righteous indignation focuses each parent only on his or her interests, too.

Former partners may find an adversarial approach emotionally appealing, but children can and do get caught in the crossfire. Hundreds of studies show that parental conflict is toxic for children in divorce (Cummings & Davies, 2010; Emery, 1982). Thus, the adversary system creates a dilemma for concerned parents—and for judges, who are legally obliged to protect children's interests in custody disputes. The cure can be worse than the disease. The adversarial

---

[1] Aristotle famously proclaimed, "The law is reason free from passion." Yet, a new law and emotion perspective suggests many reasons why emotions are relevant to legal considerations. For example, see *Virginia Journal of Social Policy and the Law* (2009), 16(2).

[2] Fortunately, family-law traditions are changing, as we explore in this chapter and throughout this book.

approach increases parental conflict, an outcome that is damaging to children's emotional well-being and to their relationships with their two parents.[3]

Children's Best Interests

A second obstacle to protecting children's interests in divorce is that the law offers only very general answers to some vexing questions, particularly how parents should rear their children across two households. (I discuss how custody law evolved to this state of indeterminacy later in this chapter.) When parents are in dispute, the law's goal of making decisions according to children's vaguely defined "best interests" can be tantamount to throwing gasoline on a fire. In the absence of clear guidelines, the de facto procedure for winning a contest over what or who is "best" for the children often boils down to this: Make yourself look like a model parent, and make your ex look like anything but (Mnookin, 1975).

The adversary system and indeterminate custody laws create problems, but they also create an opportunity to do things differently. Parents can do what no lawyer or judge or mental health professional can do as well as they can: decide what is best for their own children.[4] Parents can negotiate more cooperatively—with a mediator, in collaborative law, on their own—in an effort to preserve their coparenting relationship even as their marriage is unraveling. Helping parents to do so is one of the overriding goals of this book, and, fortunately, it also is becoming a new tradition in innovative legal practice (see Figure 9.6).

Empowerment

Empowerment is the word that best describes this opportunity. Parents can decide and create their own terms for their divorce. The law—the issues that former partners need to decide—is not all that complicated. If parents can find a way to control their powerful emotions, they also can control the terms of their divorce. This is why five chapters on emotions

---

[3] In an instructive contrast, American courts have consistently *refused* to hear disputes between married parents precisely because doing so would harm children, parents, and families (Emery & Emery, 2008).

[4] Unfortunately, neither wise judges nor skilled mental health professionals have secret or scientific answers about what is "best" for individual children in divorce (Emery, Otto, & O'Donohue, 2005).

and renegotiating family relationships preceded this chapter on legal issues.

I examine some legal technicalities in this chapter, but consistent with a focus on empowerment, I also offer more common sense, demystifying explanations about the law, the sort of explanations I hope parents can readily understand. Here is my first: Parents have two big things to sort out in divorce: (1) what to do about their children, and (2) what to do about their finances. This chapter reviews these two broad topics, focusing on children's issues and translating legal concepts into easily understood terms.

THE CHILDREN:
DECISION MAKING AND A SCHEDULE

The parents' task in deciding what to do about their children also encompasses just two issues. The first is how to make childrearing decisions. The second is creating a schedule for sharing time with the children. In the law, the first issue often is termed *legal* custody, while the second often is called *physical* custody.

A Note about Terminology

Legal terms differ from state to state and from country to country,[5] and different terms can be loaded with symbolism. For example, many parents object to the (older and dying) term "visitation," which refers to a schedule for the "noncustodial" parent to spend time with his or her children, for example, every other weekend from Friday evening until Monday morning plus overnights every Thursday. Symbolism matters. The same parent who rejects the "visitation" option may embrace a "joint custody" schedule of every other weekend from Friday until Monday plus overnights every Thursday.

Because symbolism matters, I advocate for "joint custody" as a term, particularly in contrast to the pejorative *visitation* and *noncustodial*. I also advocate for joint custody as a concept. But for reasons outlined in this chapter, I expect the great majority of divorced parents to successfully share joint *legal* custody, while joint *physical* custody appears to work only for a minority.

---

[5] States control family law in the United States, so the law differs from state to state. And while the United States has the highest divorce rate in the industrialized world, divorce rates have risen in all industrialized nations, making renegotiating family relationships a worldwide challenge.

A Parenting Plan

Many mediators (including the author) and lawyers are less concerned with terminology than with the details of a "parenting plan." A *parenting plan* is a carefully specified agreement about children's schedules and parents' decision making. In fact, some states have completely dropped the terms "custody" and "visitation" or "legal and physical custody." Instead, statutes now refer to "parental rights and responsibilities," "residence and decision making," or simply a "parenting plan" (American Law Institute [ALI], 2002). For the sake of clarity, I use "legal custody" and "physical custody" when referring formally to the law, but I use "parenting plan," "parental decision making," and the "children's schedule" when discussing the same issues more informally.

Details Matter

Let me add one more note about parenting plans. Details matter. Spelling out details is, in fact, a major reason behind the legal system's embrace of parenting plans (Ellis, 1990). A few decades ago, judges commonly awarded "primary custody" to one parent and "liberal rights of visitation" to the other—leaving parents to sort out the details. Many experts and state laws now insist that parenting plans contain a great many specifics about the schedule and decision making. The overriding goal in doing so is to minimize parental conflict by spelling out rules in advance. We now turn to consider what details divorcing parents need to consider, whether they address them formally in a parenting plan or informally as a mutual understanding.

LEGAL CUSTODY: PARENTAL DECISION MAKING

What is the best way for divorcing parents to make childrearing decisions? There are three basic legal and practical issues to consider: (1) sharing (or not sharing) major decisions about their children's lives; (2) respecting the other parent's autonomy in his or her own home; and (3) developing a means of communicating about important childrearing issues, while generally working to coordinate (but not control) parenting across two households.

Sole versus Joint Legal Custody

Typically, whether parents will share major decisions about the children is the only one of these three issues addressed in the law. Legally, one parent can have *sole legal custody*, which gives that parent the authority to make major decisions on their own, or parents can share *joint legal custody*, which obliges them to make some major decisions jointly.

In considering joint versus sole legal custody, it is essential to recognize that the list of potentially shared decisions is a very short one. Major decisions usually include only: (1) elective medical care, (2) religious upbringing, and (3) schooling.[6] This means, for example, that parents with joint legal custody need to decide together whether their children see a psychologist or get braces; they must agree whether their children will be raised Christian, Jewish, Muslim, or in some other religious tradition (or none at all); and they make joint decisions about whether their children will attend a public or a private school. However, joint legal custody does *not* mean that one parent needs the other's permission to take a sick child to the doctor, that parents must agree on whether or not to say a blessing before dinner, or that both must sign off on children's participation in school activities. Conversely (and this is frequently misunderstood), when one parent has sole legal custody, the other still has the legal right to access to the children's medical, religious, and school records and activities unless the parents have agreed, or a judge has ordered, otherwise.

The concept of joint legal custody is relatively new in the law. Broad interest in joint custody (legal and physical) arose in the 1970s, 1980s, and 1990s in the United States (Melli & Brown, 2008), earlier in more-progressive states than in more-conservative ones.[7] Divorced parents and innovative professionals initially promoted the concept, while the law reacted with considerable skepticism. This difference was reflected in my research. When I conducted my randomized trials of mediation and litigation in Virginia in the 1980s, joint legal custody was a novel idea that was not defined by state statute and was used rarely by legal practitioners. The parents who mediated in my studies agreed to joint legal custody significantly more often than the litigation parents, but only a minority of mediation cases opted for joint legal custody while no litigation cases did (Emery & Wyer, 1987a; Emery, Matthews, & Wyer, 1991).

Trends in Joint Legal and Physical Custody

Joint legal custody rapidly has become the norm in the United States, but joint physical custody has not. Unfortunately, no national, historical data

---

[6] A few less-common parenting decisions are also shared, such as obtaining a passport and taking a child out of the country.

[7] The concept of joint legal custody has yet to be "discovered" in countries where divorce rates increased more recently, for example, South Korea (Chung & Emery, 2010).

exist on developments in joint custody in the United States as a whole. Figure 6.1 provides an instructive example based on perhaps the best available data, the Wisconsin Court Record Database (WCRD), a random sample of divorce settlements in 21 Wisconsin counties from 1980 to 2001. Figure 6.1 shows three notable trends. First, joint legal custody increased from a relative rarity to become the default arrangement, specifically, from 18% of cases in 1980/81 to 87% of cases in 2000/01. Second, joint physical custody also increased notably but less dramatically, from 2% of cases in 1980/81 to 32% in 2000/01.[8] Third, joint physical custody increased dramatically following a revision of Wisconsin child support guidelines (in 1987) that lowered child support payments for parents who each had children at least 30% of the time (Berger, Brown, Joung, Melli, & Wimer, 2007).

We consider various pros and cons about joint legal and physi-

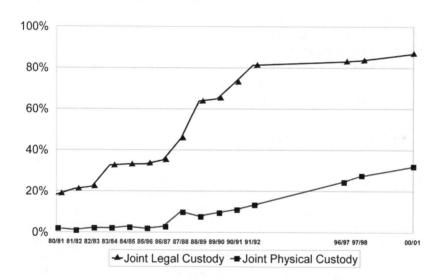

FIGURE 6.1. Growth of joint legal and physical custody: Wisconsin, 1980–2001. Joint legal custody became the norm in Wisconsin in recent decades. Joint physical custody also increased but much less dramatically. Data from Berger, Brown, Joung, Melli, and Wimer (2007).

---

[8] The U.S. national rate of joint physical custody is likely considerably lower than this Wisconsin estimate. Wisconsin law encourages joint physical custody, and these data are based on legal agreements not actual parenting. In fact, WCRD researchers themselves estimate a 20% U.S. national rate of joint physical custody (Melli & Brown, 2008).

cal custody shortly. For now, let me make two further points. First, the trends in Wisconsin appear to reflect similar trends in other states (Kelly, 2006) and in the United States as a whole: Joint legal custody has become the rule, while joint physical custody remains the exception. Based on an analysis of four U.S. national samples, for example, Amato, Meyers, & Emery (2009) found that nonresident father–child contact grew from 18% weekly in 1976 to 31% in 2002.[9] Smyth (2004) similarly found that the most common contact schedules in an Australian national sample were no contact (19%), daytime-only contact (17%), and one to two overnights every other week (13%). Ten percent of cases involved joint physical custody.

Second, the surge in joint legal custody suggests that, in contrast to what some feared, sharing parental decision making has not caused increased conflict between divorcing parents. In fact, available data indicate that the opposite is true. Joint legal custody is associated with *increased* nonresident parent–child contact and *increased* compliance with child support orders (Huang, Han, & Garfinkel, 2003; Seltzer, 1998). Although cause and effect cannot be concluded because no study has employed random assignment, this correlational evidence, high rates of joint legal custody, and the symbolic value of the term, all support joint legal custody as the default option for the substantial majority of divorcing families.[10]

Respecting Parental Autonomy

Legal custody typically is the only decision-making issue addressed by the law. However, I routinely include additional issues in mediated agreements or at least discuss them with parents. In particular, I urge each parent to respect the other's autonomy and authority in his or her own household, while also developing a means of communicating about important childrearing matters and generally working to coordinate rules across two households. I began addressing these issues decades ago based solely on my experiences in mediation (Emery, 1994; Emery et al., 1987), as did many other professionals. Today, the parent-

---

[9] Weekly contact does not necessarily imply joint physical custody. A schedule of every other weekend plus dinner on the "off" Wednesday is weekly contact. Also of note, the percentage of fathers with no contact with their children declined from 37% in 1976 to 29% in 2002 (Amato et al., 2009).

[10] Experienced divorce professionals will hardly be startled by this conclusion. Joint legal custody is now widely embraced. Yet, today's conventional wisdom was unconventional not very long ago.

ing plans used in various jurisdictions include these issues as a part of their standard templates.

Consider this. Married parents often disagree about parenting. Some disagreements are minor; others are more fundamental. What may seem vital to one parent—not too much candy, limited television, no toy guns—may seem trivial to the other. Over time, married parents generally learn to pick their battles, insisting when a rule seems essential and giving in when it's not. Parents still disagree, yet judicious parents present a united front to the children and only voice their disagreements in private.

For all kinds of reasons, divorced parents can struggle to reach or regain similar accommodations. Their anger and pain can make them want to fight about *everything*. Or they may have lost confidence and trust in one another, or perhaps in themselves. And it is complicated to coordinate parenting across two households. One parent may decide that the parenting compromises made in marriage no longer apply; the other may insist that *his or her* rules, old and new, must be upheld in the *other* parent's home.

The issues and emotions involved in a parenting dispute may need to be addressed at multiple levels, but a simple principle can help parents to anticipate and avoid many conflicts. Each parent must respect the other's autonomy in their own household. That is, when the children are with him or her, each parent has the authority to make day-to-day decisions about day-to-day matters such as the children's clothing, diet, discipline, and so on.

Responsibility: A Corollary of Autonomy

Responsibility is a corollary of autonomy. The parent who is scheduled to be with the children is responsible for them. That parent cannot delegate their responsibilities to the other parent. This includes finding alternative care for the children, when needed, even if the other parent wants "right of first refusal." That is, a parent may want to be given the option of providing substitute care when the other parent must be gone during his or her schedule timed with the children, but providing substitute care is an option, not an obligation.

Lost Control

Recognizing the other parent's autonomy also means accepting a loss of control yourself. Many parents struggle with this, so I often address this hidden loss early and head on. Before it becomes an issue, I note that a degree of lost control over your children is an inevitable consequence of living in two households, an unfortunate reality that the parents will eventually need to accept.

Communicating and Coordinating

Even as they accept a degree of lost control, many parents rightly point to the wisdom of consistency in parenting. Children benefit from consistency in discipline, in routines, and in living circumstances, and parents can make positive efforts toward providing their children with such consistency in two homes. In particular, they can develop a means of communicating about the children, as needed, and they also can work toward coordinating discipline and daily routines.

If divorced parents want to be effective, they need to communicate about, and perhaps discuss and coordinate their efforts regarding many "midlevel" parenting issues. These include matters too small to constitute legal custody decisions but too large to ignore as a part of each parent's province of autonomy. Examples of midlevel issues include school performance (e.g., report cards), activities of importance to the children (e.g., extracurricular involvements and events), health (e.g., medications that need to be taken across households), discipline (e.g., information on misbehavior and punishments), and daily routines (e.g., bedtimes).

A Planned Telephone Call

Many divorced parents have trouble communicating, of course, and as noted, others use "concerns about the children" to cross boundaries that have nothing to do with the children. For these reasons, I urge parents to set up a structured method for communicating about the children. For most parents, I recommend a weekly telephone call timed shortly before or after a regular exchange of the children. The call should take place at a time of day that allows the parents to talk outside of earshot of the children. The conversation should be brief and focused purely on the children. Thus, a common recommendation is that the parents speak on the telephone about the children for 5 to 10 minutes every Thursday evening at 9 P.M.

Brief Messages

Some parenting matters cannot wait; for example, a school activity that was just rescheduled until *tomorrow*. Other issues do not require a telephone conversation, such as a soccer game that has been rescheduled to a week from Saturday. E-mail, texting, or phone messages are handy ways to exchange this sort of information, and it is worth discussing preferred methods of communication and appropriate topics. Some parents will want to include a line or two about these issues in a written agreement.

One principle here is timeliness. Parents can indicate the preferred and fastest way to reach them. Another principle is "keep it brief." E-mails or phone messages should be short. Limit e-mails to two or three lines and voice mails to about 30 seconds. And this is *not* the forum for venting angry concerns. The other parent is likely to return the favor, while both parents can now reread each other's rants over and over. And a truly nasty message could end up as evidence in court. Finally, complicated matters (e.g., should a 13-year-old be allowed to date) are better discussed live.

While coordinating across households is a good idea, rules and routines in each home do not have to be precisely the same. Children can manage differences between parents, and even learn from them. Consistency is a goal, not a requirement, and the goal is subordinate to respecting autonomy. If parents disagree so vehemently that they end up in court with a childrearing dispute, in my view this almost certainly is an indicator that one parent should have sole legal custody.[11] For reasons discussed below, I hold the same position even more strongly regarding joint physical custody.

PHYSICAL CUSTODY: CHILDREN'S SCHEDULES

The law in every U.S. state and in many other industrialized countries indicates that custody determinations are to be made according to children's (and only the children's) "best interests."[12] This leads to an obvious and very important question: What schedule best meets children's needs?

What Does "Best" Mean?

I will address this question, but we first need to consider some key problems in trying to answer it. First, the law offers only a very general definition of "best." Table 6.1 summarizes the criteria from the Uniform Mar-

---

[11] There also are other options if high conflict continues, in particular, appointing a "parenting coordinator" (Coates, Deutch, Starnes, Sullivan, & Sydlik, 2004).

[12] In theory, what parents prefer does not matter. Judges can even throw out an *agreement* between divorced parents about what is best for their own children. Today, most judges happily sign off on uncontested custody agreements; however, some will overturn consent agreements, for example, due to skepticism about joint physical custody.

TABLE 6.1. Factors Defining Children's Best Interests

- The wishes of the children's parent or parents as to their custody.

- The wishes of the children regarding their custodian.

- The interaction and interrelationship of the children and their parent or parents, their siblings, and any other person who may significantly affect the children's best interests.

- The children's adjustment to their home, school, and community.

- The mental and physical health of all individuals involved.

Most states use these factors as a basis for their custody laws. As if these considerations are not vague enough, some statutes add even more general criteria. For example, the last criterion in the Virginia statute is "Such other factors as the court deems necessary and proper to the determination." Data from Uniform Marriage and Divorce Act, 9A Uniform Laws Annotated, Sec. 316 (1979).

riage and Divorce Act (1979), the basis for most state laws in the United States. As we discuss shortly, these broad criteria leave *plenty* of room for disagreement between different judges, different custody evaluators, different parents, and different readers of this book. One could argue that "best" means the happiest child, the most productive student, the most economically secure family, or children having close relationships with one parent or with both parents. These alternatives, and innumerable others, are not perfectly compatible, of course, so the debate is without end. Ultimately, defining "best" is a value judgment. My definition of "best" in the following discussion is when children have fewer psychological problems. I choose this definition because it is used in most psychological research, but I make no claim that this is the best definition of "best."

A second problem with defining what schedule is in children's best interests is that there is very little research on alternative custody arrangements and existing research is flawed. One inherent and essential flaw is that no one can randomly assign families to different custody arrangements. This makes it impossible to distinguish correlation from causation, a dilemma further complicated by powerful selection biases. For example, parents with joint physical custody are known to have higher incomes and/or education, better coparenting relationships, and better relationships with their children, and they differ from parents with sole physical custody in numerous other ways, both measured and unmeasured (Melli & Brown, 2008; Smyth, 2004). Any benefits found to accompany joint physical custody may well be selection effects, not consequences of the arrangement.

Third, although the law focuses only on children, parents' interests can affect custody preferences and outcomes, and perhaps they should. In addition to their desires and concerns for themselves and their chil-

dren, parents' physical custody preferences may be influenced by financial considerations, such as receiving more child support (or paying less),
tax breaks, or perhaps remaining in the family home. Parents' wishes,
whether personal or political, may be legitimate and valuable reasons
for preferring one custody arrangement over another. Personally, I am
not persuaded by either "mothers' rights" or "fathers' rights" arguments
about altering custody standards. Instead, I am an advocate for parental self-determination (including eliminating judicial review of consent
agreements, for reasons discussed later in this chapter).

Parental Self-Determination

I am hardly alone in advocating for parents' authority—and responsibility—
to decide what is best for their own children in divorce. In its proposal for
revising child custody law, the ALI (2002) argued that parental self-
determination should be an overriding principle. ALI raised many arguments to support this position, but four stand out. First, society has no
demonstrable way of determining what is "best" for children either in the
exercise of judicial discretion or in the tests and insights of custody evaluators (Emery, Otto, & O'Donohue, 2005). Second, adversary procedures
for resolving custody disputes increase parental conflict, which decidedly
is *not* in children's best interest (Sbarra & Emery, 2008). Third, evidence
indicates that both traditional and alternative dispute resolution procedures like mediation can and increasingly do allow divorcing parents to
decide what is best for their own children (Emery, Sbarra, & Grover,
2005b; Maccoby & Mnookin, 1992). Fourth and more philosophically,
expecting courts to decide what is best for children in divorce is an intru-
sion on parental autonomy on the part of the state and an abdication of
responsibility on the part of parents.

Another argument in favor of parental self-determination is that
research has identified no "best" custody arrangement for children, individualized or otherwise, but evidence clearly points to family relationship
qualities that predict better or worse child adjustment to divorce. My
mediation research shows that parental self-determination promotes precisely the sort of family relationships that can lead to positive outcomes
for children—less parental conflict, more parental cooperation, more
cooperative involvement on the part of both parents, and higher-quality
parent–child relationships.

Of course, an embrace of parental self-determination begs the question of what principles should guide custody decisions when parents *cannot* agree, even after multiple dispute resolution efforts. Actually, one
alternative is to do nothing. Perhaps courts should treat divorced parents
exactly like they treat married parents and refuse to hear their parent-

ing disputes, because such efforts ultimately create more problems than they resolve (Emery & Emery, 2008). This suggestion is only partially rhetorical. I return to consider it more specifically toward the end of the chapter.

Joint Physical Custody

No one parenting plan works best for all children, but joint physical custody still deserves close examination. Joint physical custody is much discussed by parents, advocates, divorce professionals, and lawmakers. Opinions—and legislative efforts—vary widely. Joint physical custody also is increasing in frequency (see Figure 6.1). In addition, joint physical custody has been the focus of a reasonable, if still small and problematic, body of empirical research.

Because the topic is controversial, I probably should be clear about my position at the outset. I am an advocate for joint physical custody. I want children from divorced families to spend significant time, and have good relationships with, both of their parents. However, I have long been on record as opposing the judicial imposition of joint physical custody in contested cases because this puts children in the middle of their parents' conflict (Emery, 1988). And while I encourage and advocate for parents to negotiate joint physical custody arrangements on their own, available research leads me to expect that only a minority of parents, perhaps 10 to 25%, will be able to make joint physical custody work over time for themselves and for their children. For these reasons, I am opposed to changing the law to make joint physical custody the preferred arrangement.[13]

In the review that follows, I reach several more specific conclusions based on available research and related considerations:

- Joint physical custody is not necessarily 50/50 time.
- Psychologically, joint physical custody is the best and worst arrangement for children—the best when reasonably cooperative parents make it work, the worst when it puts children in the middle of a war zone.
- Joint physical custody is being used to settle high-conflict disputes.

---

[13] I favor the ALI's proposed approximation rule, indicating that postdivorce parenting plans should approximate, as far as possible, predivorce parenting involvement. This pluralistic rule, in fact, would lead to joint physical custody for most divorced parents in the United States (Emery, 2007).

- Some parents insist on joint physical custody for the purpose of lowering their child support payments.
- Joint physical custody is less stable over time than sole mother or father custody.
- Even under legal regimes that encourage joint physical custody, only a minority of families successfully maintain the arrangement.

Defining Joint Physical Custody

There is no universal definition of joint physical custody. Some view a 50/50 arrangement as the only true joint physical custody (Kruk, 2005). The "week on, week off" schedule probably is the most common way of achieving 50/50, but there are more creative and complicated options. For example, a child may spend every Monday and Tuesday with one parent, every Wednesday and Thursday with the other, and alternate every other long weekend with each parent.

Others define joint physical custody more broadly—and quite variably. Ironically, perhaps the best example of variability comes from different child support laws in the United States. In 2006, two-thirds of U.S. states reduced support levels if parents shared joint physical custody. The lowest threshold for doing so was 52 overnights per year (in Indiana); the highest was 164 overnights (in North Dakota) (Brown & Brito, 2007).

Many researchers use a threshold of about 25% of parenting time or about 90 overnights to define joint physical custody (e.g., Bauserman, 2002; Buchanan & Jahromi, 2008; Trinder, in press). Dozens of arrangements other than 50/50 meet this criterion, for example, two overnights every week; every Thursday plus every other weekend Friday through Monday; a 10-week summer vacation plus 20 overnights during school vacations.

I prefer the broader definitions of joint physical custody for two reasons. First, I fear that parents who insist on precisely 50/50 time are focusing on their model of fairness rather than on their children's needs. Second, what is important to children is having a psychologically significant relationship with both of their parents. This can be achieved with 25% time (or 50% time), but a broader definition of joint physical custody offers more options to work around possible obstacles for parents (e.g., work schedules) and children (e.g., school calendars).

The Best and the Worst Arrangement

Does joint physical custody benefit children? The best answer to this question appears to be yes—and no.

A much-cited meta-analysis of 33 studies comparing the psychological adjustment of children in joint versus sole custody concluded, "Children in joint physical or legal custody were better adjusted than children in sole-custody settings … " (Bauserman, 2002, p. 91). At first blush, this conclusion, based on 33 studies, seems like a strong endorsement for joint custody. But meta-analysis, particularly this one, suffers from what I call the "Chicken McNugget" problem: The amalgam is a tasty bite—until you think about what's inside. What's inside the Bauserman (2002) meta-analysis is:

1. As the above quote indicates, the effect of joint *legal* custody was equivalent to joint *physical* custody, opening the door to the argument that joint legal custody (i.e., symbolism) is just as beneficial as 25–50% shared parenting time.
2. The effect size ($d = 0.23$) is modest, equivalent to an IQ score of 103 versus 100.
3. Better parents self-select into joint custody; thus the "effect" surely reflects (partially or completely) nonrandom selection into joint custody, not a consequence of the arrangement.
4. Many of the studies in the meta-analysis were of dubious quality (22 of 33 were unpublished doctoral dissertations).
5. Another meta-analysis of 63 studies of nonresident father contact and children's adjustment found negligible effects for contact *frequency* but larger (if still small) effects for relationship *quality* (Amato & Gilbreth, 1999).

A sixth and very important concern centers on Bauserman's (2002) findings about parental conflict and especially how they have been interpreted. Bauserman found that parental conflict did not account for the advantages of joint custody over sole custody. This is surprising, because both past and present conflict was substantially lower in the joint custody families (proving nonrandom selection). Moreover, the effect sizes for conflict, that is, the differences between joint and sole families, were greater than the $d = 0.23$ obtained for the child adjustment measures. Statistically, at least, conflict therefore should have accounted for the group differences in child adjustment, but it did not (perhaps because effect sizes for joint custody were larger in the subsample of studies that also included conflict measures).

In any case, the null result does *not* support the conclusion that children do equally well in joint custody whether parental conflict is high or low. In fact, Bauserman (2002) did not compare child adjustment in high and low conflict joint custody arrangements, but several studies have done so. As a whole, these investigations have found that, when parental conflict is high, joint physical custody is associated with *more* psychological problems among children, while it is linked to *fewer* problems when conflict is low (Buchanan, Maccoby, & Dornbusch, 1996; Johnston, Kline, & Tschann, 1989; Lee, 2002; McIntosh & Chisholm, 2008). (One exception found that both contact and conflict were independently related to college students' reports of psychological distress [Fabricius & Luecken, 2007].) While there certainly are methodological problems with this research, too (e.g., children are not randomly assigned to live in low- vs. high-conflict joint physical custody), the interaction between conflict and custody arrangement is consistent with the broader literature indicating strong negative effects of conflict (Cummings & Davies, 2010; Emery, 1982) and weak positive effects of contact (Amato & Gilbreth, 1999).

Thus, joint physical custody appears to be the best *and* the worst arrangement for children, depending on whether parent conflict is low or high. An important question, of course, is how much conflict is too much? Research offers little guidance here, but one operational definition of high conflict that I endorse is when parents contest custody in court. Thus, in my view, a judicial order for joint physical custody targets the right solution at precisely the wrong cases.

Using Joint Physical Custody to Settle Conflict

Other experts similarly recommend against imposing joint physical custody in contested cases (e.g., Buchanan & Jahromi, 2008; Gilmore, 2006; McIntosh & Chisholm, 2008; Trinder, in press). Unfortunately, evidence indicates that judges are doing exactly this. Perhaps the best data on this worrisome pattern come from Australia,[14] where a law enacted in 2006 urged judges to consider ordering equal division of children's time with each parent, and if not equal, "substantial and significant" time (McIntosh & Chisholm, 2008; Smyth, 2009). A study of 77 high-conflict, contested Australian cases found that fully 46% left court with a joint physical custody arrangement (McIntosh & Chisholm, 2008). This compares with a rate of 17% of joint physical custody based on general population estimates (Smyth, 2009). Unlike some hoped (Bauserman, 2002), moreover, McIntosh and Chisholm (2008) found that joint physical custody did not resolve the parents' conflict. Four months after the court action, at least one parent reported that the co-parents "almost never" cooperated in 73% of the joint physical custody cases.

Investigators have found similar results in U.S. studies. A California

---

[14] Unlike in the United States, family law is national in Australia.

study found substantial or intense legal conflict in 36% of cases with joint physical custody (Maccoby & Mnookin, 1992). In their Wisconsin data, Melli and Brown (2008) found that 10 to 20% of joint physical custody families were high conflict, depending on the measure used. In a North Carolina study, judges ordered joint physical custody in 15% of 122 cases decided through litigation, even though 99% of the mothers and 77% of the fathers had filed for sole physical custody (Reynolds, Harris, & Peeples, 2007).

While "fathers' rights" advocates argue in favor of joint physical custody, unsurprisingly, "mothers' rights" advocates argue against it. A particular objection is that mothers need the protection of the adversary system, because mediators are biased in favor of joint physical custody and will push the option on women who do not really want it (Fineman, 1988; see generally Reynolds et al., 2007). Yet, exactly the opposite was found in a North Carolina study of contested custody cases. Fewer mediation cases ended in joint physical custody (11%) and more ended with sole mother physical custody (83%) in comparison with litigated cases (15% joint physical; 66% sole mother physical). Joint physical custody was even more common among cases settled through attorney negotiations (19% joint physical, 69% sole mother) (Reynolds et al., 2007).[15] While cases were not randomly assigned to attorney settlement, mediation, or judicial determination, all cases were contested. The mediation cases were mandatory and court ordered, and a filing for a contested custody hearing preceded settlement in the attorney-negotiated cases.

In summary, evidence indicates that joint physical custody is being used to settle contested, high-conflict cases by judges, attorneys, and, to a lesser extent, mediators. This is troubling given the "best and worst" for children conclusion.

Negotiating for Lower Child Support?

Some evidence supports the much-voiced worry that parents sometimes negotiate for joint physical custody for the sole purpose of lowering their child support. Joint physical custody awards have been found to increase following the enactment of laws lowering child support for parents who share physical custody (see Figure 6.1 on p. 105; Berger et al., 2007). When modifications are allowed, moreover, joint physical custody dramatically affects child support. In a large, representative Wisconsin sample, a child support order was entered in 91% of mother custody cases,

---

[15] Alternatively, joint *legal* custody was much more common following mediation (90%) than either litigation (50%) or attorney settlement (71%) (Reynolds et al., 2007).

but mothers were ordered to receive support only in 49% of joint physical custody cases (Melli & Brown, 2008).

Do some parents agree to joint physical custody and no child support, but then fail to follow through with actual shared parenting? (That is, do they strategically bargain for joint physical custody *in the agreement only*, and only for the purpose of lower child support payments?) I could locate only one study that even partially addressed this issue. Actual contact was substantially lower than negotiated contact among 20–31% of Wisconsin families three years after agreeing to joint physical custody (Berger et al., 2008).

The evidence is troubling, but my concern is less with percentages and more with laws that may encourage strategic, inauthentic bargaining. As Brown and Brito (2007) recommend, perhaps the best solution is a formula that adjusts child support in cases of joint physical custody, but that decreases payments gradually beyond a set threshold (e.g., by a small percentage for each additional overnight beyond 90). Most state laws currently produce a "cliff" effect, so that child support declines dramatically once a threshold is reached (Brown & Brito, 2007). The more gradual adjustment, which is employed by a handful of states, recognizes the expense of joint physical custody, but provides a much smaller economic incentive for bargaining for time as a trade-off for support (Brown & Brito, 2007).

Joint Physical Custody Arrangements Change

Several studies indicate that joint physical custody is less stable over time than either sole mother or sole father physical custody, both of which are relatively stable. One study of two California counties found that, 3 years after initial settlement, 84% of families maintained sole mother custody, 70% maintained sole father custody, and 54% maintained joint physical custody (Maccoby & Mnookin, 1992). Other studies from the United States, Canada, Australia, and the United Kingdom also show considerable change over time in joint physical custody, notably more so than sole physical custody (Smyth & Moloney, 2008). Wisconsin is one exception, as research there finds considerable stability in sole *and* joint physical custody 3 years after initial court filing (Brown et al., 2006; Berger et al., 2008; Krecker et al., 2003). These findings must be interpreted within the context of state law, however, as Wisconsin discourages changes in custody in the first 2 years following settlement.[16]

---

[16] Wis. Stat. §767.325(2); Wis. Stat. §767.329. If a motion is made *within* 2 years, the moving party must show by substantial evidence that the modification is necessary because the current custodial conditions are physically or emotionally harmful to the children. After 2 years, changes only must meet the typical (and much lower) "best interests" or "substantial change of circumstances" thresholds.

Is instability bad? Is change good? I have argued that parenting plans should be "living agreements," which parents can alter to better suit their own and their children's needs. Yet, renegotiating half of all joint physical custody arrangements within a few years, as has been found in the samples outside of Wisconsin (Smyth & Moloney, 2008), is a high rate of change.

Joint Physical Custody for Infants or Toddlers?

A particularly controversial issue is whether joint physical custody is appropriate for infants and toddlers, or indeed, whether overnight visits are healthy—or unhealthy—for very young children. Unfortunately for those who wish to reach evidence-based conclusions, the range of opinion about this important topic is large, while the number of empirical studies is small.

Opinions about schedules for infants and toddlers are based primarily on attachment theory, as well as extrapolations from attachment research in other contexts (e.g., infant day care). Different researchers clearly translate this research in different ways. At one end of the continuum are attachment researchers who emphasize the importance of the primary attachment, typically the mother–infant bond. A guideline based on the input of a number of leading attachment researchers suggested that, for 2-year-old children, "overnights are not recommended. ... For children closer to 3 years, only when the nonresidential parent has been a regular and significant caretaker, one or two overnights per week can be possible. ... Two overnights in a row are not recommended (Child Centered Residential Schedules, 1996, p. 18). At the other end of the spectrum are experts who emphasize the importance of multiple attachments to both parents. One influential representation of this point of view suggested, "The ideal situation is one in which infants and toddlers have opportunities to interact with both parents every day or every other day in a variety of functional contexts (feeding, play, discipline, basic care, limit setting, putting to bed, etc.)" (Kelly & Lamb, 2000, p. 304). This position explicitly favors regular overnights for infants, and in the ideal circumstance, might support a plan where an infant alternated successive overnights with each parent (Solomon & Biringen, 2001).

Only three studies have empirically addressed the issue of overnights for very young children. Solomon and George (1999a) studied 126 infant–mother dyads and found significantly more disorganized/unclassifiable infant–mother attachments among babies who spent overnights with their father, in comparison with infants who saw their father but had no overnights and also in comparison to infants living in intact families. In a 1-year follow-up study when the children were now 2½ years old, toddlers who had overnights as infants showed more distress when separated from their mothers in a laboratory assessment (Solomon & George, 1999b).

A 1½-year follow-up study of 132 families with children who were 6 years or younger at an earlier assessment found consistent and statistically significant *benefits* for overnight contact among 4- to 6-year-old girls. No significant differences were found for boys. Results were inconsistent and generally not statistically significant for infants/toddlers aged 0 to 3. However, more frequent overnights were associated with more behavior problems for some analyses (but again, the results were not statistically significant) (Pruett, Ebling, & Insabella, 2004).

The best investigation of overnights and young children is a recent Australian study. This research used data from a national study instead of potentially biased, self-selected convenience samples. The study also involved fairly large sample sizes. Among 248 infants whose parents lived apart, those 63 children who had one night or more per week were more irritable and displayed more vigilant visual monitoring of and proximity to the primary parent. Among 587 2- to 3-year-olds whose parents lived apart, the 26 with five or more overnights out of every fortnight demonstrated less persistence and displayed more distress in parent–child interaction. Finally, among the 1,015 4- to 5-year-olds whose parents lived apart, the 71 who spent five or more overnights per fortnight showed no more nor no less signs of adjustment difficulties (McIntosh, Smyth, Kelaher, Wells, & Long, 2010).

"More research is needed" is the most unambiguous conclusion that I can draw from this small set of studies. Still, based on these early research findings, my own reading of the attachment literature, and my professional and personal experience, I am cautious about overnights with children under the age of 1 and opposed to joint physical custody at least until the preschool years. The small numbers of "shared care" arrangements in the Australian national sample (where shared care is the legal ideal) suggests that many parents are cautious, too. As I have outlined in my book for parents (Emery, 2006) and discuss in more detail below, research and experience lead me to advocate for an evolving parenting plan: Infants should spend almost all of their overnights in one home, but overnights can become regular during the toddler years and perhaps evolve into true joint physical custody by the time a child reaches preschool or school age.

Joint Legal—the Rule; Joint Physical—the Exception

This brings us back to our point of departure: I want to encourage parents to work cooperatively to construct parenting plans that give them each at least a quarter of overnights with their children. Still, joint physical custody seems likely to work for only a minority of families for the reasons noted and because of the logistics involved (e.g., the parents' need to live near one another; they need to communicate and cooperate frequently; they need to manage a more complicated life for their children living in two homes). When parents are able to work together, the benefits outweigh the costs in terms of children's emotional well-being and the quality of their relationships with both parents.

Still, it is essential to note that only a minority of parents choose joint physical custody (and fewer maintain the arrangement over time). Estimates from the United States (Melli & Brown, 2008), the United Kingdom (Peacey & Hunt, 2008), and Australia (where the law clearly encourages joint physical custody; Smyth, 2009) all indicate a *maximum* national prevalence rate of 20% or less. There has been a notable increase in joint physical custody, but unlike joint legal custody, which is now the rule, joint physical custody remains the exception.

If Not Joint Physical Custody, What?

There has been even less research on other custody arrangements. No consistent pattern of findings has emerged from the small number of studies comparing mother and father custody, for example, or from matching children with their same–gender parents (Emery, 1999). Research does show that children adjust better if parental conflict is controlled, economic security is stable, and children maintain a good relationship with at least one, but hopefully both, of their parents (Emery, 1999). Based on this evidence, and on research indicating that mediation makes these outcomes more likely (Emery et al., 2005b), I have developed the following set of principles to guide parents in constructing their own, individualized parenting plans (for more details, see Emery, 2006).

- There is no single "best" schedule for children, so parents can "brainstorm" many alternatives that might work for them and for their children.[17]
- Rather than trying to intuit what will work, parents can experiment by trying a reasonable schedule but reevaluating and per-

---

[17] In my book for parents, I offer dozens of options to help parents to begin to think creatively and concretely (Emery, 2006).

haps altering the routine after a month or two. Before formalizing their plan in a signed document, they may choose to experiment for a longer period of time.

- More creative schedules can work if the parents have a cooperative relationship, fewer if their relationship is distant, and fewer still if their relationship is conflicted.
- A child's age is important to consider in crafting a schedule. As a rule, infants and toddlers benefit from having a "secure base" with one parent and relatively brief but hopefully frequent contact with the other parent. Preschoolers and school-aged children can have increasingly "even" contact with each parent, if desired, and tolerate longer separations with the benefit of fewer transitions. Teenagers typically are focused on their own schedule, which may make more complicated arrangements less workable, yet teens also have more flexibility (e.g., perhaps being able to drive), which can create new opportunities for contact.
- Because children (and workable schedules) change with age and because parents' lives change with time, a schedule should be construed in terms of months and years, not days and weeks. A parenting plan should be a "living agreement" that parents alter according to their children's and their own changing needs.
- Siblings can create opportunities and problems for a schedule. For example, older children often are a source of security for younger ones, so "moving in a pack" can make more "even" schedules more workable for young children. On the other hand, a teenager may not like the back and forth that is fine for a 10-year-old. Finally, many children want "one-on-one" time with each parent, a complication and an opportunity for families with multiple children.
- Parents want to consider what is best for their children and perhaps get the children's direct feedback about possible schedules. But in the end, deciding upon a schedule is the *parents'* responsibility, not a child's.
- While joint physical custody is much discussed, every-other-weekend schedules, often with contact on the "off" week, remain the most common arrangement for parenting plans that include overnights (Smyth, 2004).

Think Like Parents, Not Like Lawyers

All of these principles, which I discuss in detailed, parent-friendly terms elsewhere (Emery, 2006), can be grouped under the heading of "thinking like a parent, not like a lawyer." Divorced parents who are thinking like parents, for example, might agree that a 3-month-old should have a home base with his nursing mom and regular daytime contacts of a few hours with his dad. The parents might also agree to begin weekly overnights with Dad when the baby is 12 to 18 months old, much sooner if Dad can stay at Mom's place. They might also agree to gradually turn the plan into more-equal shared parenting during the preschool years, perhaps eventually getting to 50/50 by the time the child approaches or reaches school age.

This seems like an eminently reasonable plan, yet good lawyers will raise cautions (as they should under current laws). The mother's lawyer might suggest that she seek sole physical custody as a nursing mother. After all, breast-feeding puts her in a strong negotiating position, and she can give her ex more time in the years to come—if *she* wants to. The father's lawyer might note that an agreement about increasing Dad's time later is unenforceable. (Parents cannot contract around the child's best interests.[18]) Furthermore, the father will be in a weak position if the mother backs out in a year or so, since she will have had sole physical custody for a long period of time. Therefore, the father should insist on joint physical custody now or he may never get it.

It is easy to anticipate the conflict resulting from good legal advice like this. Parents need to understand the risks, but I want them to think— and act—like parents, not like lawyers. This means taking the long view, treating their parenting plan as a living agreement and doing what they truly think will be best for their children.[19]

EVOLVING CUSTODY LAW

If joint physical custody is unlikely to become the new custody standard, then what is? Some commentators are content with the current, general guidelines outlining children's best interests (see Table 6.1), arguing that they give judges wide discretion to carefully individualize custody arrangements on a case-by-case basis (Warshak, 2007). Others embrace the focus on children's best interests, but they worry that the unpredictability of current guidelines encourages parental conflict and litigation,

---

[18] Like the ALI (2002), I support the principle that parental agreement is in children's best interests, and therefore, judicial authority to overturn consent agreements should be eliminated. Allowing and enforcing agreements like the one outlined seems like a logical and useful extension of the principle of parental self-determination.

[19] Again, it will help if the law supports such choices by honoring and enforcing parental agreements.

overburdens courts, and increases the potential for bias in judicial decisions (ALI, 2002; O'Connell, 2007; Emery, 2007).

A Brief History of Custody Standards

Custody law was not always as vague as it is in the United States today. For most of history, men automatically gained custody under *chattel rules* which viewed children (and wives) as men's property.[20] By the 19th century, chattel rules weakened in the United States, but courts still awarded custody primarily to fathers, often referring to a man's role as head of his family (Grossberg, 1985). This preference for fathers was challenged and eventually replaced by the *tender years presumption,* which held that mothers were best suited to care for children of "tender years." A historical outgrowth of industrialization and gender role specialization, "tender years" expanded in the 20th century to include not only very young children but also older children and adolescents, making mothers the preferred custodial parent unless they were deemed "unfit" (Weiss, 1979b).

The *best interests* standard dates to the early 20th century, an outgrowth of the *parens patriae* (the state as parent) role of newly established juvenile courts (Grossberg, 1985). Until the 1970s and 1980s, however, children's best interests were assumed to be served by mother custody under the tender years presumption. The presumption was gradually abandoned as a result of changing gender roles and legal questions of gender bias. This created the dilemma that continues today: What is "best" for children? As Robert Mnookin (1975) put it:

> Deciding what is best for a child poses a question no less ultimate than the purposes and values of life itself. Should the judge be primarily concerned with the child's happiness? Or with the child's spiritual and religious training? Should the judge be concerned with the economic "productivity" of the child when he grows up? Are the primary values of life in warm interpersonal relationships, or in discipline and self-sacrifice? Is stability and security for a child more desirable than intellectual stimulation? These questions could be elaborated endlessly. And yet, where is the judge to look for the set of values that should inform the choice of what is best for the child? (p. 260)

Few would object to the ideal of putting children's interests first in divorce. Unfortunately, the unclear legal definition of "best" creates an impossible conundrum, one that helps to make custody disputes one of

---

[20] Chattel rules continue to guide custody decisions in many countries today.

the most common causes of legal action in the United States today (Schepard, 2004). A clearer standard would offer parents some guidance, guidance that they may or may not choose to follow in negotiating their own agreements. A clear standard also would provide predictable guidance in contested cases, thereby discouraging destructive custody contests.

The Approximation Rule

One promising new standard is the *approximation rule,* which would make parenting time after divorce approximate, as much as possible like parental involvement during marriage. Equally involved married parents would have 50/50 joint physical custody; breadwinner–caretaker couples would have more traditional arrangements (without consideration of gender); and variations in between would have appropriately varied parenting plans. Originally conceived by law professor Elizabeth Scott (1992), the ALI (2002) embraced the approximation rule in its proposal for revamping custody standards. It is critical to note, however, that the ALI made parental agreement its *highest* priority. The ALI strongly encouraged mediation and other forms of private dispute settlement and would no longer give judges the authority to override parental agreements (whether or not they conformed to the approximation rule).

The mostly untested[21] approximation rule is promising for several reasons. The rule is pluralistic—it is not a "one size fits all" proposition, yet it is clear and therefore should reduce conflict (Atwood, 2007; Emery, 2007). To those who object to a custody "formula," I am reminded of controversies over child support formulas that were adopted in the late 1980s (see below). Today, child support formulas are virtually automatic and greatly reduce potential conflict (ALI, 2002). And while some view the approximation rule as harming the negotiating position of divorced fathers (Warshak, 2007), national data indicate that, on average, married mothers provide about twice as much direct child care as married fathers (Bianchi, 2000). Under the approximation rule, this would result in joint physical custody for the typical American family (two-thirds time to mothers, one-third to fathers).

To be sure, there are some trouble spots for the approximation rule. One concern is that some parents want to become more involved with their children after divorce. A second is that fathers generally become more involved parents as children grow older. A third is that divorcing parents of infants and very young children have little, or no, predivorce

---

[21] As of the end of 2010, West Virginia was the only state to have adopted the approximation rule, and I have been unable to locate any evidence on its effectiveness there.

parenting to approximate. A fourth is that manipulative parents might strategically increase their parenting time in anticipation of a future divorce. These and other concerns would need to be accommodated and resolved as far as possible. In fact, the ALI (2002) recommended eight factors that "trump" the rule (e.g., ensuring a parenting time minimum). Still, approximating childrearing during marriage seems, at the least, to be a reasonable starting point in parents' negotiations.

MONEY: FINANCIAL ASPECTS OF DIVORCE

Divorcing parents have two big issues on which to decide: what to do about their children and what to do about their money. Many mediators only negotiate matters related to the children, leaving financial negotiations to attorneys. Nevertheless, it is important for mediators to know about the financial aspects of divorce for several reasons. First, divorcing parents naturally are very concerned about money. Second, disputes over money often are intertwined with conflicts about children, for example, physical custody and child support (or remaining in the family home or taxes). Finally, many ADR professionals do negotiate finances, including the author (although not in my mediation studies).

Two Economic Facts about Divorce

We begin our overview of divorce economics by noting two important facts. First, almost everyone suffers financially as a result of divorce. Second, on average, women and their residential children bear the brunt of the hardship.

Unless a family is very wealthy, it is virtually certain that their standard of living will decline as a result of divorce. In fact, a family may need as much as 30% *more* income in order to maintain the *same* living standard. Why? Because lost economies of scale make it far more expensive to live separately than together. For example, a married family with two children needed $21,834 to live at the poverty level in the United States in 2008. A single parent with two children, and one parent living alone, needed $28,547—over 30% more income (see Figure 6.2). No wonder everyone feels financial pressure in divorce.

Abundant empirical evidence also demonstrates that mothers and their residential children typically bear the brunt of the economic strain. On average, women's standard of living declines by about 25% following divorce, while men's living standards actually increase by about 10% (Peterson, 1996; Jansen, Mortelmans, & Snoecky, 2009; Uunk, 2004). The primary reasons for the gender difference are the differential earning

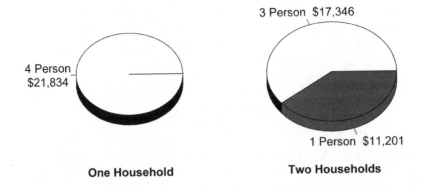

FIGURE 6.2. Increased income needs owing to lost economies of scale in divorce. Using official U.S. poverty thresholds, this figure illustrates how needs rise and therefore living standards fall as a result of divorce. At the 2008 poverty level, parents with two children would need over 30% *more* income to maintain the *same* standard of living ($28,547/$21,834).

power of women and men and the "opportunity costs" involved in rearing children (e.g., lost work experience).

The disparity may be shrinking with gains in women's employment (McKeever & Wolfinger, 2001), but even equality in earnings cannot eliminate the problems of economies of scale or the direct and indirect costs involved in raising children. Remarriage or repartnering is perhaps the only "solution" to the economic strain of divorce for women, as their family incomes recover to predivorce levels following remarriage/repartnering (Jansen et al., 2009). Of course, remarriage is not a potential legal or policy solution, and remarriage can introduce many new emotional, interpersonal, and economic conundrums for parents and children.

The three big "money" issues that must be addressed in divorce—property division, alimony, and child support—all are potential ways to reallocate finances between former spouses.[22] As we will see, however,

---

[22] As noted in Chapter 1, I use "divorced" to refer to cohabiting parents who split, as well as to formerly married partners. However, this linguistic convenience needs to be parsed when considering finances. Unmarried parents incur the same child support obligations as married parents, but in the United States, cohabiting couples generally are not required to pay alimony. Unmarried couples also can keep their property separate, while property acquired during marriage becomes jointly owned. The ALI would change this. Cohabiting couples would be treated like married couples, provided they lived together in a marriage-like relationship for a period of time. That is, property would be jointly owned and alimony might be required. Contemporary "common-law marriage" does precisely this in New Zealand and elsewhere (Lind, 2008).

alimony is the only transfer that is philosophically designed to accomplish this goal.

Property Division

Property division is the allocation of marital assets. In most states, the law divides marital property based on the principle of what is *equitable* or fair (Oldham, 2008). A small handful of states divide property *equally*, and "equal" often, but not always, is the operational definition of "equitable" in attorney negotiations and judicial decision making in other states (Kisthardt, 2008).

A major issue in property division can be determining what constitutes *marital property*, that is, jointly owned property. Historically, most states determined property based on who held title, so, for example, a house, a business, or a pension might have been titled to only one spouse, who could claim sole ownership upon divorce. Equitable distribution laws changed this, so that all property acquired during a marriage (including things like individual retirement accounts) is considered marital property—except gifts or inheritances in some states (Oldham, 2008). Even inheritances and gifts may be treated as marital property if the money is pooled with the couple's other assets (e.g., in an investment account), because such comingling can make it impossible to distinguish separate from marital property. In its proposal for legal reform, the ALI (2002) suggested a further and dramatic step: Separate property should gradually become marital property with increasing duration of marriage.

A couple's home, if they own one, often is their most valuable marital asset, and it frequently must be sold in order to accomplish property division. One investigator found an order to sell the family home in one out of every three cases (Weitzman, 1985). Many feel that it is desirable to maintain this source of stability for children during divorce, although few current or proposed laws support this objective (ALI, 2002; Oldham, 2008). One consequence is that bargaining for custody can be complicated by competing desires about the family residence. Some couples find a way to trade assets—a home versus a large pension, for example. Others retain joint ownership for a period of time in order to provide continuity for their children. Perhaps the most creative and complicated arrangement in this regard is "bird nesting" where the children remain in the family home, while the parents move in and out according to a prearranged schedule.

Alimony

Alimony (or spousal support or maintenance) is a payment made from one spouse to another for the purpose of maintaining the standard of living enjoyed during the marriage. The concept of alimony, typically a transfer from a former husband to a former wife, seems anachronistic to some, especially given contemporary visions of gender equality in the workplace. It is perhaps because of this conflict that the rules for determining alimony are so vague (Eekelaar, 1991; Oldham, 2008).

One of the few consistent innovations in alimony has been to limit its duration, particularly following shorter marriages (Oldham, 2008). But some evidence suggests that alimony is rare in any case. Perhaps one in five divorced women in the United States report receiving alimony, a fact that caused at least one commentator to declare an "alimony myth" (Weitzman, 1985). The low percentage is attributable to several factors, including: most divorces take place after brief marriages involving young partners who earn relatively little income; the duration of alimony often is limited, as noted; some opt for "lump sum" alimony payments (e.g., a bigger share of the property settlement); and some women are "at fault" in divorce, a factor that prohibits alimony in some states (Oldham, 2008).

Alimony laws can be simultaneously complex, vague, and unpredictable (Kisthardt, 2008). As with custody law, the ALI (2002) recommended creating clear and predictable rules based on (1) the partners' income disparity, (2) the duration of the marriage, and (3) years spent in childrearing. The ALI also changed the rationale for alimony from the goal of maintaining the former standard of living to compensating for lost human capital.

While the ALI did not offer a specific alimony schedule, the American Association of Matrimonial Lawyers (AAML) recently did, and their schedule is a useful illustration. The AAML would set alimony *amounts* to equal 30% of the payer's gross income minus 20% of the payee's gross income. The AAML would calculate alimony *duration* by multiplying the length of marriage by the following factors: 0–3 years (0.3); 3–10 years (0.5); 10–20 years (0.75); over 20 years, permanent alimony (Kisthardt, 2008). So, for example, a husband who earned $100,000 would pay a wife who earned $50,000 an amount of $20,000 per year in alimony for 4 years if they had been married for 8 years.

Alimony terminates when the recipient remarries. This creates for the recipient a financial disincentive for remarriage, and in the contemporary climate, many divorced adults cohabit rather than remarry. For this reason, a cohabitation clause might be added to a separation agreement, terminating alimony if the recipient cohabits in a marriage-like relationship or under other specified conditions.

Child Support

Child support is money paid from one parent to the other for the purpose of contributing to the costs of raising children. In the United States today, all states use schedules to calculate child support. Schedules differ from state to state, but most allocate a percentage of each parent's income to child support. Amounts are adjusted for different numbers of children, and sometimes are based on the number of overnights with each parent, as well as specific, additional costs such as medical expenses (including medical insurance) and work-related child care. The philosophy behind the calculations is to share the expenses parents would spend on children if they were living together.

All U.S. states' adopted child support schedules as a result of federal legislation passed in 1984 and 1988. Without a doubt, the schedules have made child support calculations easier, and thus have reduced parents' money conflicts considerably. Still, controversies can arise when there are questions about a parent's income (e.g., large disparities between before- and after-tax earnings), the payer has a substantial debt or additional children, or the parents share joint physical custody. The ALI (2002) recommended continuing current formulas but adding further considerations for children's needs and parents' respective earnings. When parents' incomes are quite unequal, these adjustments would substantially alter child support calculations, upward or downward.

Apart from the schedule, modifying child support over time can be an important issue. Like custody, child support is always open to modification (because both are based on the children's best interests, not the parents' contract), but negotiations and procedures can be complicated. Still, recalculating child support can lead to substantial changes in the dollar amount, because parents' incomes may change significantly, often as a result of altered employment or inflation over time. One option for anticipating such adjustments is to build automatic recalculations into an agreement, perhaps occurring every year or two shortly after taxes are filed (and therefore income data are handy).

The federal government has long been interested in increasing child support awards and compliance, because this would reduce Temporary Assistance for Needy Families (TANF, formerly AFDC) payments. This motivation led to the schedule requirement in the 1980s, as well as to various efforts to improve child support enforcement. According to census data, however, change has been slow. In 2005, 57% of custodial parents in the U.S. (61% of mothers, 36% of fathers) had a child support agreement or order, percentages not significantly different from 1993 levels. The proportion of parents receiving full payments did increase significantly over this time, from 37% to 47%. Another 30% of parents received partial payment in 2006. Importantly, the poverty rate among custodial mothers declined from 37% in 1993 to 28% in 2005 (Grall, 2007).

Taxes

A number of additional financial considerations are relevant in divorce. Taxes are one of the most important. In the United States, alimony payments are treated as a tax *deduction* for the payer and a tax *liability* for the recipient. Child support receives the opposite treatment. Child support is tax free to the recipient but is not a deduction for the payer.

Thus, the after-tax value (and before-tax cost) can be very different for the same dollar amount of alimony versus child support. Someone in the 20% tax bracket must earn over $1,200 to pay $1,000 in child support, but needs to earn $1,000 to pay $1,000 in alimony because of the tax deduction.[23] The recipient of $1,000 in child support keeps the full amount but must pay $200 in taxes on $1,000 in alimony (if they are in the 20% tax bracket).

Dependent care deductions are another important tax consideration. According to U.S. Internal Revenue Service rules, the dependent deduction goes to the parent who has a child for more time unless the parents agree otherwise. As long as the parents agree, the IRS places no restriction on assigning the dependency deduction.

Head of household status, which reduces the marginal tax rate, is treated differently—and can be more valuable than the dependency deduction. Among other conditions, an unmarried, separated, or divorced parent can qualify as head of household only if a child lived with them for more than half of the year. Parents with 50/50 joint physical custody cannot both be head of household for the same child. If they have two or more children, however, each parent may be able to claim head of household status if different children spend a few extra nights with each of them. Adding such details to an agreement potentially can be valuable to both parents in a 50/50 custody arrangement.

College and Other Special Expenses

Most laws do not address some expenses that many parents consider to be routine costs of child care. Examples include elective health care that is not medically necessary (e.g., braces, psychotherapy), extracurricular activities (e.g., summer camp), or private school tuition. Parents sometimes agree to share these expenses, perhaps dividing them in proportion to their incomes. Even if parents choose not to share such costs, raising the issues in advance can help to avoid future conflict.

---

[23] Workers actually must earn more to pay both child support and alimony, because FICA and Medicare are due in both cases.

For many families, the cost of a college education is the most important expense not addressed by most laws. Because college is so costly, divorced (and married) parents need to plan long in advance if they wish to save for children's tuition and living expenses. Divorced parents might agree to contribute a monthly, fixed dollar amount to a tax-free college savings program, for example, or they might each commit to paying a fixed percentage of the future cost of a college education at a designated university. Again, raising the topic can help to avoid conflict and hopefully can assist each parent in planning for the future even if they chose not to address college expenses in their agreement.

NO-FAULT DIVORCE AND PRIVATE ORDERING

We bring our consideration of legal issues to a close with a broad and brief look at how governments have regulated marriage and divorce, and how the deregulation of divorce fits with current efforts to promote the private ordering of divorce settlements.

In Europe, marriage originally was a private contract between two family groups, as it was (and to a lesser extent still is) in parts of the world today. The civil regulation of marriage and prohibition of divorce in Europe dates only to the Middle Ages, an outgrowth of advocacy by the Catholic Church (Eekelaar, 1991). After the Reformation, civil laws granted divorces (contrary to Catholic doctrine) but only if there was "fault," usually a finding of adultery, cruelty, or desertion.

During the 1900s, the judiciary regulated divorce less strictly, accommodating changing social attitudes with broad interpretations of grounds such as "cruelty" (Plateris, 1974). "No-fault" laws enacted in Great Britain in 1969, in California in 1970, and currently in all 50 U.S. states dramatically altered divorce. A no-fault divorce may be granted when both spouses request it and/or when the spouses have lived apart for a fixed waiting period. Some states retain fault grounds along with no-fault divorce, and for this strategic reason, as well as for emotional ones, fault can be an issue during negotiations even under no-fault divorce laws.

Still, no-fault laws represent a huge, historical change toward the deregulation of divorce. Adults in most industrialized countries not only are allowed to choose whom to marry, but they also can freely decide whether to divorce. Marriage and divorce increasingly have been privatized. Cohabitation is perhaps an even stronger indication of the privatization of intimate relationships, although new "common law" marriage laws reveal governments' interest in regulating marital dissolution (Lind, 2008).

Still, the sweeping deregulation of intimate relationships offers another impetus for mediation and ADR. Husbands and wives, mothers and fathers increasingly have both the right and the responsibility to make decisions about whether and how to marry or divorce. Mediation can be viewed as a way to help parents exercise their right to order their own affairs, and when it comes to children, their responsibility to do so.

SUMMARY

Many parents turn to the law for direction and protection in divorce, but find too little of both. The adversary system is supposed to offer protection, and it may be emotionally appealing to hurt and angry former partners. But adversary procedures can undermine the ongoing relationships between parents and their children—and between former partners who remain parents.

The law also offers parents little direction with respect to how to best parent children across two households. Suggesting that judges will make decisions according to children's best interests sounds reassuring, but it is an empty promise. Psychological research does not point to a single custody arrangement that best meets all children's psychological needs, and neither wise judges nor experienced mental health professionals have demonstrated an ability to make better decisions than parents.

Evidence indicates that most parents can successfully share major decisions (joint legal custody). However, joint physical custody can be the best—or the worst—arrangement for children, depending on the parents' conflict. In any case, to date, only a minority of parents successfully maintain joint physical custody. Recognizing the potential and pitfalls of custody arrangements can help parents plan wisely in advance; for example, clearly delineating shared and separate decisions and many other details in a parenting plan. For parents who cannot agree, the law needs a clearer standard for deciding custody disputes such as the proposed "approximation rule."

Money is the second major legal issue in divorce. Child support formulas have reduced conflict and helped to lift many residential mothers and their children out of poverty. However, many important expenses involved in raising children, for example, the cost of college, are not addressed by the law. Equitable property division has made the definition and allocation of marital assets fairer and easier to complete. Alimony remains an enigma in theory and in practice, although there are some rumblings of reform. Still, no legal remedy can overcome lost economies of scale, as a divorce can increase expenses by as much as 30% and almost inevitably lowers living standards.

No-fault divorce has eased the legal complications involved in ending a marriage. Cohabitation is another effort to make relationships more of a private agreement. Mediation and ADR are consistent with these broad trends, helping parents to reach settlements more on their own terms.

7

NEGOTIATING AGREEMENTS I

*Setting the Stage
and the First Mediation Session*

Take the first step in faith. You don't have to see the whole
staircase, just take the first step.
——Martin Luther King, Jr.

How can divorcing parents craft a sensible legal agreement when they
are being tossed about in the emotional cross-currents of divorce? Often,
they can't. This simple fact leaves parents with three options. They can
deal with their emotions first and do the details of a divorce later. They
can hand off the negotiations to someone else, most likely their lawyers.
Or they can rely on a third party to help them separate their emotions
from the issues involved in working out an agreement.

There are good reasons to consider all three options. Working
through the emotions first surely is the best alternative. But both parents
must be willing to take the time to deal with their own and each other's
feelings, either while still living together or separating informally. Hand-
ing negotiations over to lawyers, and perhaps leaving final decisions up
to a judge, may sound appealing in the chaos of divorce, and sometimes
this is the only option. However, sooner or later divorced parents must
deal with each other, and doing so sooner—and avoiding the adversarial

system—improves the chances of successful coparenting later. The third alternative is the focus of this and the next chapter, which detail how mediators can guide parents through their emotions and into a parenting plan. These "how-to-do" chapters serve as a treatment manual for anyone wishing to replicate or better understand my randomized trials of mediation and adversary settlement (Chapter 9). They also describe techniques and concepts that collaborative law professionals, therapists, traditional attorneys, and others can adapt in their various efforts to keep parents' emotions in check during divorce negotiations.

In Chapter 9, I review other evidence-based approaches to mediation together with a variety of approaches to settling divorce and custody disputes. I should be clear about two aspects of that discussion now. First, a wide range of dispute resolution alternatives—ranging from negotiating around the kitchen table to formal litigation—is needed to resolve or at least manage various divorce and custody disputes. Second, mediation is not just for "nice" divorces. Not every dispute can be successfully mediated, but, contrary to what some may think, mediation often is particularly helpful and appropriate for emotionally difficult divorces.

The present chapter focuses on setting the stage for mediation and conducting the first, critical mediation session. The education, policies, and procedures that set the stage for mediation are essential both to the negotiations and to the acceptance of mediation by the legal community. Getting the process off to the right start in the first session also is critical, as the meeting typically is affectively charged and full of hidden agendas, as parents look to the mediator for understanding, guidance, and, perhaps, an ally.

SETTING THE STAGE

In the first edition of this book, I noted that, because divorce mediation was new, mediators must be clear about their policies and procedures, and they should collaborate with legal professionals in developing them (Emery, 1994). In many parts of the United States (e.g., California) and countries around the world (e.g., Australia), divorce mediation is no longer new, having been available, even mandated, for 30 years or more. Yet, controversy continues about various policies even in established programs, and divorce mediation still is a new concept in many communities and countries. Of course, mediation almost always is new to clients, who typically do not get married with an exit plan. So it remains critical for mediators to have clear policies and procedures, to enlist the legal community in developing them, and to educate professionals and the public about what mediation is and how it works.

Judicial Support

Judicial support is critical to the success of any mediation program. Judges can insure that parents try mediation by making referrals themselves, or better yet, by helping to get cases to mediation early. For example, a judge might enter a standing order for a couple to attend a mediation orientation session (to occur at the time of filing or prior to a hearing), or judges can otherwise indicate their support to court and social service agencies, clerks' offices, the general public, legislators, and perhaps especially, the bar. Judicial support is critical to the acceptance of mediation by the local bar. Trial lawyers tend to agree with the judges who hear their cases.

Family court judges should be supportive of mediation for several reasons. First, like mediators, judges are in the middle in a custody dispute, and the position offers insight into the predicament of children caught in their parents' conflict. Second, judges see many families whose custody dispute is one of several problems, all of which may involve more psychological than legal issues (e.g., substance abuse, poverty). Third, these same families also may be involved in multiple, related court actions that judges must treat separately but potentially can be addressed together in mediation. Fourth, large and growing numbers of parents are unmarried, making their obligations to each other and their children even murkier— in the law and in their personal commitments. Fifth and finally, all of this is further complicated by increasing numbers of *pro se* cases. Facing case after case like this, judges are inclined to like that mediation promises to be helpful—and to reduce their overcrowded dockets.

These judicial perspectives were forcefully represented in a commentary by retired Judge Leonard Edwards (2007), who had two decades of experience as a California family court judge (where mediation has been mandatory since 1980). Responding to a commission that recommended revamping New York State's approach to custody disputes, Judge Edwards highlighted parent education and mediation as the most important proposed innovations based on the California experience:

> An important element of these programs is the attempt to focus parents' attention on the needs of their children during the separation and divorce process. The perception of those who work in the family courts is that divorcing parents are in a state of crisis and that the parents' personal needs often come before the needs of the children. For that reason, much time and effort in the court process is spent educating and reminding parents of the child's perspective. Mediators and court administrators have also learned that resources and interventions provided at the front end of the custody resolution process are more likely to result in the parties resolving the case themselves than those provided later in the process. (2007, pp. 24–25)

Edwards (2007) went on to say that, if New York implemented a unified approach to mediation:

> Judges … would have to start looking at the court system as a series of educational steps and procedural opportunities for parents to resolve their child custody disputes. The judge would become more of a case manager and less of a trier of fact. The judge would develop an attitude that while the court remains ready to provide a trial, if necessary, the preferred outcome is for parents to reach an agreement without resort to the formal court process. (pp. 54–55)

While support for mediation should be widespread among the bench, different judges surely have their own concerns or preferences about such matters as the content of agreements, the style in which they are written, how mediators relate to the bar, and what happens when mediation produces only a partial agreement or no agreement at all. Therefore, obtaining judicial input is essential not only for garnering strong support for mediation but also for developing workable policies and procedures.

The Bar

It is equally critical to involve members of the bar in shaping mediation policies. Most family lawyers are negotiators, not litigators, and they too are concerned that adversary procedures can inflame an already difficult situation, particularly for children. As long as they are treated as partners in the effort, most attorneys are likely to support mediation as a valuable option in an array of alternatives that include traditional legal practice, collaborative law, and lawyer–mediators (see Chapter 9). A very effective way to build ongoing collaboration is to establish multidisciplinary practice groups of divorce professionals that meet informally to get to know and educate each other about professional roles and responsibilities, local preferences, and innovative ideas and approaches.

Key questions and issues to raise (or reconsider) in setting policies and procedures are summarized in the following sections.

What to Mediate?

As noted in Chapter 6, the issues that must be negotiated in a divorce settlement can be reduced to two main topics: children and money. *Custody mediation* is limited to negotiating children's issues, specifically legal and physical custody and perhaps child support. *Comprehensive mediation* also incorporates financial issues.

A common "bargain" in practice is for mediators to negotiate custody, while attorneys work out finances (Ricci, 2004). Because an essential goal of mediation is helping children and divorced families, custody mediators often are mental health or social service professionals, particularly custody mediators who work in publicly supported programs. Attorneys typically have expertise in financial matters, but not in the psychological aspects of divorce, thus this division of labor is often sensible.

An argument for comprehensive mediation is that disputes about money and the children often are intertwined. The simplicity of resolving disputes in a single setting also is a potential benefit (Kelly, 1989). Many lawyer and non-lawyer mediators offer comprehensive mediation in private practice. Sometimes lawyers and mental health mediators work together, an approach that offers many potential advantages, particularly if the co-mediators are female and male. Despite these potential benefits of comprehensive mediation, custody mediation is likely to remain the focus of public programs, which have the goal of protecting children (Emery & Wyer, 1987a).

Voluntary, Discretionary, or Mandatory?

There continues to be debate about whether participation in mediation should be purely voluntary, whether cases should be ordered into mediation based on judicial discretion, or whether an attempt at mediation should be mandated before a court hearing is held. Like others (Edwards, 2007; McIssaac, 2010), my preference is to mandate an effort at mediation, which means that parents must attend at least one session, perhaps separately, to learn about the process but with no obligation to continue. My reasons for this preference include: (1) my desire to protect children; (2) the fact that mediation is an "emotionally unnatural" choice for parents in the short run but a demonstrably better alternative for most in the long run (Emery et al., 2005b); and (3) the likelihood that mandatory mediation encourages a less adversarial approach throughout the range of dispute resolution alternatives (see Chapter 9).

Obviously, mediators have no direct control over whether the process is voluntary, discretionary, or mandatory, and we must work with voluntary clients unless a mediation service is court-connected. (Some courts refer mandatory mediation cases to private mediators instead of maintaining their own service.) Still, mediators have an important role in educating clients, and the public, about the meaning of these alternatives. Education can help to correct one common misunderstanding: that mandatory mediation somehow requires a settlement as opposed to an effort. People cannot be denied access to the courts, and they can refuse to continue with mediation even in mandatory programs, which typically only require attendance at a single education session.

What Cases to Exclude?

Concerns about excluding cases from mediation typically are based on either the participants' inability to represent themselves or their dramatically unequal bargaining power. Serious mental illness, intellectual disability, or substance abuse may impair a parent's ability to represent him- or herself, and it typically is uncontroversial to exclude cases for these reasons. Much more controversial is when to exclude cases based on unequal bargaining power, particularly as related to questions of family violence.

Both child abuse and intimate partner violence require careful consideration as screening criteria before mediation. Child abuse obviously is of great importance in determining custody arrangements, as nothing is more important than a child's physical safety. The intimidation of a former partner by a perpetrator of violence in mediation, and beyond, similarly is a major concern, particularly since a history of some type of violence is found in about half of all cases (Holtzworth-Munroe, Beck, & Applegate, 2010). Difficulties in defining and substantiating abuse greatly complicate the development of screening criteria, as does the possibility of false allegations of abuse.

Much has been written about whether mediation should proceed in the face of partner violence (Salem & Dunford-Jackson, 2008; Ver Steegh, 2003), whether mediation is more or less appropriate in cases with different types of intimate violence, particularly "coercive controlling violence" (Kelly & Johnson, 2008; Moloney et al., 2008; Ver Steegh, 2005), how to assess intimate partner violence and its subtypes (Ellis & Stuckless, 2006; Holtzworth-Munroe et al., 2010), and how to protect victims when either terminating or continuing mediation upon learning of a history of violence (Beck, Walsh, Mechanic, & Taylor, 2010). The various issues and debates are too numerous to summarize here. Some mediation programs routinely exclude cases if there is a substantiated history of family violence. Others (including California's mandatory program) do not, but address concerns about abuse and unequal bargaining power, in part, by allowing partners to come for separate sessions, perhaps with an attorney or other support person, and to end the process for whatever reason (Edwards, 2007; Ricci, 2004).

Although opinions differ about how mediators should address domestic violence, there is widespread agreement about three procedures. First, mediators should routinely assess for partner abuse using interviews, written measures, or both. Second, mediators retain the right to end mediation themselves if they determine that bargaining inequities are too great as a result of partner abuse, intimidation, or any other reason. Third, pending charges of child or spouse abuse are *not* negotiated in mediation. When formal charges are pending, mediation can be suspended until an independent legal determination has been made. Mediation may or may not proceed at a later date, depending upon that outcome.

In my research, we excluded cases from mediation if (1) the woman was a resident at a battered woman's shelter, (2) there was a pending charge of domestic abuse, or (3) the mediators, based on their best judgment, determined that substance abuse, mental illness, intellectual disability, or unequal bargaining power made mediation unfair or perhaps impossible. We did not routinely exclude cases with a history of violent acts or informal complaints of current abuse. However, we did adopt various safeguards including (1) separate mediation sessions ("shuttling") if this option was believed to be less threatening either by a party or the mediators; (2) keeping the parties separate in other ways when necessary, for example, walking a parent to their car; (3) allowing either party to end (or not begin) mediation at any time for any reason (including feeling threatened); (4) the mediators ending the process if they were concerned about bargaining inequities; and (5) the mediators strongly urging parents, in writing, not to sign agreements before obtaining independent legal review.

How Neutral Is Neutral?

Mediators are supposed to be neutral, but exactly what does this mean? Surely neutrality means that mediators should not advocate for one party over the other. But can neutral mediators hold (and offer) opinions about issues like the benefits and risks of joint physical custody, the workability of "bird nesting," or the tenability of a parent's apparently untenable position? Consistent with widespread opinion, I just suggested that mediation should stop when a mediator judges a power imbalance to be too great. Yet, how can a mediator decide whether to withdraw without evaluating the parties, their negotiations, and a potential agreement? Mediators must overlook *any* power imbalance, ignore *any* accusation, and accept *any* agreement—or admit to limitations on their neutrality.

In practice, mediators adopt very different stances about neutrality, as is evident in a common distinction between three approaches to mediation. *Facilitative mediation* limits the mediator's role to facilitating communication, aspiring to remain neutral with respect to the content of agreements (Mayer, 2004). *Evaluative mediation,* in contrast, expects the mediator to offer opinions, make concrete suggestions, and even be confrontational at times (Lowry, 2004). *Transformational mediation* is intended to alter parties' relationship, not merely negotiate an agreement (Bush & Pope, 2004), an approach that blurs the boundaries of mediation and family therapy.

These three styles often are discussed as qualitatively different approaches—you have to pick one over the others. However, they were originally conceived as dimensions, not categories (Riskin, 1996). Mediators can be more or less facilitative, evaluative, or transformational, and it is perfectly possible (and wise in my view) to be a little bit of all three. My approach to mediation certainly includes aspects of all three approaches, although like most family mediators (Mayer, 2004), I probably am more facilitative than evaluative or transformational. Yet, I think it is far too restrictive—and, as I have suggested, impossible—to ask facilitative mediators to avoid all evaluation or any effort to probe their clients' relationship more deeply. Moreover, mediators are experts who have experience with important issues like different custody schedules. I am very willing to share my experiences with clients, as well as to discuss research on different schedules (see Chapter 6). However, I do not try to "muscle" clients into accepting any particular custody arrangement.

Since complete neutrality is not possible, mediators instead should strive to recognize and admit to their biases, including to their clients. This is a goal that lawyers surely will help mediators to achieve. Over time, attorneys pick up on patterns and "shop" for mediators (and judges) who tend to hold positions favorable to their clients.

Mediation or Family Therapy?

Like some forms of family therapy, mediation is a short-term and problem-focused intervention designed to resolve a family conflict. Unlike therapy, however, the overriding goal of mediation is to negotiate a fair, acceptable agreement (Kelly, 1983). Improving family relationships and promoting mental health are not explicit goals, except in transformational mediation which explicitly seeks to change the parties' relationship first and resolve disputes second (Bush & Pope, 2004).

Of course, mediators hope that positive individual and family change will be an *indirect* benefit of the process. Moreover, mediators often address various emotional issues (e.g., the pain behind anger) in the service of reaching an agreement. However, emotional or relationship change is not an end in itself.

A related issue is whether mental health mediators can move from therapy into mediation or from mediation into therapy. The simplest rule is to avoid such transitions. Still, this does *not* mean that couple therapy should automatically end when a couple decides to separate. A couple therapist often can help guide the partners through their emotional separation and into appropriate ADR (Emery & Sbarra, 2002). When both partners clearly want the former therapist to become their mediator, it may be possible to move into this new role. This is unlikely to happen following a one-sided separation, however, since the partner who has been left is likely to see therapy as a failure.

Moving from mediation into what may look more like divorce or family therapy is probably a more common, natural evolution of the process. Many parents return to mediation periodically for help in renegotiating agreements or resolving other, related conflicts. I strongly believe that such returns to mediation are *not* failures, but instead show the success of the process in creating a forum for discussing, planning, and renegotiating a "living agreement" (and perhaps other matters). As a rule, however, I prefer to construe these additional meetings as mediation, not therapy. Doing so preserves the mediator's role and special aspects of the mediator–client relationship, for example, confidentiality (which by law may be better protected for mediators than for therapists). In follow-up mediation sessions, I also limit the number of meetings, and maintain a focus on parenting and coparenting, even when new issues arise such as remarriage. I also may see one parent alone for a session or two after the original mediation ends, but I do so only with the knowledge and permission of the other parent, who remains my client, too. In short, mediation does not (and should not) become therapy, but, over time, mediators may address topics similar to issues more commonly addressed in family therapy (e.g., discipline or a troubled parent–child relationship).

Is Mediation Confidential?

When mediation ends without an agreement, a controversial question is whether the mediator should maintain confidentiality. This controversy continues to divide various courts involved in California's mandatory mediation program. Mediation is confidential in some California counties. In others, mediators offer the court an evaluation and often an explicit recommendation when mediation ends without an agreement (Edwards, 2007; Ricci, 2004).

Mediation essentially becomes arbitration when the process is not confidential. Reflecting this, mediators who do not offer confidentiality may reveal their opinion intentionally, especially if mediation is breaking down, in an effort to push parents into agreement (Welch, 2004). Such strong-arm tactics do produce agreements, and this is a potential advantage of nonconfidential mediation. However, parents may be inhibited in their discussions when mediation is not confidential. In this circumstance, parents can focus more on winning the mediator's support than on negotiating with each other. Many mediators, including the author, believe that the heart of mediation is giving parents an unimpeded opportunity to talk to each other and hopefully resolve their differences. From this perspective, the process of learning to work together is as important as the outcome.

Whether mediators can guarantee confidentiality (when they want to) is a question that can be clouded by legal considerations. Unless communication in mediation is privileged by statute, as it is in many states, a judge potentially can order that a mediator's testimony is in the children's best interests, even if the parents have signed a confidentiality agreement. This is because, in the eyes of the law, parents cannot contract around the principle of children's best interests, and a judge might decide that this means ordering mediator testimony regardless of whether or not a confidentiality agreement exists.

Should Attorneys Review Mediated Agreements?

If they are not represented by an attorney, I routinely urge parties in mediation to seek legal representation, and especially to have independent attorneys review an agreement before it is signed. This is a wise safeguard for parents and for mediators. In addition, the mediator's need to protect against inequities is less when each partner has an independent advocate.

As they prepare to ask their lawyers to review their mediated agreement, I often remind clients of two things. First, most attorneys view their job as finding holes in a potential agreement, not rubber-stamping something they have not negotiated themselves. A lawyer's input into a tentative agreement can be very helpful for spotting problems, but not every potential legal problem is a parenting problem. For example, a few lines in an agreement where parents commit to work together to coordinate parenting across households may be legally unenforceable, but such statements still can be helpful to parents. Or agreeing to revisit a parenting plan that places an infant primarily with its mother until the baby turns 18 months old probably weakens *both* parents' (potential) legal position, yet this still may be a good compromise for the couple who negotiated it. For reasons like this, I urge parents to remember that the mediated agreement is *their* agreement. In other words, listen to the legal advice but make your own decisions, particularly when it comes to your children.

Second, I tell parents that, while they want to craft a solid, legal agreement, I believe their moral commitment to parenting and coparenting, hopefully as demonstrated in mediation, will be stronger and more enduring than any legal agreement could be. I believe this to be true, and sincerely hope that my clients do, too.

How Long Should Mediation Last?

The use of time limits is a simple but critical consideration in setting the stage for mediation. In my research, mediation could last no longer than six 2-hour sessions. One rationale for the time limit was to study an intervention of a practical length for court programs; a second was to have a clear ending when mediation was unproductive; a third was to take advantage of the subtle pressures created by a ticking clock. The sessions did not necessarily take place on consecutive weeks. We often gave parents extra time to gather information, consult with attorneys, think through the implications of an agreement, ponder other major life decisions, and perhaps experiment with childrearing arrangements—maybe for a couple of months before signing the final agreement. In the end, parents in the studies spent an average of between 5 and 6 hours in mediation (Emery et al., 1991).

Public and private mediation programs experience opposite economic pressures regarding time limits in mediation. Because of financial constraints, some court mediators may be given as little as an hour to negotiate an agreement. In my view, this simply is not mediation. Such a short amount of time places all of the emphasis on getting agreements—keeping cases out of courts, rather than helping parents to coparent and order their own affairs. While some cases may settle in an hour, courts need to give mediators the opportunity to meet with clients for at least 2 hours on at least two or three occasions, the average time used in my studies.

In contrast to publicly supported programs, the economic incentive for private mediators (and lawyers) is to drag out cases. Notwithstanding the need to make a living, private mediators should carefully consider setting a time limit for the reasons outlined above. Comprehensive mediation might require more time than custody mediation, perhaps 8 or 12 2-hour sessions. And if more time is needed in an individual case, it is far easier to make an exception and relax an established time limit than to impose a seemingly artificial time limit when the process is dragging out unproductively. And as noted, successful mediation cases commonly return for help in addressing routine or more difficult issues. In addition to new difficulties created by remarriage, relocation, or developmental change, I see a number of clients once a "semester": in August to plan for the fall, in January to plan for the spring, and in April to plan for the summer.

How Should Mediators Be Trained?

How mediators should be trained remains a controversial topic. A handful of universities offer formal degree programs, while courses in ADR have become more common in law school curriculums, and to a lesser extent, in the education of social service and mental health professionals. However, most mediation training surely takes place in workshops offered privately or by the leading organizations such as the Association of Family and Conciliation Courts.

A number of states now certify mediators. An excellent example is California, which sets a high bar. Court mediators must have at least a master's degree in behavioral science, 2 years of prior mediation experience, and knowledge of the court system, family law, and community resources (Ricci, 2004). Family Mediation Canada is another example of a rigorous training and certification process (English & Neilson, 2004). Other states require no degree, and certify mediators based on minimal training (e.g., attending a 20- or 40-hour training program). Still other states do not control the title "mediator" at all. While standards of practice have been developed by organizations such as the Association of Family and Conciliation Courts (AFCC) and the American Bar Association (ABA), these do not address mediator training. Thus, there continues to be great variability in the background and training of mediators, a fact that surely impedes broad acceptance about the field of practice. My personal view is that mediation should be a practice specialty within an established legal or mental health profession.

Solo or Co-Mediation?

Co-mediation with an experienced—or equally inexperienced—mediator of the opposite sex is one of my preferred techniques for training, and practicing, mediation. Co-mediation balances the genders of the mediators and the clients, and it is reassuring to have another mediator in the room when learning about the process. Co-mediation also allows one mediator to direct the content of a negotiation, leaving the other to observe the process. The mediators can reverse roles; for example, the mediator who has been quieter can comment on the process or redirect the content to an overlooked topic. Co-mediators can also play "good cop/bad cop," as one mediator can confront an issue head on, while the second addresses the same issue from a more empathic stance.

Children, Stepparents, Grandparents, Lawyers?

Should mediation include children, stepparents, grandparents, and/or lawyers? Mediators differ in how they answer this question. Some mediators routinely include interviews with children, for example, and one very important Australian study found that "child-inclusive" mediation led to better outcomes for children and family relationships in the short run and at 4-year follow-up (McIntosh, Long, & Wells, 2009; see Chapter 9). Other mediators regularly involve lawyers in the process, or are required to do so by law or local rule. My standing policy, however, is to exclude everyone from mediation except for the two biological (or adoptive) parents.

What role children should play in custody disputes is controversial in mediation, in litigation, and in other settlement procedures. Initially, I believed that children should play a central part in mediation, since the ultimate goal was to promote children's best interests. However, I quickly reversed my position for precisely the same reason.

Instead of being given the *right* to have input into where they will live, too many children end with the *responsibility* to make custody decisions in the name of "hearing their voice" (Emery, 2003). And being responsible for choosing between two warring parents is the epitome of being caught in the middle of their disputes. In contrast, the implicit and explicit message in mediation is that *parents* have the right, and the responsibility, to make decisions about what is best for their own children. As a part of their decision making, parents can, and surely should, incorporate the children's preferences.

Thus, we rarely obtained children's independent input in our mediation studies, and I continue this practice today—even though I am impressed with the very careful inclusion of children and the positive results of "child-inclusive" mediation (McIntosh et al., 2009; see Chapter 9). We also routinely excluded stepparents, grandparents, and lawyers from mediation, not because they are unimportant, but because the responsibility for making custody decisions rests with the biological parents, not with these other adults. (I continue this practice, too.) As important as stepparents, grandparents, and lawyers may be, the biological parents assume responsibility for determining and defining the basis of these roles.

Every rule has exceptions (and it is easier to make an exception than to set a rule *post hoc*). Some children, especially teenagers, have clear preferences about where they want to live, they are able to articulate their desires, and they can offer good reasons for their choices. In such cases, involvement in mediation can help the children to give voice and weight to their opinions, particularly in speaking to a parent who may feel rejected. The goal in such a case is to help the teenager to be clear and convincing, and to minimize the feelings of guilt and rejection that may be felt by the adolescent and the parent, respectively.

We also may include stepparents or grandparents in mediation for a session or two if they are very involved in childrearing, or clearly play a central part in a dispute. Generally, these meetings do not include both biological parents, as one parent is likely to feel outnumbered in the presence of extended family from the other side. Rather, we hold a separate session for one biological parent and his or her relatives. The goals are to give the stepparent or grandparent some voice in the process, but simultaneously to support the biological parent's responsibility (or authority) to make decisions about their children's lives.

Setting the stage for mediation involves a number of essential considerations, as the above sections begin to introduce. Mediation policies can have a profound effect on the dynamics of the process, which is why I have noted the procedures followed in my studies. Mediators can find further guidance in the standards of practice adopted by AFCC and ABA. We turn now to an overview of the first mediation session, a description detailing the methods used by several different pairs of co-mediators in my research studies, all working in a court setting. I still use most of these same techniques today, although I have adapted them for solo mediation and work outside of a court service unit.

THE FIRST SESSION

Unlike later meetings, the initial 2-hour mediation session is highly structured. The meeting has five distinct parts: an introduction to mediation, child focus, problem definition, individual caucuses, and problem redefinition (see Figure 7.1). The structure allows the mediators to present some important didactic information; reassures parents with a safe, organized framework for discussing emotionally charged issues; and guides parents through some important emotional and substantive topics. By the end of the session, parents have resolved few of their conflicts, but they have learned about mediation and are becoming emotionally prepared to use it.

Introduction to Mediation

The mediators open with the simple warning that the first 10 to 15 minutes of mediation will be largely didactic. But they quickly follow with an acknowledgment of the many emotions involved in getting to mediation. One mediator might say something like, "We assume that you both have many strong feelings about your relationship, past and present, including sadness, fear, hurt, pain, and anger." In so doing, we want to acknowledge, legitimize, and normalize the parents' emotions, but we don't want to discuss them at this time. Instead, the mediators compliment the par-

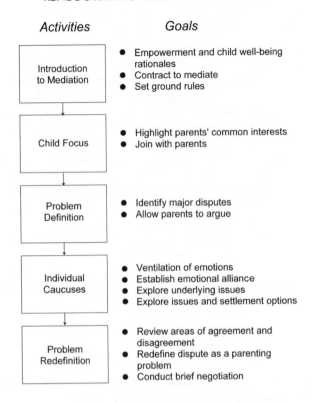

Activities

Goals

Introduction to Mediation
- Empowerment and child well-being rationales
- Contract to mediate
- Set ground rules

Child Focus
- Highlight parents' common interests
- Join with parents

Problem Definition
- Identify major disputes
- Allow parents to argue

Individual Caucuses
- Ventilation of emotions
- Establish emotional alliance
- Explore underlying issues
- Explore issues and settlement options

Problem Redefinition
- Review areas of agreement and disagreement
- Redefine dispute as a parenting problem
- Conduct brief negotiation

FIGURE 7.1. Five phases and major goals of the first mediation session.

ents for trying mediation (perhaps despite their many difficult feelings), and begin to educate them about the process. They contrast mediation with a custody hearing. A key is to indicate, accurately, that parents can control their own future in mediation, whereas a decision will be made for them in court. One mediator might say, "Some decision is going to be made about your children. It's up to you whether to make the decision yourselves or have a judge decide for you." This confronts parents with the reality that a decision *will* be made, and often motivates them to want to make their own decisions about their own children.

Empowerment, Responsibility, and Blame

We *want* to motivate parents to make their own decisions. After all, empowering parents is a key goal of mediation. Yet, the philosophy is about "should" not just "can." From the outset, the mediators adopt the stance that parents have the right—and the *responsibility*—to make decisions about their children's upbringing. This position might be left implicit, or it may be stated explicitly. Still, the mediators are likely to have to remind parents about their responsibility by asking them more than once (and in various ways) whether they think it's best for them or a judge to decide how their children should be raised.

While we are on the topic of responsibility, let me interject a note about responsibility and blame for a marriage breaking down, an issue that commonly arises in mediation, sometimes from the outset. Divorce is a heavy burden to shoulder, and many former partners try to lighten the load by shifting all the blame onto their mates. Arguments about who is at fault for a breakup commonly erupt in the first session (even though we live in a no-fault divorce era). "We're only here because HE had an affair." "I had an affair, because you rejected me for YEARS." "Rejected you? You were never around to reject!" And so it goes.

Mediators do not want to get caught up in this blame game, which is a trap with no end. Instead, one mediator might say something like, "I am sure there is plenty of blame to go around." Or "I've never seen a breakup where each person shares the blame 50/50, but I haven't seen one where it's 100/0 either." A comment like this can be quickly followed by a statement like, "But in any case, we're here to talk about the present and the future, not the past."

The Children's Interests

Although self-determination is important, the main reason for pursuing mediation is its potential to benefit the children. The mediators might note how children are hurt by their parents' anger and fighting—something a great many parents in mediation have witnessed for themselves. But the emphasis should be on the positive: how parental cooperation can benefit children, no matter what the specifics of a parenting plan. This discussion usually does not need to involve authoritative pronouncements or guilt trips. Most parents clearly realize that their conflicts are destructive. Despite their own sometimes overwhelming pain, many parents also sense the need for cooperation in coparenting in the future. Still, a statement such as "I am here for the same reason you are. I'm interested in your children's well-being" can remind parents of their mutual interest in their children. It also can help the mediator to ally with the parents in attempting to meet the shared goal of promoting their children's welfare.

Parents can be empowered further even as the mediators raise concerns about the children. The mediator's positive focus on parenting and coparenting tells parents that they *can* promote their children's positive mental health. Contrary to what parents may have read or been told by family and friends, divorce does not doom their children. They can still have a happy, healthy childhood, and divorced parents still can have control in promoting this. Despite the divorce, they can make sure that their children get to be "just kids" not forever "children of divorce." The way to do so is to work to improve relationships, each of their relationships with the children and, to the extent possible, their relationship with each other.

Thus, the two major themes of mediation are established from the outset of the first session:

- Parents know what is best for their own children, and they can and should make these critical decisions themselves.
- The parents' present and future actions, together and separately, can ensure that their children will thrive, even as they adjust to a divorce.

The Mediation Contract

After outlining the rationales, the mediators shift the topic to how mediation works. They briefly explain the process, and if the parents have no questions, the mediators ask the parents to sign a contract highlighting several points (that were just explained). The document states that the parents are in mediation voluntarily, can end the process at any time, and are encouraged to consult an attorney independently. It also states that, should mediation fail to end with a written agreement, neither parent will subpoena the mediators to appear at any subsequent hearing. The contract to mediate also notes various limits on confidentiality, which will differ from state to state.[1]

Originally, I thought of the contract to mediate as a protection for the mediator, but it also benefits parents. The mediators therefore should point out that the contract assures them that the mediators are not conducting a custody evaluation, passing judgment, or making decisions for the parents. Rather, the mediators are there to help the parents talk about some very difficult issues, and perhaps offer some reflections and perspectives, in the hope that the parents can arrive at their own resolution to their disputes. This discussion, and the signing of the contract, seems to make parents more committed to pursuing mediation in good faith.

---

[1] Virginia's statute privileging communications in mediation had not been enacted when my research was conducted (VA Code §8.01-576.10). Readers in jurisdictions that do not privilege communications in mediation should know that such contracts can be challenged. See Folberg (1988) and "Protecting Confidentiality in Mediation" (1984).

Ground Rules

Once the contract is signed, the mediators outline several ground rules for present and future sessions. They tell the parents that they are in charge of the sessions and expect the parents to respect their authority. The mediators warn parents that they may be interrupted, asked to stop talking, or perhaps asked to leave the room. They also tell the parents that they want them to focus on the issues at hand rather than the emotions behind them. (One of my preferred lines: "We don't want this to be like a rock and roll song, where the music is so loud that you can't hear the lyrics. We want you to focus on the lyrics, not the emotional music.") Finally, the mediators note that they will focus on the present and future, not the past. The mediators might also say that it can be hard to follow the rules, but they will enforce them nevertheless.

In establishing ground rules, the basic message is that the mediator is in control. This is conveyed, in part, to underscore the mediator's authority. It also is intended to reassure the parents that mediation will be a safe place for them to discuss emotionally charged issues. It is extremely difficult for many separated parents to exchange ideas without becoming upset, and the mediator must be both authoritative and empathic. One way a mediator can begin to do this is to end the discussion of ground rules by telling the parents that either one of them is free to take a break if mediation becomes too difficult. At this point, the mediator might also say that mediation is not for everyone. However, the comment often has the paradoxical effect of enhancing the parents' desire to make mediation work for them.

Flexible Structure

Mediators should not expect parents to fully follow the ground rules. After all, the stakes are high and parents' emotions are powerful and complex. In fact, the rules are not intended to be rigid. Instead, they set expectations in a way that allows mediators to redirect conversation or short-circuit arguments, as needed, later in the process. Once a rule has been established, it either can be enforced or, if it appears important to do so, the mediator can make an exception. Without an established rule, however, parents may feel that they are being treated unfairly when the mediator interrupts them and asks them to focus on issues rather than emotions or to look to the future instead of the past. As with setting a time limit, the rule seems far less intrusive if it is established at the outset rather than imposed in response to a difficult interaction.

This example illustrates a more general point about flexible structure in mediation and in following a parenting plan. Divorcing parents need a clear structure—explicit boundaries—but once a pattern is in place (new boundaries are established), they can be more flexible in following the rules.[2] A key example I invariably explain later in the process is that, once parents have followed their parenting plan religiously for at least several months, they may become more flexible in following the spirit rather than the letter of their agreement. Just like the ground rules provide a structure to fall back on when problems arise in mediation, the details of the parenting plan serve the same purpose when problems arise with more flexible coparenting.

Setting Limits

The mediators bring the introduction to mediation to a close by outlining a few more points that set limits on the process. They tell parents that it usually takes 4 to 10 hours for parents to reach an agreement in mediation, and that mediation is limited to no more than 12 hours. They also may comment about limiting communications with the mediators between sessions. Telephone calls and e-mails can be frequent between mediation sessions, far more so than between sessions of psychotherapy, and these contacts can place demands on both the mediator's time and neutrality. Mediators can help to limit these contacts by setting a rule in advance, or by charging for the time (a standard practice for attorneys).

Finally, the mediators outline their goals for the first session. They tell the couple that the mediators will work primarily with them together, but they also will meet with each parent separately in the first and perhaps future appointments. The mediators make it clear that the main goal of the first session is to find out whether mediation is appropriate for the parents. The parents similarly are encouraged to use the first session to find out more about mediation and the mediators, and to make a decision about whether they want to continue. Finally, the mediators remind the parents they are free to terminate mediation for whatever reason, including if it seems unproductive or because the "fit" with the mediators does not feel right. Parents seem to particularly appreciate this last suggestion, which encourages them to be good consumers in shopping for professional services.

Child Focus

The introduction to mediation usually takes 10 to 15 minutes. During this time, parents often seem to become more relaxed and less angry,

---

[2] I rarely use terms or concepts like "boundaries" with parents in mediation. I think in those terms, but generally talk with my clients about "rules" or "routines" instead.

sometimes even a little bored. In an attempt to create an atmosphere that is conducive to negotiation, the mediator's verbal and nonverbal behavior can be deliberate, quiet, and calm. This tactical slowdown may be particularly effective when parents seem especially nervous or agitated at the beginning of mediation. Many parents come into the session prepared to "argue their case," but before they do so, they have to wait through the mediator's presentations. Parents may be ready to launch into their disagreements after the introduction to mediation, but they are not allowed to do so quite yet. The first thing the mediators ask parents to talk about is not their disagreements, but an area of agreement: the things they like about their children.

Mediators transition to this child focus with a statement such as "As we discussed, a major reason for trying mediation is your children's welfare. We would like to know a little more about what your children are like before we talk about the disagreements you are having about them." This opening surprises many parents who are preparing to air their grievances at last. In fact, the comment often leads to an animated conversation between the parents. If it is managed well, this discussion can be fun for the parents and the mediators. Parents may dig pictures out of wallets, and tell tales of their children's antics. The conversation seemingly reminds the parents of their common interests and history in raising their children. If so, the mediator can direct the conversation to focus on the children's strengths, and commend the parents for their individual and joint success in rearing their children. This can help parents who may feel like failures to remember their successes in raising their children.

On the process level, the mediation session becomes more open and unstructured while discussing the relatively safe issue of the children's strengths. As the discussion proceeds, the mediators can become less directive, and share a genuine interest in the children's well-being. The mediators should try to ignore or block negative comments by either parent, at least until the parents engage in at least some mutual, positive dialogue about their children. After a few minutes, the mediators can bring the discussion to a close with a statement about using mediation to find a way for each parent to continue to be an effective support for the children.

Unfortunately, some parents' emotions are so intensely negative that it is impossible for them to have even a brief, amicable discussion about their children. If angry enough, divorcing parents can turn any topic into a blame game. When attempts to find common ground about the children repeatedly fail, the mediators should bring the child focus to a premature end. The mediator can ask whether the fighting is typical of the parents' relationship, and raise questions about its effect on the children. Although the child focus is negative and unpleasant in this case, the underlying messages are the same as when a supportive conversation takes place. The parents each are concerned with their children's welfare. Their behavior has and will continue to influence their children's emotional health. Their job is to find a way that they can assure that their parental influence will be a positive one, both individually and jointly.

Problem Definition

Parents finally get to "argue their case" about 20 minutes into the first session. After ending the child focus, the mediators ask each parent to present their perceptions of their differences about the children. They also ask the parents to briefly share some of their ideas about possible solutions. Before the parents start talking, however, the mediators request that the parents speak in a highly structured manner. They give each parent about 5 minutes to offer "your side of the story," uninterrupted by the other parent. Typically, the mediators let the parents decide who will go first, but they may suggest that one parent begin if there seems to be a reason for doing so (e.g., that parent has been especially quiet). As an aid in maintaining silence, the mediators may give the other parent a pad and pencil for notes. When it is this second parent's turn to speak, the mediators thank him or her for being quiet, remind the other parent to please do the same, and tell the parent who now has the floor that the mediators are not looking for a rebuttal but instead want to hear that parent's concerns.

As each parent speaks, the mediators use reflective listening, empathy, and a few questions to summarize and clarify the issues. In so doing, the mediators have several goals. The most important is simply to ensure an accurate understanding of the topics of dispute. The areas of disagreement that the parents outline at this point typically become the major topics of discussion in future mediation sessions. Thus, the information is extremely important to gather and comprehend. This also is a time for the mediator to begin to obtain information about the parents' current arrangements for spending time with the children, work schedules, child support, and other practical matters that will bear on later negotiations.

Another important goal of the mediators' summary is to begin to redefine the issues at hand. Part of this redefinition involves semantics, as language that is intensely symbolic is replaced with more neutral terms. The mediators substitute terms such as "time sharing," "decision making," and "parenting plan" for terms like "custody," "visitation," and "separation agreement" (see Chapter 6). Yet another part of the redefinition is more substantive, in particular, reframing the nature of the parents' disputes. In subtle ways, the mediators hint that part of the problem appears to be the parents' inability to agree on how best to parent their children. "It sounds like the two of you share similar goals—you both want your children to have strong relationships with each of you. But you disagree about the best way to make that happen." All of this helps to make abstract legal disputes more concrete and controllable. (As an important aside, note how sample statements include qualifiers such as "sounds like" and "similar," a tactic that makes it harder to disagree with the summary. Getting parents to agree on the problem, even generally, is a prerequisite for moving them toward a solution, and many parents come into mediation prepared to disagree about everything.)

Reframing the custody dispute as a parenting problem not only turns legal abstractions into manageable parenting issues, but also it is akin to the structural family therapy concept of redefining children's psychological difficulties as problems of parenting (Minuchin, 1974). The mediators suggest that the parents' issues are not just a matter of custody. Certainly a parenting plan needs to be agreed upon, but perhaps more importantly, the parents need to find ways to work together no matter what the eventual plan may be. The reframing is put gently at this point. However, the mediators become more emphatic as the first session moves toward its close, as we discuss shortly.

Anger and Arguments

The discussion of their disputes and preferred solutions often ignites each parent's anger. When the mediators lift their prohibition against interrupting the other parent (after giving each parent at least one turn and doing some initial reframing), it is not unusual for the discussion to become embroiled.

The parents' conflict can be instructive to the mediator in many ways. Their style of arguing offers some insight into their past and current relationship. Both parents may be intensely caught up in the dispute, for example, or one partner may be "hysterical," while the other is cool and reserved. Or the discussion may be passive or intellectualized, but punctuated with sarcastic comments. Some parents avoid conflict altogether.

The intensity and topics of angry dispute often signal which issues raised previously are most important and probably most difficult to address. Parents also may raise new, key concerns during this anticipated fight (e.g., an affair). The conflict may be affectively charged and all inclusive, suggesting broad issues in the parents' relationship. Or it may focus on a particular topic. Parents may have a generally cordial relationship, but they become heated in discussing an issue that is a source of intense disagreement, for example, one parent's planned remarriage or relocation. In many cases, the angry dispute focuses on issues only indirectly related to custody. The parents' argument about a parenting plan quickly turns into an even more vehement dispute about an affair, a mental health or substance abuse issue, or perhaps one partner's callous rejection of the marriage versus the other's inability to face reality.

Managing and Tolerating Conflict

Mediators must learn to manage conflict and have confidence in their ability to do so, but they also must learn to tolerate even angry arguments. On the one hand, the mediators may lose credibility and dash any hope of reaching an agreement if they cannot control the parents' intense emotions. On the other hand, rapport may be destroyed if the mediators squash any expression of difficult but critically important feelings. When and how to stop parents from fighting therefore is a matter requiring careful judgment. Alternative strategies range from detached listening to firm directives to stop talking to telling one parent to leave the room.

Managing Conflict by Not Trying

When learning to mediate, I experimented with a number of methods for avoiding a fight at this early point in the first session. Frankly, the intensity of parents' conflicts made me anxious, and I was concerned about demonstrating my ability to control angry disputes (especially since the mediation conference room was directly over the judges' chambers when I began my research studies). Over time, however, I became convinced that a dispute at this early point in mediation actually facilitated later problem solving. Thus, my preferred conflict management technique when this first fight erupts is simply to observe the parents, allow them to fight, and when they finally turn to the mediators in frustration, ask whether this is typical of their encounters.

There probably are several reasons parents benefit from fighting early in mediation. Some parents may want the mediators to see and hear just how bad things are. Others may think more clearly once their emotions have been discharged. Or maybe parents need to experience one more failed attempt to negotiate before they are willing to accept the mediators' help. In any case, when parents turn to the mediators in frustration, they are inviting them into the disputes. Mediators thus are wise to follow up parents' likely admission that, yes, such angry disputes are typical, but suggesting that this is why the parents can benefit not only from mediation but also from finding new ways of relating to each other outside of mediation (although, at this point, we do not suggest what those new ways of relating might be).

Just as some partners fail to have a cordial discussion during the child focus phase, others do not argue during the problem definition phase of the first session. In these cases, parents are allowed to proceed with their even-handed discussion. Most couples eventually will have an angry exchange, and I typically respond to that first fight in the same way—managing the conflict by not trying to manage it. In fact, parents who are very calm and controlled at the beginning of mediation often turn out to be so strategic—or so firmly locked into their bargaining positions—that they refuse to compromise in later discussions. Contrary to what some expect, mediation often seems to be more successful with parents who initially are more acrimonious than with partners who, on the surface, seem to be cooperative.

The mediators bring the problem definition stage to a close after they have been "invited" into the parents' dispute. Wrapping up, the mediators may offer a bit more reframing, while briefly summarizing the parents' areas of agreement and disagreement. They then promise to address all of the issues, but before moving on, the mediators interview each parent individually, as they said they would do.

Initial Caucuses

Both co-mediators interview each parent alone in the initial caucus. All subsequent caucuses follow this same format. It would be more efficient to have each mediator caucus separately with each parent, but concerns about forming alliances between one parent and one mediator outweigh the desire for efficiency. If a 2-hour interview has been scheduled, which is typical, caucusing with each parent alone takes place about 45 minutes into the first mediation session. If a 1-hour session is held, caucusing is postponed until a second meeting, where parents may come at different times.

Just before breaking for the caucus, the mediators tell the parents that they wish to gather more information about each of their views. Often, it seems more important to talk with one parent first, perhaps because that parent is particularly distraught. Typically, I pick that parent by making an innocuous excuse; for example, I ask the other parent to step out because they are closer to the door. When the caucus begins, the mediators indicate that information obtained in caucus will be held in confidence, unless the parent gives permission otherwise. Then, one mediator invariably says, "We would like to know more about the things that may have been difficult to discuss in front of [the other parent], but might help for us to know about."

This statement usually opens the floodgates. Parents typically have just had an angry dispute, and they no longer need to keep their emotions pent up. While the previous fight may have been intense, the parents (or the mediators) kept the "discussion" in check when the parents were together in the room. Now that they are separated, the mediators allow each parent to express his or her emotions fully. Thus, shortly after having their hurt, pain, fear, and anger aroused, parents can vent in a safe setting. Very commonly, parents begin the caucus by continuing to give voice to their anger—and are in tears a short time later.

In addition to the emotional venting, the caucus gives the mediators a chance to establish rapport with each parent as an individual. The mediators can empathize with each parent's emotions, yet still remain neutral on the issues. That is, they can establish an *emotional alliance* with each parent, while avoiding a *strategic alliance* with either one. Parents gain some trust in the mediators and the process when they feel they are heard, respected, and understood. They thereby begin to build a small degree of trust in each other.

Underlying Issues

Of course, the caucus also serves informational purposes. A bridge between the emotional and the substantive is to use the caucus to begin to discover "real" or underlying issues in the parents' disputes. For example, what appears to be a difference about overnight visitation may prove to be a disagreement about "overnight guests" when the children also are in the home. Such underlying issues may be addressed directly, or more obliquely, in later negotiations. The choice depends on the sensitivity of the issue, and whether it can be resolved indirectly or must be agreed upon explicitly.

Reconciliation Possibilities

A key issue underlying many predissolution negotiations (and some postdivorce negotiations) is the possibility of reconciling. The mediators typically raise this topic (if the parents don't beat them to it) so they can better understand each parent's agenda. In some cases, *both* partners are uncertain whether they want to divorce (see Chapter 1). In such a circumstance, what appeared to be the initiation of mediation may, in fact, be the beginning of couple therapy. Divorce therapy is another alternative that some parents choose instead of mediation. Unlike marital therapy, the goal of divorce therapy is not reconciliation. Like couple therapy and unlike mediation, however, divorce therapy gives the partners a forum for exploring and expressing their own feelings, and for better understanding each other's feelings.

If only one partner expresses a desire to reconcile, the mediators remind him or her that mediation is *not* couple counseling. They can soften the blow by noting that, whether or not the parents eventually reconcile, they hope mediation will help the partners and their relationship by sorting out arrangements for their children. For a partner who maintains a fervent desire to reconcile, the possibility of an improved coparenting relationship might allow them to hold on to some small hope for reconciliation (which does indeed happen sometimes).

Of course, the mediators must remain sensitive to one partner's hope of saving the marriage during subsequent negotiations. The possibility of reconciliation may not be discussed directly, but the partner's hopes often are apparent in his or her behavior, for example, being repeatedly hurt by the other parent's obvious desire to move on. Mediators may convey empathy nonverbally or indirectly at such times. The mediators also need to be alert to the possibility that a partner who wants the relationship to continue may attempt to undermine mediation. As noted earlier, the leaver is likely to be eager to "do business," while for the left party, doing business means accepting the end of the relationship. Showing empathy for the left partner can be particularly important, because it may feel like the mediators are on the leaver's "side." After all, the mediators are helping the leaver achieve his or her objective: to negotiate an agreement.

As mediation continues, caucuses may be needed to help the left partner cope with the increasing awareness that reconciliation fantasies are, in fact, just fantasies. Such issues, or perhaps obstructionist ones, can be acknowledged far more tactfully in caucus than in joint sessions. Furthermore, a caucus is usually the appropriate forum for making a referral for individual therapy if the mediators believe this will be beneficial.

Overlapping Options

One reason why mediation is a valuable forum for divorcing partners is because many legal disputes really are about one or both of the parents' underlying emotional concerns. Of course, there are important substantive issues to address, and these are a second, key focus of the initial caucus. The mediators can explore each parent's perspective on their disputes more freely without the other parent in the room, and parents also are generally more comfortable sharing their ideas about potential solutions when talking to the mediators alone.

In exploring these issues, the mediators restate their understanding of the key issues and ask each parent about his or her hopes for a settlement. The mediators also inquire about any legal information or advice the parent has obtained. Some parents naively reveal strategic behavior in response to the latter question, for example, "I'm only here because my lawyer thought I might get a better deal in mediation." Other parents reveal clearly unrealistic but firmly held positions, for example, an uninvolved or impaired parent might be demanding 50/50 joint physical custody. In such a circumstance, the mediators might encourage parents to consult their lawyer about what would be likely to happen in court. The suggestion itself may imply that the position is untenable, but in any case, the parent soon is likely to be confronted with a bit of reality delivered from a credible source—his or her own attorney. Of course, by not directly suggesting that the position is untenable, mental health mediators avoid the unauthorized practice of the law, and lawyer mediators avoid dual representation.

While exploring potential solutions with each parent alone, it is not unusual for the mediators to discover an overlap in the two parents' positions. Communication can be that bad, or if they have engaged in positional bargaining to this point, each parent may have "hid the ball" and be unaware of the overlap in the range of acceptable compromises. Discovering such mutually acceptable solutions is, of course, one of the goals of the caucuses. Yet, while knowledge of overlapping positions obviously is of critical importance, the mediators still must use the information cautiously. They promised that the caucuses would be confidential, and there often is still considerable room for negotiation about exactly how much each parent might or might not compromise.

It is also common, of course, for the mediators to discover no overlap in the parents' positions during the initial caucus. Still, points of agreement inevitably are uncovered during the joint and individual discussions that have taken place to this point. It is important for the mediators to review these areas of agreement, as well as of disagreement, as they begin to bring the first meeting to a close.

Problem Redefinition

The first mediation session ends with a review and redefinition of the substantive differences that have been raised up to that point. The review is based primarily on information obtained during the problem definition discussion. Thus, in a 1-hour session, the problem redefinition can occur without the caucuses. In reviewing the disputes, the mediators explicitly acknowledge that the parents' differences are substantial and important. Still, they highlight the parents' areas of agreement, even if only their shared love and concern for their children. The goal of emphasizing areas of agreement is to underscore the parents' common interests and convey at least some optimism about reaching a resolution.

After reviewing specific areas of agreement and disagreement, the mediators then suggest that the parents' inability to negotiate their differences is the paramount problem. Their inability, to date, to find a way to work together as coparents is the most basic issue for them to address and hopefully change. This reframing of the dispute may take the form of a general suggestion that the parents need to find a way to resolve their disagreements about the children now and in the future, since they will always be connected through the children. Depending on what has occurred earlier, however, the redefinition may be more direct, specific, and painful to hear. For example, the mediators may forcefully state that it appears that the parents are trying to hurt each other through the children—and the children are the ones who are really being hurt. Such difficult feedback might be paired with the mediators discussing how hard it was for *them* to be in the middle of the parents disputes, and by inference, how much harder it must be for the children to be caught in the middle.

Whether the feedback is gentle or confrontational, the mediators balance the discussion of the parents' differences by returning to an optimistic portrayal of the parents' ability to control their own future. There are always many areas of agreement, even when custody is disputed with rancor, and neither the parents nor the mediators can afford to lose sight of this fact. The mediators might note that the parents may have irreconcilable differences in their relationship, but they have resolved many differences about parenting in the past—and, again, this is one area where they agree about many things. So, they have the opportunity, and the responsibility, to do their job, to find ways to work together in the present and in the future, so their children can thrive. And as always, part of the job of being a good parent is putting some of your own feelings second and putting the children first.

As the first session is coming to a close, the mediators ask the parents for feedback about the accuracy of their summary of the parents' areas of agreement and disagreement. They also ask about the parents' thoughts about how they see the core problem, that is, the redefinition of the custody dispute as a basic coparenting issue. At this time, the mediators may clarify or simply acknowledge differences in perception. The mediators can then ask the parents if they wish to continue with mediation. If they are hesitant, the parents might be encouraged to mull the decision over for a few days. The mediators still schedule a second appointment, but they tell the parents that they are free to cancel for any reason. As the mediators invite the parents to consider their decision, they might tell them that the first session was unusual. Future sessions will emphasize problem solving far more than information gathering.

Depending upon the family's circumstances and the amount of time left, the mediators often will begin a brief negotiation at this point. The negotiation typically involves a temporary agreement, one that can be implemented before the next scheduled session. A visit for the coming weekend might be arranged, for example, or the parents might negotiate a united response in regard to discipline or some other issue concerning the children. This brief interchange almost always results in an agreement, because the parents are only asked to follow it until the next appointment. In so doing, however, the parents are given a taste of successful negotiation. Hopefully, this will foreshadow what they will succeed in doing in subsequent meetings.

The mediators bring the first session to a close by again praising the parents' laudable efforts in coming to mediation, congratulating them for their obvious concern for their children, and offering a directive. The mediators strongly recommend that, while the process is ongoing, the parents refrain from talking with each other about their disagreements outside of mediation. This prescription is designed to protect the progress that has been made thus far. If the parents do not talk outside of mediation, they are following the mediators' advice. If the parents talk outside of mediation but get into an argument, they observe the problems that result from *failing* to follow the mediators' advice. Finally, if the parents talk outside of mediation and have a fruitful interchange, so much the better.

SUMMARY

A number of policies and procedures must be carefully evaluated and implemented before beginning mediation. These issues involve important legal and ethical questions, and they can substantially shape the process of mediation itself. The following are among the most important questions for mediators to ask and answer about their own policies:

1. What disputes will be mediated?
2. How will clients be referred to mediation?
3. What cases will be screened out of mediation?
4. Will mediation be confidential?
5. What will be the role of attorneys in reviewing agreements?

Mediators are wise to consult members of the local bar, and especially the bench, in developing answers to these questions. It also is essential to inform clients and members of the legal community about final policies and procedures. In setting the stage for mediation, additional crucial decisions include mediator training, whether to attempt co-mediation, and establishing time limits on the process.

The first mediation session is crucial. The highly structured first session outlined in this chapter includes five major sections: (1) an introduction to mediation that has the goals of explaining rationales and setting ground rules; (2) the child focus, a time when parents are asked to share information about their children's strengths and remember their common interests in promoting the children's best interests; (3) problem definition, when disputes are outlined first in a structured manner, but later arguments are expected to erupt; (4) individual caucuses with each parent, which offer mediators the opportunity to explore the range of possible solutions, to uncover underlying issues in the parents' relationship, and to establish an emotional alliance with each parent; and (5) problem redefinition, when the mediator reframes the custody dispute as a basic conflict resolution problem in the parents' ongoing relationship. The first session allows the mediators to explore the parents' issues, and their emotions, thus setting the stage for intensive problem solving in subsequent mediation sessions. These sessions are the focus of the next chapter.

8

NEGOTIATING AGREEMENTS II

Identifying Issues, Brainstorming Options, and Drafting Parenting Plans

My interest is in the future because I'm going to spend the rest of my life there.

—CHARLES KETTERING

The first mediation session gives parents a chance to voice their concerns, and helps to prepare them emotionally and practically for the negotiations to come. Hopefully, the meeting also gives them some confidence in the mediation process, helps them to better appreciate their children's interests, and encourages them to look more toward the future than the past. Having learned about the dispute, the individuals involved, and the nature of their relationship, the mediators also are ready to move forward after the highly structured first meeting.

The second and all subsequent meetings are much less structured than the initial one. As mediation proceeds, the parents are increasingly responsible for negotiating themselves, with the mediators assuming a more facilitative, "coaching" role. Because these subsequent sessions are less structured and thus more variable, the middle and later phases of mediation are best described in terms of common themes and substantive topics. In this chapter, we focus on several process themes, including

164

(1) separating issues from emotions, (2) brainstorming alternatives, (3) identifying interests and evaluating options, and (4) experimenting with parenting plans. Our substantive foci are the topics that form the sections of a parenting plan, including legal custody (decision making), physical custody (residence), holidays and vacations, parenting rules, methods of communication, financial matters (at least those related to the children), and procedures for resolving disputes or renegotiating the agreement in the future.

If mediation is successful, its focus eventually shifts to the details of drafting, reviewing, and implementing a written agreement. A few process concerns commonly arise at this time. For example, as parents are about to reach a final agreement, a minor dispute may escalate into a major conflict, one that threatens the entire plan. We consider why events like this happen and what to do about them.

Throughout this chapter, we use brief case studies to illustrate both process themes and various substantive topics. We also discuss specific mediator strategies and alternative settlement options in some detail. Our goal in doing so is to give a sense both of the range of clients and problems seen in mediation and of the common themes that emerge across cases and individuals.

PROCESS THEMES IN THE MIDDLE MEDIATION SESSIONS

A number of prominent mediators have elaborated on themes that characterize their approaches to negotiation in mediation (Coogler, 1978; Folberg, Milne, & Salem, 2004; Haynes, 1981; Irving, 1980; Johnston & Campbell, 1988; Saposnek, 1983). While the differences are notable, the similarities across approaches are much more important. And there are remarkable similarities in various approaches to mediation. The common themes perhaps have been characterized most clearly, and certainly most popularly, by Fisher and Ury (1981) in their influential book, *Getting to Yes*.

Fisher and Ury (1981) offer a four-phase model of "principled negotiation." In their terms, the tactics of principled negotiation involve (1) separating the people from the problem; (2) focusing on issues, not positions; (3) inventing options for mutual gain; and (4) using objective criteria to evaluate options. In brief, these four phases refer to helping disputants to view their disputes more objectively; focusing on broad goals rather than fixed negotiating positions; being creative in considering possible resolutions; and using objective criteria in evaluating options.

Unaware of Fisher and Ury's (1981) approach, I initially conceptualized the process of negotiation in mediation in terms of the general problem-solving model (D'Zurilla & Goldfried, 1971). The problem-solving model includes the steps of (1) identifying the problem, (2) brainstorming alternatives, (3) evaluating possible solutions, (4) selecting and implementing one alternative, (5) evaluating the outcome, and finally, (6) returning to the beginning of the iterative process if the selected outcome proves to be unsatisfactory. After practicing as a mediator for a number of years and reading the work of other mediators (much of which did not exist when I began mediating in 1981), it became clear that the problem-solving model shares a number of similarities with other methods of mediation, particularly Fisher and Ury's (1981) general principles of negotiation. I want to note these commonalities, even though I use my own terminology and techniques to describe the mediation process (see Figure 8.1).

Focusing on Issues, Not Emotions

The first step in the problem-solving model is to identify the problem objectively—a goal similar to Fisher and Ury's (1981) separating people

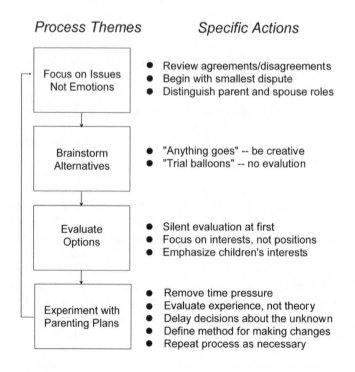

FIGURE 8.1. Themes and activities in later mediation sessions.

from their problems. Both approaches attempt to keep personal feelings from intruding on negotiations. Both also assume that problems can be resolved more readily if they are viewed more dispassionately.

In my approach to mediation, much of the first session is designed to facilitate this important goal, which I term more specifically as "focusing on issues not emotions." The mediators recognize and legitimize the parents' powerful, complex, and easily aroused feelings—they are riding an "emotional roller coaster." From the outset, however, the mediators also make it clear that the issues at hand, not the emotions behind them, will be the focus of mediation. Indeed, the mediators urge the parents to focus on issues, not emotions, throughout the process and into the future in their ongoing, coparenting relationship (as illustrated by the metaphor of becoming partners in the business of parenting).

The mediators describe the goal of separating issues from emotions didactically, and they reinforce it with their focus and actions throughout the process. As mediation proceeds, for example, the mediators frequently ignore emotions that surface, and instead redirect the discussion back to substantive topics. They may do this unobtrusively by ignoring emotional provocations and selectively attending to substantive topics, or perhaps by making an empathic statement in response to a strong feeling but simultaneously reminding one or both parents about the limited goals of mediation. At other times, the mediators may need to offer more forceful reminders, and these often are best delivered during a caucus. ("I can see how hurt and angry you are, and as we discussed last time, I am sorry for all you have lost. But we're here to focus on your children and a parenting plan. Do you still have the name of the therapist I gave you?") Whatever the technique, the mediators' redirection is much more likely to be accepted when each parent feels understood. Thus, the emotional alliance established in the first session is critical to the mediators' success in helping parents to focus on issues and not emotions in subsequent negotiations.

Despite the emphasis on issues, mediators may have to unearth underlying emotions, offer interpretations, or encourage the expression of feelings in later sessions. When to do so is a judgment call. Perhaps the parents cannot control their conflicts, even in the face of the mediators' efforts. Or parents might refuse to make reasonable compromises, or one parent may shift positions in a way that appears more emotional than strategic. In some cases, parents ask for an opportunity to vent.

Whatever the circumstance, however, the goal of these interventions is *not* therapeutic. Rather, as with the first session, the goal is to prevent strong emotions from clouding substantive discussions by allowing the parents to ventilate their feelings in a controlled manner. In so doing, the mediators must limit both the frequency and the length of discussions of emotional topics. Some people will refuse to focus on the issues at hand if the mediator fails to enforce ground rules. Others may give up on the process if it begins to seem more like therapy than mediation.

Setting the Agenda

Mediators can use several strategies to help parents to keep their focus on solving problems. One standard procedure in the middle sessions is to begin each meeting by setting the agenda. The mediators summarize the agreements that were reached last time, outline disagreements that need to be discussed now, and ask if the parents have any new or pressing issues to add to the agenda. The mediators may review these topics verbally, write them on a flip chart, or they may already be summarized on a spreadsheet.

In addition to facilitating record keeping, a particular benefit of a written document, especially a flip chart, is that it can become the focus of attention during mediation sessions. The parents and the mediator may literally turn to face a flip chart during the negotiations. This action symbolizes the goal of separating issues from emotions. Rather than the parents opposing each other, the flip chart becomes a shared problem, one that brings the parents and the mediator together in an attempt to resolve it.

Smaller Problems First

In working through a list of issues, mediators generally should begin with smaller, more readily solved problems and progress to larger, more intractable ones. They begin this pattern during the first mediation session. The negotiation at the end of the first meeting intentionally is framed as needing only a temporary resolution. Thus, parents hopefully have resolved a small dispute before they begin to address bigger ones in subsequent meetings.

Many mediators advocate working from smaller to bigger problems, but some use other tactics. "Logrolling" is an alternative where several disputes are considered simultaneously, so the parents can trade off compromises (Moore, 1986). I also use elements of logrolling, particularly as we address more and more aspects of a parenting plan (or a financial one). Yet, moving from smaller to bigger problems has clear advantages early in mediation. The small victories provide motivation and optimism about settling bigger disputes. And even if parents cannot reach an agreement about everything, the strategy can at least leave them with something. Mediation may end with a partial agreement, if not a complete one, thus narrowing the scope of disputes to be addressed through other means.

Disentangling Marital and Parental Roles

An educational aspect of focusing on issues not emotions involves continually helping the partners to distinguish and disentangle their marital (romantic) and parental roles. In a two-parent family, spousal roles and parental roles become intertwined over time. When a couple divorces, these roles must be separated. Even though the spousal role ends, the parental role continues. As discussed at length in Chapters 1 through 5, many former partners fail to prevent the hurt and anger they legitimately feel toward one another as spouses from disrupting their effectiveness as parents.

A common and particularly important circumstance is when one or both partners remain emotionally attached to the former spouse. For most parents in mediation, the problem is *not* that they care too little about each other. Rather, the problem is that they care too much and express their feelings in inappropriate ways. That is, more couples are enmeshed than disengaged (see Chapter 4).

The children are one of the few things that tie former spouses together, and one or both partners in an enmeshed relationship may use a dispute about the children as a (deliberate or unintentional) means of maintaining contact with the other. The anger masks their (more honest) longing, while the children provide a legitimate reason for contact in the parents' eyes. A fight over the children also is a ready excuse to new lovers or spouses who may otherwise question the need for contact between the former partners.

An angry dispute about the children may not seem much like a romantic relationship, but fights can be both informative and engaging for one or both former partners. Intense emotional reactions may show that a former partner is "still hooked" ("I can still get a rise out of him!"), even when the affect expressed is anger instead of love (Emery, 1992; see Chapter 4). This irrationality of emotions is at the heart of the truism, "love and hate are not far apart," and was brought to life to me in one of my first mediation cases.

T. J. and Millie had been divorced for nearly 4 years when T. J. petitioned the family court for a custody hearing. T. J.'s petition was unusual. Rather than making a specific request for a change in custody or visitation, it simply requested that a hearing be held.

The parents' court record indicated a long history of disputes. During the 5 years since the separation, their three teenage children, two boys and a girl, had lived with the two parents in almost every conceivable combination. They had lived primarily with their mother for a time, but all three also had lived primarily with their father. The two boys had been with their father, while the daughter was with her mother. The mother kept the two youngest for another period, while the father had the oldest. The different arrangements went on and on, and none had lasted longer than several months. During all of this confusion about custody, both parents had gotten remarried, which added some support, but mostly further complications, to a family circumstance that already was chaotic.

Millie and T. J. came together for their first mediation session, which was held inside a courthouse, an imposing building in the heart of the community. The conference room where the mediation sessions were held also was impressive. The room contained a long conference table surrounded by about 20 chairs. The formal setting lent considerable authority to the mediators during what were often difficult and heated negotiations.

T. J. and Millie seemed decidedly unimpressed by the setting, however, at least as evidenced by their arguments. From the time that T. J. announced something had to change about their custody arrangements—he was not sure what—he and Millie argued loudly and ceaselessly. They hurled accusations back and forth at one another, and waved pencils in each other's faces. (The pencils were carefully placed on the conference table along with pads of paper, so that parents could jot down ideas during their "rational" problem solving.)

The inexperienced co-mediators could make little sense of these endless arguments. It was obvious the parents were working against each other in rearing their children, and it was equally clear that the children were suffering as a result. Discipline was nonexistent. If one parent tried to crack down, their efforts were soon subverted when the teenager complained to the other parent. That parent would then agree that the other was unfair, and he or she promised that things would have been different if the child was with them. In fact, several changes in custody were made at a child's initiative, apparently as a way of avoiding discipline.

The mediators could see the problems caused by the parents' constant bickering and subversion, and they tried numerous strategies for controlling the conflict. However, no technique, whether subtle and mild or strong and direct, had a discernible effect on Millie and T. J.'s fighting. When allowed free reign, the frustrated parents did not stop fighting. When told firmly to be quiet, each partner would do so for a few minutes. Soon the debates began again. The arguments lasted for most of the first 2-hour session, and they dominated the second. No progress was made, and the mediators were discouraged.

The loud, apparently angry fighting continued through the first half of the third mediation session. Then, in desperation, one of the mediators remarked that T. J. and Millie seemed to be enjoying themselves. The arguing stopped almost immediately, and the pencils stopped waving. T. J. and Millie slowly broke into smiles. They agreed that they were having fun. Their fighting in mediation reminded them of life when they were married. They liked it. It was energizing. More important, it proved to each of them that the other was still "hooked." After all, Millie observed, if T. J. did not care, why would he get *so* angry? T. J. grinned as Millie said this. The change in the atmosphere in the room was remarkable, and wholly unexpected by the mediators.

Following this breakthrough, Millie and T. J. spent the remainder of the third and most of the fourth mediation session discussing their feelings about their marriage, their divorce, and their children. During these emotionally intense and strikingly honest discussions, it became obvious to them and to the mediators that they still cared deeply for one another. Because they had acknowledged these warm feelings directly, they no longer needed to test each other indirectly by fighting. Sadly, T. J. and Millie also admitted to each other that reconciliation was impossible despite their warm feelings. They had to let go and get on with their lives.

Having addressed, if not fully resolved, their real feelings, Millie and T. J. were able to agree that they had to do a better job with their children. They admitted that the children had manipulated them. They acknowledged that their inconsistent parenting and chronic conflict were causing problems for their children at home, in school, and with their peers. They agreed that they needed to reestablish their joint authority as the children's parents.

As parents working together for the first time since their divorce, T. J. and Millie decided to involve their children in mediation in an unusual way. They brought their three teenagers with them to the final mediation session. The children sat on one side of the long conference table, and the parents sat together on the opposite side. The mediators sat off in a corner. Rather than asking their children where they wanted to live, the two parents told the children what their living arrangements would be. They also outlined a set of rules for both homes that would be enforced from that day forward. When the parents had finished their lecture, the oldest mumbled, "I guess anything is possible." But the children looked relieved, as well as skeptical, about their parents' resumption of their role as parents.

Millie and T. J.'s lingering attachment was atypical, because reconciliation is a real possibility when *both* partners remain emotionally attached. If they had not already remarried, perhaps T. J. and Millie would have reconciled. More typically, only one partner remains emotionally invested, usually the party who has been left (see Chapter 3). Still, whether one- or two-sided (or ever-changing), I have repeatedly observed a pattern of interaction similar to Millie and T. J.'s in heated custody disputes, as have other investigators (see Bickerdike & Littlefield, 2000). Real differences about their children notwithstanding, many parents' intense anger in custody disputes (including anger stemming from the pain of rejection) really reflects their continued emotional investment in their lost romantic relationship. As I said in Chapter 1, the parents may be fighting about the children, but what one or both are *really* fighting about is the end of their marriage.

One-Sided Attachments

An obvious question is: How can someone maintain a one-sided attachment? After a few, perhaps many, attempts at provoking a reaction without success, the emotionally attached partner should simply stop trying. In many divorces, this is what happens. However, other factors can make attachments linger. The left partner may be so devastated by the separation, or so afraid of being alone, that their hopes for reconciliation last much longer than they would ordinarily. In other cases, the emotional attachment is a sign of psychopathology, often a personality disorder (Johnston & Campbell, 1988). Or the attached individual might provoke a strong reaction from their former partner that really is anger about the children, but is misinterpreted as a sign of emotional investment.

Perhaps the most common explanation of one-sided attachments, and the chronic fighting they engender, is the development of a pursuer–pursued relationship, as former spouses attempt to redefine their boundary of intimacy (see Chapter 4). After failing to provoke a reaction, the partner who is more attached stops pursuing and disengages completely from the relationship. When this happens, the partner who is no longer invested in a romantic relationship may turn from being the pursued to being the pursuer. He or she still wants to "be friends," perhaps for the children's sake, because of his or her own guilt, or maybe for manipulative reasons. Whatever the motivation, the partner now attempts to engage the other in a friendly way. Eventually, the "friendly" effort is successful—and misconstrued by the attached partner as a sign of intimate interest. As a result, the partners reverse roles again in a two-step that can last for years.

Partners in the Business of Parenting

The mediators' goal is clear when former partners like Millie and T. J. are in conflict over redefining their boundary of intimacy: Help them begin to develop a new, business-like relationship—to become partners in the business of parenting their children (see Chapter 4). Often, the mediators will discuss this goal in general terms with both parents together. They may draw Figure 4.2 (p. 72) on a flip chart, explain why a business-like relationship is preferred ("You now have a job to do, not a relationship to resolve"), and outline some rules for interacting in a business-like way.

Unlike what happened with Millie and T. J., the mediators rarely discuss the issue of unresolved attachments with the parents together. Mental health mediators may be tempted to explore such emotions directly, but this is exactly the wrong approach for most parents who come to mediation. It is essential for mediators to *recognize* the emotional dynamics involved in a custody dispute, and it is important for mediators to convey their understanding to each parent. But when working with the parents together, it is far more productive for the parents *and* the mediators to focus on the issues rather than the emotions behind them.

On the other hand, the mediators do—and should—typically broach the topic in caucus with each parent alone. In so doing, the mediators empathize with the left partner's grief, and encourage him or her to seek support from friends, family, or a therapist, while also moving forward with business-like coparenting—for the children's sake. ("You need to love your kids more than you may hate your ex.") The mediators also empathize with the leaver, but encourage him or her to be patient, explaining why, right now, the goal of being friends is unrealistic, even hurtful. ("Maybe he [or she] shouldn't be, but your ex is a long way behind you in grieving the loss of your marriage.") Even in caucus, however, the focus on emotions is brief and has the goal of moving everyone back to dealing with the issues. Mediation is not therapy.

Focusing on issues not emotions facilitates problem solving, and it also can help the parents begin to define a clear boundary of intimacy. From the first session, the mediators establish formal, structured rules for how the parents are supposed to interact, and they encourage business-like, child-focused interaction throughout. Hopefully, this will become a model for their future coparenting relationship.

Of course, parents may eventually develop a more friendly relationship. Doing so may be ideal, but if it is going to happen, it will take time, willingness on the part of both parents, and the right life circumstances. Mediators cannot expect divorcing parents to become friends at this chaotic time, so they must have more limited goals. In the short term, helping parents begin to create a working partnership is much more realistic and reasonable.

Brainstorming Alternatives

Brainstorming is a key component to my approach to mediation, as it is in the general problem-solving model. In brainstorming, the mediators encourage parents to temporarily suspend judgment. They ask parents to propose creative solutions to their disputes, not necessarily workable ones. They may urge parents to be outlandish, and perhaps may propose unusual alternatives themselves as a way of stimulating creativity or sending a veiled message. And the mediators tell parents that the rules of brainstorming forbid them from evaluating the various alternatives until they have come up with a long list of novel possibilities. Simply put, anything goes during brainstorming.

Creative Solutions

As in other circumstances, brainstorming can stimulate creativity in mediation. Emotional conflicts are at the heart of most mediation cases, but some parents are facing tricky, complicated problems. Brainstorming can help these parents (and, as we will see, parents in emotionally complicated circumstances, too). Consider the following case:

> Jonesy and Robert had a custody arrangement that was working very well for both of them and for their 7-year-old daughter, Althea. Two years earlier when Jonesy and Robert were divorced, they agreed that Jonesy would have legal and physical custody. Althea would spend every other weekend and one evening during the school week with Robert. The arrangement was working smoothly. Althea was doing well personally, with friends, and in school. The parents had adjusted to their divorce and their new lives. Robert had remarried, and Jonesy said she got along fine with his new wife, especially because she was so kind to Althea and respectful of Jonesy. Robert regularly paid Jonesy a generous amount of child support. In fact, the family was a good reminder to the mediators. Like most professionals, they typically saw families who were struggling through a difficult divorce. Althea, Jonesy, and Robert, like most divorced families and individuals (the ones we usually do not see), were happy, well functioning, and got along reasonably well with one another.
>
> So why were they in mediation? They were facing a tricky problem. After 2 years of working in a low-paying clerical job, Jonesy decided that she needed to go back to school so she could improve her job prospects. Her plan was to move back to her hometown and get a nursing degree (RN) at a university there. She had thought through her plan very carefully. Her parents still lived in the same town, and Althea's grandmother had volunteered to take care of her when Jonesy was in class. In fact, Jonesy was planning on living with her parents for at least several months to get settled, save money, and have time to find her own place close to her parents' home. Not only that, but Robert's parents also lived in the same town. Jonesy got along with them well, and she was more than willing to promote Althea's relationship with her paternal grandparents.

Unfortunately, Jonesy, Robert, and Althea were now living 350 miles away from their hometown, a 7-hour drive.

It is not surprising that Robert exploded when Jonesy told him in May that she wanted to move after Althea finished second grade in early June. She wanted time for them both to get settled during the summer, before the fall semester. Robert argued that he had been fulfilling his part of the separation agreement. He couldn't just quit his job. In fact, he had anticipated the possibility of Jonesy wanting to move. Their separation agreement included a clause indicating that if Jonesy relocated more than 30 miles from their current home, this would lead to a change in custody from Jonesy to Robert. The legal validity of the clause was uncertain, thus making the issue all the more contentious. The parents' cooperative relationship was deteriorating as a result of their legitimate but incompatible desires, which seemed to boil down to two alternatives: move or not move.

Brainstorming helped these parents to consider a much wider range of options. While it took some time to get past their initial anger and fear about the process, the rules of brainstorming eventually opened up their creative thinking. Jonesy could move with Althea but return after graduating in 4 years. Jonesy could move without Althea but resume custody when she returned. The grandparents could move and care for Althea here. Robert could pay for child care and tuition so that Jonesy could go back to school here. Althea could go to boarding school (the mediators' suggestion). Everyone could move to a neutral site. The mediators wrote these and many other ideas on a flip chart in an atmosphere that was eased by the rules of brainstorming but remained tense nevertheless. Playing the brainstorming game for real is very different from playing it for fun.

After a few meetings and a lot of mulling and careful thought outside of mediation, Jonesy and Robert agreed to a creative, integrated compromise. Jonesy would not move during the next year. Instead, she would go to the local community college to take the basic, high school biology and chemistry courses she needed before she could begin nursing school. To help encourage this, Robert agreed to pay for the (modest) tuition. He also agreed to watch Althea for a second weeknight while Jonesy attended evening classes. At the end of a year, however, Robert agreed not to oppose Jonesy's move with Althea.

The compromise gave Jonesy most of what she wanted, that is, a chance at a better life and support in getting there. It also gave Robert some desirable options. He would have another year with his daughter while she was at an impressionable age. He also could begin job hunting in his former hometown with a year, not a few weeks, to find work. And, as he whispered to me privately, when we were shaking hands at the end of mediation, "You know what I'm *really* hoping for don't you?" "No," I said, puzzled. "I'm hoping she'll meet someone, fall in love, and never want to leave here!"

It is difficult to imagine how Jonesy and Robert could have negotiated such an integrated compromise outside of mediation. If they had discussed options on their own, they probably would not have been as creative, or their discussions might have become embroiled. The enforceability of the relocation clause was a major focus of their attorneys' negotiations (the lawyers referred Jonesy and Robert to mediation), and any decision made in court likely would have been limited to one of the two outcomes that the parents had conceived initially: move or not move. With mediation the parents were able to brainstorm an option that was imperfect, but far more creative and acceptable than anything they had considered previously.

Of course, brainstorming in mediation is not as easy as this case study may make it seem. The first bit of brainstorming occurred when Jonesy said, "You could let me move," and Robert retorted, "Sure, and Althea can stay here with me." When they failed to move beyond these options (while giving each other the silent treatment), the mediators suggested sending Althea to boarding school. The suggestion was a way to break the tension, get started on generating some new, creative options, and remind the parents that there may not be a perfect solution but there were *worse* alternatives.

Trial Balloons

Another benefit of brainstorming is that it can allow parents to raise options that may be very difficult to suggest otherwise. That is, parents can safely "float a trial balloon." The mediators tell the parents to be creative, to share even wild possibilities, and not to consider how realistic the various options might be. This encourages parents to raise alternatives that they have been weighing but have been hesitant to discuss. For example, parents may suggest that a possible solution to a custody dilemma is reconciliation. I can recall only one time where the partner agreed with the suggestion—a mediation case with a truly happy ending. But even when reconciliation is quickly rejected, the rules give the partner the information they were looking for and an out, a chance to save face. "He said, 'anything goes'!"

Brainstorming allows parents to float other sorts of other trial balloons. One example is when a mother does not want a major role in post-divorce childrearing. We *hope* that fathers will be very involved with their children after divorce, but we expect this from mothers. Such expectations make it exceedingly difficult for a woman to admit to herself that she may not want to play a primary role in childrearing, let alone to suggest this to her former husband. Brainstorming allows parents to raise alternatives like this, ideas that they have considered secretly, but never voiced. Once the topic is broached, it can be discounted as an exercise in creative thinking—or discussed seriously later when all the options are evaluated.

Evaluating Alternatives

The third step in the problem-solving model is to evaluate the various alternatives identified during brainstorming. When they are still generating options, the mediators generally block any evaluative comments or discussion by the parents. But this does not mean that the parents have not been thinking. They cannot help but to mull over the options privately.

This can be helpful. The silent evaluation prevents parents from immediately rejecting ideas that may have merit, and instead gives them time to consider the options at length. As they mull over an idea, parents may find that what seemed unacceptable at first is more appealing after further consideration. Or they may think up variations on the theme that are more acceptable. For example, a suggestion of sharing joint physical custody may seem totally unacceptable to a parent who wants sole custody. As he or she weighs the option, however, they may appreciate some potential benefits. The children may like having more frequent contact with the other parent. Both parents might like sharing the responsibility of raising children—and having more free time. Or a parent might still think that joint physical custody is not the best option during the school year, but he or she may be willing to share (or switch) custody during the summer. In short, the delay in evaluating alternatives allows both parents to "sleep on it" without the mediators explicitly suggesting that they do so.

Interests, Not Positions

A technique that can help parents to continue to be creative when evaluating their alternatives is to focus on underlying interests, not just bargaining positions (Fisher & Ury, 1981). A *position* is a proposed solution, and it often includes strategic elements such as overstatement. An *interest* is the underlying goal that the position is designed to fulfill. Insisting on moving to further your education is a position. The goal of having enough money and parenting support to allow you to further your education is an interest.

Positions are fixed, or they are altered grudgingly, thus inhibiting creativity. Interests can be fulfilled in a number of different ways, and encourage creative thinking. "We need to share time exactly 50/50" is a position, one that a parent may refuse to modify. "I want to have a lot of time with my children and be a major influence in their life" is an interest that can be fulfilled in many different ways.

When the focus is shifted from positions to interests, areas of agreement may be uncovered and creative solutions may become apparent. One couple I saw, for example, easily reached an agreement about physical custody. They also negotiated the details of most holidays with relatively little difficulty. The parents became embroiled, however, in fighting over whether their son should spend every Thanksgiving holiday with his father, or whether he should alternate Thanksgivings with each parent.

I eventually asked the parents to discuss their interests: Why did Dad want every Thanksgiving? He said he wanted to establish a Thanksgiving ritual where he and his son would visit the boy's paternal grandparents who lived several hundred miles away. In fact, he had spoken with his mother about this possibility several times. He had assured her that he would not agree to any plan unless it contained this arrangement. Surprised, the mother said she had pictured her son spending every Thanksgiving alone in his father's apartment. That is why she was objecting. When she heard about the goal, she readily agreed to the father's Thanksgiving plan. She actually was pleased with the prospect of her son maintaining contact with his grandparents.

The Children's Interest

The children's well-being is an interest shared by all separated or divorced parents. Thus, the child focus established in the first session remains a theme throughout mediation. If the mediator allies with anyone, it is with the children (Saposnek, 1983), and this alliance is used to push the mediation process forward when it gets bogged down. As they consider the alternatives, parents may be reminded to consider the child's interests when discussing a complex, 50/50 joint physical custody arrangement; they may be asked to speculate on their children's feelings when discussing whether visitation should be scheduled or unscheduled; or, when they seem ready to give up, they may be reminded that they, the parents, can be the ones to decide what is in their children's future best interests.

Criteria for Evaluation

Another helpful technique in evaluating options is to decide the criteria for evaluating them in advance. Some mediators recommend that disputants adopt a standard of fairness before reviewing various alternatives

(Haynes, 1981; Moore, 1986). Others urge negotiators to use objective criteria in evaluating outcomes (Fisher & Ury, 1981). These strategies can be especially helpful when negotiating finances. For example, negotiations proceed much more smoothly once a couple agrees that their standard of fairness will be a 50/50 division of assets. Similarly, agreeing to value their home based on the average of two objective appraisals reduces haggling over its worth.

Standards for evaluating alternative parenting plans are not as clear. Promoting children's best interests is the overriding goal, but there is no objective way to determine children's best interests—not even extensive and expensive custody evaluations (Emery et al., 2005a). Mediators can provide information about research on children and divorce (e.g., on joint physical custody), as well as share their own experiences. Still, parents retain the responsibility for evaluating children's best interests in mediation. Mediators can remind parents to keep the children's perspectives and interests in mind, but ultimately it is up to the parents to determine those interests.

This shift in responsibility often requires mediators from a mental health background to take a new approach. Mental health professionals assume more authority and responsibility for decision making in assessment and therapy, including in custody evaluations, than mediators assume. Thus, mental health professionals must learn to give up a degree of control when they mediate. They can raise questions and offer opinions, but they must remember that the paramount goal of mediation is to encourage and respect the parents' authority and responsibility. At the margin, if not always in the individual case, doing precisely this is what is best for children and for divorced family relationships (see Chapter 9). Moreover, mental health professionals must remember that there is no scientific evidence that they do, in fact, know which parenting plan is best for individual children in divorce (Emery et al., 2005a).

Experimenting with Parenting Plans

The final step in the problem-solving model is experimenting with one alternative, reevaluating it, and, if necessary, returning back to pick (or create) a new option to try. As with other techniques, unique issues and benefits arise when applying this procedure in mediation.

Few mediators discuss experimenting with a parenting plan for a trial period as an intervention technique. However, this is a basic aspect of my approach, and it offers a number of potential advantages to the process and to parents. A trial allows parents to evaluate a plan based on the most objective possible criteria: how it actually works for their children and themselves. Suggesting a trial period also relieves the immense pressure on parents to create and agree to a permanent schedule. (Agreeing to a parenting plan to last throughout childhood is akin to deciding where a preschooler will go to college, an analogy that I sometimes use with parents in mediation.) More generally, the practical "let's try this out" approach encourages parents to view their parenting plan as a "living agreement."

As parents are weighing alternatives to try, it often is a good time to discuss the "living agreement" approach (see Chapters 5 and 6). A living agreement means that the parents can, and should, revisit and revise the schedule based on changes in their own lives, their children's changing developmental capacities (e.g., the best schedules for infants differ from the best schedules for adolescents) (Emery, 2006), and how well the schedule is working for everyone, particularly the children. We found that parents randomly assigned to mediation did, in fact, make more changes in their basic parenting plan over the course of the subsequent 12 years. They made an average of a little more than one major change in the course of the decade, typically negotiating the new schedule informally or in mediation. Litigation families rarely changed their parenting plans (see Chapter 9).

A concern about experimenting with parenting plans is that children benefit from stability in postdivorce family life (Emery, 1999). Research shows, however, that custody arrangements often change over time (Smyth & Moloney, 2008; see Chapter 6). A more formal trial period—deliberate experimentation—can actually add structure to this practice. Like T. J. and Millie, many embroiled and confused couples constantly jockey for position with their children. Even if they change their parenting plan, the "try it" approach has the benefit of helping distressed parents come to *some* agreement. An agreement, even a temporary one, can help parents to separate physically, and perhaps help them to begin to separate emotionally. And while I do not have statistics to back this up, my experience is that a temporary schedule, or something close to it, often becomes the final schedule (but still remains a "living agreement").

The strategy of experimentation is not limited to schedules. For example, I have worked with a number of parents who disagree about where to send their children to school. In this situation, it often is easier for parents to agree on a plan to try one school temporarily, perhaps reviewing the choice as the first semester is coming to a close. Such a trial is more palatable to disputing parents, and it also gives them information, not just speculation, on which to base future decisions.

These kinds of compromises, whether made formally or informally, parallel the sort of wait-and-see decisions that married parents make routinely. Considering how parents in married families make decisions is always a good point of perspective for mediators and for parents. With some parents, in fact, I ask how they would make a decision if they were still married. Of course, I do not ask this question of parents who are likely to use the opportunity to revisit debates about their marriage and why it unraveled.

Many temporary agreements involve a trial of perhaps a few weeks or a few months. Others involve much longer time intervals. A review may be scheduled for a year or more in the future—for example, when a toddler reaches preschool age. Or a choice between public and private education may be deferred until a child completes elementary school. Again, the delay—putting off a final decision—parallels what married parents do in reevaluating major decisions throughout their children's development. True, divorced parents run the legal risk that their agreement may be unenforceable (because it is trumped by the children's best interests). And a temporary agreement may set a legal precedent that could affect future judicial rulings. Parents need be aware of these risks. Nevertheless, many parents still decide that the legal impediment is not going to stop them from agreeing and doing what *they* think is best for their children.[1]

DETAILS OF A PARENTING PLAN

Custody mediation does not occur in a substantive vacuum. Mediators must develop considerable expertise in the legal, economic, social, and psychological aspects of divorce. This is true despite the fact that mediators often encourage their clients to seek independent advice from lawyers, accountants, and mental health professionals. We need to be able to guide our clients and to recognize the limits of our expertise, that is, to know when to make a referral.

In custody mediation, the most important expertise is knowledge of various time-sharing and decision-making aspects of a parenting plan. We covered key issues in detail in early chapters. Here, we briefly review some major topics from the practical perspective of how they arise and may be addressed in mediation.

---

[1] In my view, laws should be changed to remove legal impediments to upholding parental agreements. Divorced parents' agreements about their future parenting should be enforceable like other contracts, rather than being routinely subject to being overturned under the "best interests" standard. This change would (1) place the authority and responsibility for making parental decisions on *parents'* shoulders; (2) avoid the illusion of secret, judicial knowledge; (3) encourage creative, temporary settlements; and (4) most important in the present context, allow parents to construct an agreement designed to evolve along with their children's development.

Global Parenting Concerns

When parents separate, communication about children commonly breaks down—in part because there is no forum for talking about them. Mediation offers a much needed forum, and "parenting" routinely is listed on the agenda at the beginning of the second mediation session. (The agenda typically is written on a flip chart.) Parenting often is at the top of the agenda, both because it is critical and because parenting concerns can be relatively easy to address. Parenting issues often are clear and are shared by both parents, who typically do not begin mediation with rigidly fixed bargaining positions about these topics.

Two general categories of parenting concerns frequently arise. The first set of issues are ones that almost all divorced parents encounter, such as communication about the children. Many parents struggle with communication, a problem that I prefer to solve with scheduled, business-like telephone calls (Chapter 5; see below). Another near universal topic is the consistency of the rules set for the children between the two different households. The children's needs for stability and predictability are important to consider, but so is each parent's desire to be autonomous in his or her own home (Chapter 6). The mediators often raise these issues, even if the parents have not brought them up. This gives the mediators a chance to offer some useful advice and hopefully begins the negotiations with some easily reached agreements.

Children Caught in Conflict

A second set of parenting issues is not as universal, but unfortunately, they are common. These involve children who are exposed to, involved in, or otherwise caught in the middle of their parents' disputes. Parents may be in a tug-of-war, each trying to pull the children to their side. They might fight openly in front of the children, perhaps during exchanges or over the telephone. The tension between them may be silent but so palpable as to fill the children (and the mediators) with anxiety. One or both parents may deride the other in front of or when talking to the children. Discipline may be inconsistent due to a failure to communicate or as a deliberate attempt to subvert the other parent. The parents may quiz the children about what happens in the other parent's home (including questions about that parent's romantic relationships), or parents may tell the children to carry inappropriate messages back and forth between households, for example, about money, changes in schedule, or other adult topics.

In circumstances like these, anger obviously is intruding on effective parenting, and the mediators need to be clear about their concern for, and alliance with, the children. A valuable tool in doing so is to use your own reactions as a barometer and a mirror. When mediators are uncomfortable with parents' anger, or feel intense pulls on their loyalty, the children are likely to be feeling the same way. After gauging their own reactions, mediators can reflect their feelings, as well as their concerns for the children, back to the parents. ("I feel like I'm jumping out of my skin just sitting in the same room with you two. I can only imagine what it must be like for your children.")

In offering this feedback, the mediators should be clear that their goal is *not* to resolve all of the parents' anger. Former partners have many reasons to be hurt and angry, and it is important for the mediators to acknowledge this. ("I know this is really hard for you, too. It's just that we need to find ways to do what we all agree is most important, protecting your children.") Mediators also should be clear that conflict is not necessarily "bad." In fact, conflict is a necessary part of negotiations and of relationships, even business-like ones. The goal for parents is to work to control and contain their anger and conflict around the children. As such, the mediators might use this opportunity to educate parents about what research shows to be more or less harmful types of parental conflict for children (Cummings & Davies, 2010; see Table 8.1).

Of course, the mediators are not responsible for resolving all of the parents' issues or emotions. Instead, their feedback about the effects of conflict is intended to be educational. Hopefully, this encourages parents to move forward in their negotiations for the children's sake, if not for their own. And while mediators will want to refer some families to a mental health professional for individual or family therapy, the major

---

TABLE 8.1. Constructive Conflict

Parental conflict is more constructive and less harmful to children when it ...

- Is less intense.
- Is less emotional.
- Is not physical.
- Is not about the children or childrearing.
- Does not occur in front of the children.
- Does not involve the children.
- Does not lead to "put-downs" of the other parent.
- Is contained between the parents in other ways.
- Does not keep parents from presenting a "united front."
- Is resolved, even if only by an agreement to disagree.

---

benefits of mediation are indirect and, as my research shows, unfold over time. Even as parents negotiate a parenting plan in mediation, they are beginning to renegotiate their relationship. Mediation is just a beginning, but it is a choice point, one that, on average, helps parents to preserve their coparenting relationship even as their marriage comes apart.

Physical Custody: A Schedule

Parenting concerns are easier to resolve, and by addressing this topic first, we frame the discussions of custody that follow as parenting issues, not (or not just) legal issues. We also use now-common terms such as *parenting plan, schedule,* and *decision making* (instead of custody; see Chapter 6) to make the issues less mysterious and ominous, and to help parents recognize that these are *their* disagreements. Parents are not debating some legal abstraction they can neither comprehend nor control. They are trying to decide how they, the parents, will rear their children.

I typically focus on the schedule (physical custody) before discussing decision making (legal custody) with parents because the schedule usually is a pressing topic (even though legal custody is easier to resolve). Parents often have some informal schedule before coming to mediation, but it may be a bone of contention—perhaps including what the schedule should be for the coming week. If there is no schedule, parents, and children, usually are in desperate need of one.

Lack of Clarity

Many conflicts arise from having a poorly defined schedule or none at all. An open-ended schedule creates all kinds of logistical problems, requires the parents to negotiate constantly, and as a result, leads to dashed expectations all around. Thus, my strong bias is to push parents to specify a schedule in detail, even if one or both parents want to be "flexible."

I have two basic reasons for encouraging specificity. The most important is that children benefit from structure and predictability. If children are expecting to spend time with a parent they have not seen for awhile, they are likely to be anxious, confused, or hurt if they have to wait and wonder about when or whether they will actually see their father or mother. They may be crushed if the plans change, even for good reasons (and plans often change for bad reasons). Even when contact with each parent is frequent and secure, very flexible schedules can disrupt children's routines with school, extracurricular activities, and friends.

A second reason I encourage a very specific schedule is to draw clear boundaries in the coparenting relationship. A schedule and other details (such as how to exchange the children) limits the need for parents to communicate, and thereby reduces opportunities for conflict. Even if parents disagree about a final parenting plan, a specific if temporary schedule clarifies expectations for everyone.

Hidden Agendas

Of course, parents often struggle in redefining the boundaries of their relationship. In fact, some parents resist a schedule precisely because they *want* a reason to be in touch with their former partner, even if only to fight (see Chapters 2, 3, and 4). Mediators need to be aware of, and try to uncover, such "hidden agendas." Other examples include objecting to a schedule when the real concern is the children having contact with a new romantic partner. Parents also may object to a schedule when they really are worried about financial matters such as child support awards or who stays in the family residence. We have discussed these and other issues earlier, together with alternative strategies for addressing the true problem. Our main point here is to remember that the schedule may not be the "real" issue, particularly when a parent seems irrationally opposed to a seemingly reasonable plan.

Alternative Schedules

A surprisingly large number of custody disputes really are about hidden agendas, lack of clarity, or other indirect concerns. Of course, many parents do have real disagreements about how to share time with their children. In this case, brainstorming and focusing on interests and not positions can be helpful techniques for creating new solutions. The concept of the children's best interests also can be used to frame these discussions. The objective of a schedule is not to "divide the child," but to devise an arrangement that benefits the children and hopefully keeps both parents richly involved in their lives. In fact, parents hopefully can learn to see each other as potential sources of support, not parenting competitors, if they both recognize the need to work together for their children's sake.

Even though parental self-determination is a guiding principle, mediators can help parents to devise a schedule by offering some substantive suggestions. After all, the mediators have dealt with these issues before; most parents have not. During brainstorming, mediators may make outlandish suggestions in order to encourage creativity or perhaps to confront parents about the absurdity of some of their disagreements. Mediators also may suggest more practical options during brainstorming or at other times. The mediators' concrete suggestions can be educational, broaden the range of options considered, and may be more acceptable because the idea is coming from a third party.

All of this begs the question "What schedules should mediators suggest?" For example, should we advocate for joint physical custody? As we saw in Chapter 6, the debates about joint physical custody are broad and complicated. In fact, mediation is less likely to result in joint physical custody in contested cases than is litigation or attorney negotiation (Reynolds et al., 2007). Then there is the question of neutrality. How can a mediator be neutral yet also advocate for (or against) certain schedules?

My view is that the best protection against bias is to be clear about our views—to ourselves and to our clients, while still honoring parents' ultimate right to self-determination. I also believe that mediators can and should help parents by using our substantive expertise about alternative parenting plans. Toward these ends, I have discussed specific alternative schedules for parents to consider based on two key considerations, their children's age and their coparenting relationship, specifically whether they have an angry, distant, or cooperative divorce (Emery, 2006). Table 8.2 offers an illustrative example. I do not review all of the options or the important reasons behind them here, since I addressed them at length in my book for parents (Emery, 2006).[2]

Principles for Evaluating Schedules

While I am quite willing to suggest alternative schedules for parents to consider—and parents often embrace one of those suggestions, I do not advocate for any particular schedule. However, I do routinely raise principles for parents to keep in mind for evaluating schedules. My key principles are:

- There is *no* single ideal schedule—not joint physical custody, every other weekend visits, "bird nesting" (where the children stay put and the parents move back and forth), or the hundreds of variations in between. Any schedule can work, or none can. Making a parenting plan work depends upon you, your ex, and your relationship.
- Neither judges nor psychologists possess special wisdom or mysterious tests that can tell you what is best for your children. You, the parents, are in the best position to make these decisions.
- View time with your children in terms of months and years, not just hours, days, and weeks. Your parenting plan can be a "living

---

[2] Reflecting increased contact over recent decades (Amato, Meyers, & Emery, 2009), the schedules I suggest today involve fathers more than those that appeared in the first edition of this book.

TABLE 8.2. Alternative Schedules Based on Child's Age and Coparenting Relationship

Infants and babies younger than 18 months

Traditional options for an angry divorce
• Every Saturday from 11:00 A.M. until 5:00 P.M., including an afternoon nap.

More integrated options for a distant divorce
• Every Saturday from 11:00 A.M. until 5:00 P.M., including an afternoon nap; every Wednesday evening from 4:30 P.M. until 6:30 P.M., perhaps spending some time at the residential parent's home.

Closely integrated options for a cooperative divorce
• Two weekdays from 8:00 A.M. until 1:00 P.M. (substituting for child care); every Saturday from 11:00 A.M. until 5:00 P.M.; Saturday overnights if the baby tolerates.

Toddlers 18 months to 3 years old

Traditional options for an angry divorce
• Every Saturday from 2:00 P.M. until 6:00 P.M. Overnight until 10:00 A.M. on alternate Sundays.

More integrated options for a distant divorce
• Every Saturday from 9:00 A.M. until 5:00 P.M., including a nap. Overnight until 9:00 A.M. on alternate Sundays. Every Wednesday evening from 4:30 P.M. until 6:30 P.M.

Closely integrated options for a cooperative divorce
• Two weekdays from 1:00 P.M. until 5:00 P.M. (substituting for child care); every Friday from 1:00 P.M. until 12:00 P.M. on Saturday.

Early school-age children 6–9 years old

Traditional options for an angry divorce
• Every other weekend from 5:00 P.M. Friday until 4:00 P.M. Sunday.

More integrated options for a distant divorce
• Every other weekend from 5:00 P.M. Thursday until 4:00 P.M. Sunday. Alternate Thursday evenings from 5:00 P.M. until 7:30 P.M.

Closely integrated options for a cooperative divorce
• Every Wednesday from 3:00 P.M. until 5:00 P.M. on Saturday with one parent; every Saturday at 5:00 P.M. until 3:00 P.M. on Wednesday with the other parent.

Late school-age children 10–12 years old

Traditional options for an angry divorce
• Every other weekend from 5:00 P.M. on Friday until 4:00 P.M. on Sunday. Alternate Mondays from 5:00 P.M. until 7:30 P.M. on the Monday following the weekend spent with the residential parent.

More integrated options for a distant divorce
• Every other weekend from 5:00 P.M. on Thursday until 4:00 P.M. on Sunday. Every Monday evening from 4:30 P.M. until 7:30 P.M.

Closely integrated options for a cooperative divorce
• Alternate weeks with each parent with exchanges on either Fridays or Sundays.

Note. For more alternatives, details, and information, see Emery (2006).

agreement," one that you alter as your children grow older and your family circumstances change.

- You probably want to experiment with a schedule at first, so you can see how your children react instead of guessing what will or won't work.
- Different schedules work better for children of different ages. In general, younger children benefit from having more of a "home base." School-aged children can manage more complicated schedules as long as the parents help them. And you need to consider a new schedule for teenagers: Their own.
- If you have more than one child, this creates both opportunities and complications. A younger child may be able to handle more complicated schedules if she is moving back and forth in a "herd." But a 16-year-old may rebel about a week-to-week schedule that works fine for his 9-year-old brother.
- Your coparenting partnership is critical to making *any* parenting plan work. You have many more options for children of a given age—and over time—if you can work to develop a cooperative, business-like relationship with your children's other parent.
- Suggested schedules are intended to be concrete *examples*. You need to think creatively about a parenting plan while considering the best options for your family.

In addition to these principles, I often will play devil's advocate about a schedule if the parents do not do so. It is far better to anticipate a problem that does not arise than to miss one that does. Thus, I commonly tell parents that complicated schedules offer benefits, but also come with costs—for example, they require more cooperation and coordination. Therefore, while I do not push joint physical custody on reluctant parents or dissuade enthusiastic parents from trying it, I am happy to discuss pros and cons with both groups of parents.

Changes in Residence

Some of the most difficult negotiations about a parenting plan occur when one parent wants to move to a geographical area a considerable distance away from the other. In this case, creativity in regard to summer vacations, school holidays, the sharing of travel expenses, and telephone contact often helps to bring the parents to an agreement. One parent still may feel more like a loser, however, even when numerous practical compromises are suggested.

For some parents, these feelings are alleviated by discussions of their sense of loss, the importance of parental influence even from a geographical distance, the possibilities of changes in the children's primary residence in the future, and the children's best interests. For other parents, their chances of winning in court are so small that they agree to a compromise even though it is less than optimal from their perspective. For at least a few parents, however, the only solution is for a third party to assume the responsibility of making a decision about relocation. Mediation does not always result in an agreement, and getting agreement is not the overriding goal of the process. Rather, the goal is to provide parents with the opportunity to discuss their options. Such discussions can be helpful even when they do not directly result in a compromise solution.

Parental Responsibilities or Decision Making

Parents also must agree about legal custody, the allocation of parental rights and responsibilities, or, more simply, decision making. The term *custody* carries tremendous symbolic importance in the eyes of many parents. Joint versus sole legal custody can have somewhat different legal ramifications (Chapter 6), but symbolism seems to be a bigger motivator. Sole legal custody may be a symbol of one parent's primary responsibility for rearing children or of the legal custodian's right to raise their children autonomously. Similarly, joint legal custody may be a public statement of the parents' commitment to raise their children cooperatively, or of one parent's continued psychological connection with their children despite reduced physical contact.

Symbolism is important. During my studies (the 1980s), many parents rejected a parenting plan if it gave the other parent sole legal custody and primary residence, but they accepted the same schedule as long as they retained joint legal custody. In fact, mediation ended in joint legal custody more often than litigation, although joint legal and especially joint physical custody were unusual in both groups (Emery et al., 1991).

I suspect that the dramatic increase in joint legal custody (Chapter 6) has caused the term to lose much of its symbolic value today. Instead, more parents now insist on joint *physical* custody, particularly reaching the threshold defined by child support statutes.[3] Of course, a skeptic might wonder if symbolism is the only motivation, since child support amounts often drop substantially when parents share physical custody as defined by child support laws (Chapter 6).

---

[3] Thresholds for adjusting child support due to joint physical custody currently vary from a low of 52 overnights per year (in Indiana) to 164 overnights (in North Dakota) (Brown & Brito, 2007). No one has compared the number of overnights specified in parenting plans in states with different thresholds, a potentially very interesting study.

Day-to-Day Decision Making and Communication

The mediators can begin a discussion of legal custody by acknowledging its symbolism, while also noting its limited implications for parents' decision making—whether to share decisions about religious upbringing, choice of schools, and elective medical care (including dental and psychological treatment). After discussing the narrow scope of legal custody, we typically note that the law does not clearly address several key aspects of parental decision making. We use this as an opportunity to anticipate and hopefully prevent many common parenting conflicts.

For one, joint legal custody is not a license to micromanage. Parents are free to make day-to-day decisions when the children are with them without being second-guessed. In short, each parent must respect the other's autonomy. A second topic we often discuss, sometimes emphatically, is that the children will benefit if the parents are pretty consistent in their household rules (e.g., bedtimes), even though each parent has final authority to make and enforce rules in his or her own household. Finally, we invariably note that the parents will need to communicate about unanticipated parenting issues, but they should keep communications to a minimum. As discussed earlier (Chapter 5), we typically have parents agree to exchange very brief phone, text, or e-mail messages about notices that cannot wait (e.g., an unexpected special event at school tomorrow), while discussing more complex parenting matters (e.g., discipline issues) in a scheduled, brief, weekly telephone call to occur at a convenient time when the children are out of earshot.

Parenting Differences

Disagreements are common during the discussion of decision making. Sometimes the dispute is caused by an underlying interest that has been unstated or unanticipated. Parents may be of different religious backgrounds; for example, one partner's insistence on sole custody (or the other's insistence on joint custody) may be designed to ensure that the children are raised according to the preferred religion. Some parents have similarly strong views about the choice of public or private schools. Although such differences may not be readily resolved, the chances of settling them are improved when all parties understand the nature of the "real" dispute.

In fact, acknowledging the existence of the underlying difference in parenting is a major step toward resolving it. In a surprising number of cases, the parents only think they disagree. When given the opportunity to talk, they discover that they do not really have a big dispute. In other cases, parents are anticipating a dispute that may or may not arise in the future. In this circumstance, the conflict often can be settled by negotiating an agreement not about the actual decision, but about how the disagreement will be resolved in the future. For example, the parents may agree to return to mediation when a child reaches a certain age in order to renegotiate the schedule at that time. Married parents continually discuss and renegotiate decisions about their children's upbringing, and mediation can be a forum where divorced parents have the same opportunity.

More minor parenting concerns also may surface. Parents may have specific worries about their children's diet (e.g., vegetarian, restricted sweets), or they may worry more generally about coordinating rules between two homes. In addition to discussing the specific issues, one common way to address such concerns is to acknowledge the parents' loss of control over their children as a result of living apart. Like parents' lost control as children grow older, divorced parents need to recognize and come to grips with this inevitability. They have no other choice.

There is little left to the meaning of the term *custody* once parents agree about how they will make major and more minor decisions about childrearing. What remains is symbolism, or perhaps, an anachronism. Like a growing number of state laws, many parents choose not to use "custody" in their mediated agreements. These parents view their own agreements about parenting as far more important than legal terminology.

Money and the Children

Mediators must be aware of parents' financial circumstances and disputes even when mediation is limited to custody issues (as in my studies). Financial arrangements with respect to the children are a particular concern, because they may play a strategic role in a custody dispute. For example, many parents want their children to remain in the same house following a divorce, at least for a period of time. In such a circumstance, a custody dispute may be about the house or related money matters as much as the children.

Custody mediators must be careful not to intrude into issues that parents (and their lawyers) have defined as separate from mediation. Still, mediators can educate parents about some financial issues related to their children. Some education may be basic; for example, unrepresented parents may know of schedules for calculating child support. Other suggestions can be aimed at helping parents anticipate future trouble spots. Work-related childcare and medical costs usually are considered to be additions to child support; extracurricular activities or camps, which can be quite expensive, typically are not. Will the parents share these expenses, and if so, how? Who will get the tax deductions for the children? Are the parents aware that tax rates differ substantially for single adults versus heads of households? The IRS rules are clear on these matters, so the parents need to be, too.

The most important financial matter to bring up probably is the cost of college education. College is a big-ticket item, one that typically is *not* addressed in the law. If parents want to pay for part or all of their children's college expenses, as many parents do, they need to plan and save in advance (unless they are very wealthy). Some options for parents to consider include opening a college savings account to which they both begin to contribute immediately; and agreeing to continue child support through the college years; and agreeing in advance to make fixed payments or proportional contributions to their children's college education, perhaps basing future payments on the cost of room, board, and tuition at a designated state university.

WRITING AGREEMENTS

There are a number of different ways in which the details of a developing agreement can be tracked during mediation, and there also are a number of different procedures for writing the final agreement. Agreements can become complicated and memories can be distorted, so it is essential to maintain an ongoing record of tentative decisions. Mediators can use case notes to do this informally earlier in the process, always taking care to review the details with the parents at the beginning and end of each meeting. As the agreement takes shape, however, a written record is preferable, because it both takes less time and is less likely to cause controversy.

Written records can take several forms. One possibility is to write various details on a large flip chart and to post old sheets on the wall at the beginning of a new session. Another option is to have one of the parents track the details of the agreement and bring in copies of their notes to each session. Similarly, mediators can write up the details of the developing agreement and share copies with the parents. A draft of an agreement that is written up by either of the party's lawyers also may be used to summarize tentative agreements.

My preferred method is to use a preexisting word processing template for drafting an agreement, together with a spreadsheet for tracking finances, as this is both convenient and helpful in pointing to topics to cover. A number of templates are posted on the Internet. Some states and jurisdictions have parenting plan templates available, or required, for filing agreements.

All agreements made in mediation are open for renegotiation until the entire package of issues has been agreed upon. At this point, an agreement needs to be drafted. The draft can be written by the mediator (typically labeled a "Memorandum of Understanding"), one of the parents, or one of the lawyers, or by the parents and mediators together in a session. My agreements typically contain a number of details about parenting that are not explicitly addressed in the law, as well as specific plans about schedules, decisions, and custody designations (see Table 8.3). They also often include a clause about how future disputes will be resolved, such as an agreement to attempt mediation before initiating legal action in the future. I use informal terminology and plain English; lawyers may or may not choose to translate this into their language.

After a draft is completed, the parents are encouraged to object to it, to change their minds, and especially to have their attorneys review it. A follow-up session is then scheduled to allow both parents time to contact their attorneys and think through the details of the agreement.

Some parents prefer to write up informal or temporary agreements rather than full-scale legal documents, and they wish to end mediation at this point. Provided that they fully understand the advice to contact counsel, I accept parents' decisions. Most parents have their agreement reviewed by attorneys, however, and changes inevitably result from this process. (I remind parents in advance that an attorney's job is to anticipate all possible problems, so the parents should expect their lawyers to voice concerns.) Sometimes the objections are minor, perhaps even silly. Sometimes they include important additions. The attorneys may renegotiate the final details themselves in some circumstances, or they may encourage the parents to resolve them back in mediation. In a few cases, an agreement completely breaks down during the course of the attorney review.

The possibility of these varied outcomes makes it essential to schedule a follow-up mediation appointment in advance. This subsequent meeting provides an opportunity for the parents to negotiate a few further points and give the mediator feedback on what has transpired. It may offer the parents one last chance to negotiate cooperatively, or the final meeting may be a time to review the accepted document and to anticipate trouble spots in the future.

The final document can vary greatly in detail, form, and appearance. Some mediated agreements are brief, use informal language, and are written by the parents themselves. Others are long, legal documents rewritten by the attorneys and containing much legal boilerplate. There are many variations in between these extremes. In my view, the best agreements contain many details about parenting, appropriate legal safeguards, and much of the parents' own wording, preferences, and philosophy.

TABLE 8.3. Sample Parenting Plan

Weekly schedule

1. Katie and Andrew will be with their mother every week Monday through Thursday.
2. Katie and Andrew will be with their father on alternate weekends from Thursday at 5:00 P.M. through Sunday at 7:00 P.M.
3. Katie and Andrew will be with their father every "off" Thursday from 5:00 P.M. until the beginning of school on Friday (or 5:00 P.M. on Friday when there is no school).

Holiday schedule

1. Holiday schedules replace the weekly schedules.
2. Beginning with Thanksgiving 2011, Katie and Andrew will be with their mother from 5:00 P.M. the Wednesday immediately before Thanksgiving Day through Sunday at 7:00 P.M.
3. Beginning with Christmas 2011, Katie and Andrew will be with their father from 5:00 P.M. on their last day of school before Christmas vacation through 2:00 P.M. on December 25. The children will be with their mother from 2:00 P.M. on Christmas Day until 7:00 P.M. on the Sunday before school resumes.
4. The schedule for Thanksgiving and Christmas will alternate yearly between the two parents.
5. Every year, Katie and Andrew will be with their father for the entire 10-day spring break and Easter weekend from 5:00 P.M. on Friday through 7:00 P.M. on the second following Sunday.
6. The parents agree to arrange to allow each parent to spend at least 3 hours with Katie and Andrew on the children's respective birthdays.
7. Katie and Andrew will spend Mother's Day and mother's birthday (February 27) with their mother, and Father's Day and father's birthday (November 13) with their father.
8. During the summer school vacation, Katie and Andrew will spend a 2-week vacation with their father and a 2-week vacation with their mother. Specific dates will be determined by April 1 of each year.

Parenting and decision making

1. The parents will share joint legal custody of Katie and Andrew. They will jointly make decisions about the children's religious training, education, and elective medical, dental, and psychological care.
2. The parents will work to establish similar rules in their households, to encourage the children's relationships with both parents, and to avoid making negative comments about one another to the children.
3. The parents agree to speak on the telephone for 5–10 minutes each Wednesday evening at 9:00 P.M. in order to exchange information about the children.

Amending this agreement

1. If either parent plans to move more than 25 miles from their present address, they will notify the other parent at least 6 months prior to the move to allow time to renegotiate this agreement if necessary.
2. If the parents are unable to resolve any differences about the details of this agreement or about rearing Katie and Andrew, they agree to attempt to reach an agreement with a therapist or mediator before initiating legal action.

ENDING MEDIATION

Ending mediation can be difficult. The writing of the agreement is a symbolic acknowledgment that the relationship has ended. More practically, it means that the sessions are ending, and many parents privately enjoy their contact during mediation. The signing of a final agreement also can be frightening because it makes changes much more difficult to renegotiate in the future. For these reasons, some people quarrel about insignificant issues as mediation is coming to an end. The goal of this quibbling often seems to be to prolong contact with the former spouse or to avoid coming to a final decision. By this point in time, an interpretation about the meaning of ending mediation is accepted by most parents, particularly if it is made in caucus, not in front of the former partner.

Even for parents who retain little emotional investment in the marriage, ending mediation can be difficult. Parents frequently express gratitude for having been given the option of mediation. However, their mixed emotions often include being tired, relieved, and typically quite sad. The partners have not reconciled; that was not their goal. What they have done is to separate in a way that hopefully was less difficult than the alternatives. Still, the grief over their multiple losses is painful. Mediation is not simply a way to negotiate an agreement. It is a way of saying good-bye.

SUMMARY

Custody mediation becomes less structured in the second session and continuing through drafting a final parenting plan. Still, certain process and substantive themes characterize these middle and late phases of mediation. The major process themes in the model outlined in this chapter include (1) identifying specific problems, while focusing on issues not emotions; (2) brainstorming alternatives, while suspending evaluation to encourage creativity and give parents time to ponder options; (3) evaluating alternatives in terms of parents' interests, not their positions; and (4) experimenting with parenting plans to see what *really* works for children, and what reduces pressure on parents. The plan must be approached as a "living agreement," one parents may change in the near or more distant future.

The substantive topics addressed include not only legal issues but also various concerns about postdivorce parenting. Custody disputes are reframed as familiar parenting and coparenting issues, which they are at the core. Legal and physical custody are described in terms of a schedule and decision making, an approach that can empower parents, limit unnecessary battles over terms loaded with symbolism, and suggest additional topics outside of the law that parents should consider—for example, how to develop similar rules across households while still respecting each other's parenting autonomy. The focus on parenting also suggests financial topics to discuss even though parents are not obligated to do so, particularly how to pay for college. As always, mediators also often must address a variety of issues on parents' "hidden agendas," ranging from a desire to reconcile to worries about new parenting figures.

Although some parents opt for informal verbal or written agreements, successful mediation usually ends with a written document that becomes a legal agreement when parents sign it. Mediators, parents, or lawyers may draft tentative agreements (often called a "Memorandum of Understanding"), but in all cases, parents are strongly encouraged to review the draft with independent attorneys before signing the document. Some parents choose to preserve some of their own language instead of substituting legal boilerplate. More importantly, mediators encourage parents to preserve not only their legal agreement but also their moral commitments to parenting made in mediation.

9

MEDIATION
RESEARCH

A 12-Year Randomized Study

> The courts of this country should not be the places where the
> resolution of disputes begins. They should be the places where
> the disputes end after alternative methods of resolving disputes
> have been considered and tried.
> —JUSTICE SANDRA DAY O'CONNOR

With the help of the people listed in the Preface, I conducted randomized trials of the "emotionally informed" approach to mediation
described in this book. My studies compared the outcomes of mediation
and adversary settlement (usually litigation) among two samples of high-
conflict families. When parents petitioned a Virginia court for a contested
custody hearing, they were randomly assigned either to try to resolve
their disputes in mediation or to continue with the legal proceedings. We
assessed these families multiple times over the course of 12 years after
they resolved their disputes in mediation, in court, or in whatever way
they could.

As detailed in this chapter, 12 years after an average of less than 6
hours of mediation, nonresidential parents who mediated saw their children far more often than parents who continued with the adversary process. Based on "grades" given by the primary residential parent, moreover, nonresidential parents who mediated also were better parents. And

of critical importance, coparents who mediated reported significantly less conflict, despite the fact that they had many more opportunities to fight. (Because both parents maintained more contact with their children, they necessarily also had more contact with each other.)

While mediation did not "work" in every case, my research showed that, relative to adversary settlement, mediation caused notably more positive outcomes for parents, children, and the court—in the short term and, remarkably, even more so over the long run. Again, because we randomly assigned families to mediation or litigation, we know that mediation *caused* these outcomes.

My primary purpose in this chapter is to summarize the methods and findings of my studies of mediation and adversary settlement. This scientific information forms the evidence base for the methods outlined in the present and the first edition of this book (Emery, 1994). The study also deserves its central focus, because the random assignment and long-term follow-up make it a unique contribution to mediation research.

Like most random assignment studies, however, my research involved a relatively small number of families. The findings certainly cannot be said to be representative of all divorcing families or of all approaches to mediation. In order to suggest such important generalizations, this chapter also references findings from various other studies and program evaluations of mediation.

Research findings are organized around three, key areas where, on average, mediation has largely been demonstrated to offer benefits relative to adversary settlement: (1) the administration of justice (e.g., settlement rates, time, and cost), (2) party satisfaction, and (3) family relationships and individual well-being.[1] While results of research are encouraging and mediation surely is the best studied legal intervention in custody disputes, I still must offer a caveat at the outset: We desperately need more research on mediation, on adversary settlement, on the many new forms of alternative dispute resolution, and on family courts more generally.

OVERVIEW OF METHODS

My graduate students and I have published a number of papers on the work summarized in this chapter. Major reports include a general rationale for mediation (Emery & Wyer, 1987b), a comparison of outcomes for an initial sample of 40 families (Emery & Wyer, 1987a), a replication study involving 31 additional families (Emery et al., 1991), a 1-year

---

[1] As we will see, mediation may not lead to mental health benefits.

follow-up of parents who participated in both earlier studies (Emery, Matthews, & Kitzmann, 1994), a report on children's psychological outcomes 1 year after dispute resolution (Kitzmann & Emery, 1994), a major report on the 12-year follow-up that especially detailed changes for family relationships (Emery et al., 2001), a report on the emotional pain reported by young people whose parents divorced 12 years earlier (Laumann-Billings & Emery, 2000), and two analyses of 12-year outcomes for parents (Sbarra & Emery, 2005b, 2008). All of these papers were published in well-respected, peer-reviewed journals, and contain far more details than can be summarized here. Still, an overview of the methods should help the reader who has not seen, or is not concerned with, all of the details found in these scientific reports.

Experimental Design

Perhaps the greatest strength of my research is that real families with real custody disputes were randomly assigned to either mediation or adversary settlement. Random assignment is critical to determining cause and effect in scientific research, a statement that is "old news" to social scientists but deserves a bit of elaboration for other readers. Random assignment ensures that families who mediated and litigated are equivalent prior to the intervention. Unlike what may happen in the real world, in my research, "nice" parents did not choose mediation; angry parents did not choose to fight it out in court.[2] Because of random assignment (the essential procedure used to determine if a new medicine or any other treatment works), families who mediated or litigated differed only on one variable: how they settled their dispute. This means that any differences we observed afterward were *caused* by either mediation or by adversary settlement.

Not surprisingly, real families with real disputes (not to mention their lawyers and judges) often object to random assignment to settlement options, which is why this essential scientific method is used so rarely in studies of court procedures. In my research, a court mediator approached families when they filed a petition for a contested custody hearing. At random, the mediator asked families either to try mediation or to participate in a study of the court (the litigation control group). Of those families, 71% agreed to try mediation and 84% agreed to participate in the court study, a total of 71 families in all (35 in mediation, 36 in

---

[2] The fact that everyone had filed for a contested custody hearing means that conflict was high for all families. They were not "nice" or highly cooperative to begin with, as some stereotypes suggest about parents who mediate.

litigation). Those who agreed to join the study were virtually identical to those who declined participation in terms of demographic characteristics and prior court records (Emery et al., 1991).

Confidence in the study's results is increased, because a replication (Emery et al., 1991) found results broadly similar to an initial investigation (Emery et al., 1987). In addition, we completed 18-month (Emery et al., 1994) and 12-year follow-ups (Emery et al., 2001) of the combined sample, carefully examining patterns of attrition to make sure there was no differential drop-out between the groups. At all points in time, we assessed families using objective, standardized measures. Finally, we used a structured, thematic intervention that we developed ourselves for the purpose of this research, so others could replicate our work (see Emery, 1994; Emery et al., 1987; as well as this volume). Several different male–female co-mediators worked with parents, so the results would not be attributable to a particular mediator's skills.

Sample and Limitations

I want to call attention to the limitations of my study, as well as its strengths. The most important limitation is the sample. Only families who petitioned the court for a contested custody hearing were included, thus we focused on a small subset of all separated and divorced families, that is, parents who have very acrimonious relationships (perhaps 10% of the total) (Maccoby & Mnookin, 1992). The parents in the sample also were young and had low income, on average, and the majority of their children were of preschool age or younger.

Because of the nature of the sample, it is an open question whether my results generalize to less angry, older, and wealthier parents of older children. In fact, one could question whether the results generalize to other parts of the country or to other countries, or indeed, if findings would differ today in the rapidly evolving world of parenting, divorce, and family law. In an effort to address these possibilities, I frequently reference findings from other studies conducted in a variety of places, often with much larger samples, when discussing the results of my research. Overall, the findings are quite consistent across studies.

Another limitation of my research is that we only studied custody mediation, not comprehensive or "all issues" mediation. The mediators negotiated schedules (physical custody), decision making (legal custody), and child support (if it was linked with a custody issue), but they did not address spousal support or property division. We also only studied the one model of mediation outlined in this book. In this chapter, I note some results of studies of "all-issues" mediation, and very limited evidence on different approaches to mediation. Hopefully, future research will refine what approaches to dispute resolution work best with what parents under what circumstances.

No study can maintain a high degree of experimental control, test different models, and simultaneously use a representative sample of the divorcing population. Researchers always must compromise between internal validity (experimental control) and external validity (representativeness). My research is uniquely strong in terms of experimental control, but open to question with respect to representativeness. In fact, I invite readers to ponder how well my results might generalize by sharing my biggest concern: I expect that my findings generalize across families and across many approaches to mediation. However, I do *not* expect that similar results would be found for very-time-limited and time-pressured mediation, for example, where mediators have an hour, perhaps 2, to "get an agreement" (Trinder & Kellett, 2007).

In my view, mediation is about parental self-determination more than about getting agreements. Mediation can be short term, as it was in my research, but mediation often requires more than 1 or 2 hours. In my studies, mediation could last for up to 12 hours, sometimes including multiple meetings spaced out over a few weeks or months. (On average, the co-mediators worked with families for less than 6 hours.) There was time pressure, but we had enough time to put parenting ahead of agreements. This is very different from courts or community centers where mediators, perhaps with limited training, all too often are given only an hour or so to "get an agreement." Or to put my concern another way, calling something mediation does not make it mediation.

ADMINISTRATION OF JUSTICE

One of the most basic questions to ask about mediation and the administration of justice is whether mediation helps parents to settle disputes—or is just an impediment, adding to the time it takes parents to get in front of a judge. When I was planning the study, some skeptical lawyers put the issue this way: "Sure. You'll settle some disputes with mediation, but we settle disputes, too. We often file a petition for a hearing only to 'up the ante' in our negotiations."

Settlement Outcomes

The point is well taken. We found that a number of lawyers did settle their cases after filing. Over a quarter of the cases in the adversary settlement group (who, like the mediation cases, were recruited at the time of filing) settled before the hearing date. However, 72% of cases randomly assigned to continue with adversary settlement appeared in front of a judge compared to only 11% of cases randomly assigned to mediation (see Figure 9.1).

The difference in custody hearings was statistically significant and is substantively important. Cases randomly allowed to continue with litigation were nearly seven times more likely to be settled by a judge as were the cases assigned at random to mediation. In fact, even when mediation did *not* end in a settlement, parents often settled subsequently, outside of court, with the aid of their lawyers (Emery et al., 1991; see Figure 9.1).

Settlement Rates in Other Programs

Do these results generalize to other settings and mediation programs? Importantly, good settlement rates have been found in large samples of families petitioning for contested custody hearings. In particular, an early "snapshot" study of California's mandatory mediation programs found that of 2,669 cases, 46% settled within 2 weeks of their first mediation, while an additional 20% scheduled appointments for further mediation

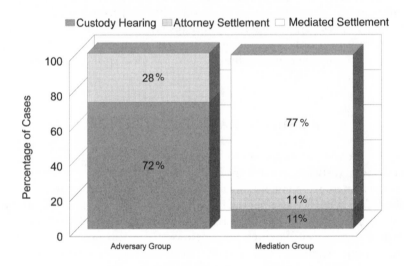

FIGURE 9.1. Settlement outcomes following random assignment. Cases randomly assigned to mediation were far less likely to proceed to a custody hearing than those allowed to continue in the adversary system.

(Depner, Cannata, & Simon, 1992). A similar, recent "snapshot" study reports agreement rates of about 50% in California's mandatory mediation program (Tyda, Chang, & Piazza, 2010). Other research shows that settlement rates typically range from 50 to 90% (Kelly, 2004; Walker, 2010).

Existing research leads to two straightforward and important conclusions about settlement. First, mediation is *not* a mere impediment to getting to trial, but an alternative that settles many disputes not resolved by attorneys and otherwise destined for court. Second, settlement rates vary widely, which raises the question: Why? Myriad factors surely contribute to the variation; some are basic and important to note. For example, one study found notably higher settlement rates for families ordered into mediation sooner rather than later in the legal process (61% vs. 24%) (Zuberbuhler, 2001). Rates also surely are higher when mediators make recommendations if mediation fails, since strongly "encouraging" settlement is one of the goals of the recommending procedure (e.g., "Here is what I will recommend if you quit mediation now. Do you want to keep trying?").

Future research surely will detect other basic influences on settlement rates, for example, whether mediation is court or community based and the strength of judicial support. Courts and judges can lend considerable weight to mediation, and I would be stunned if settlement was not found to be substantially higher in court settings and with strong judicial support. Finally, one basic issue that does *not* appear to influence settlement rates is whether mediation is limited to custody or includes "all issues." To date, comparisons of the two alternatives have shown mixed results (Walker, 2010), sometimes favoring comprehensive mediation (Walker et al., 1994) and sometimes favoring custody mediation (Davis et al., 2000).

Beyond Settlement

Settlement is a very important index of the success of mediation, particularly from the perspective of administration of justice. However, settlement rates are not the only or even the most important index of mediation's success. Even when parents fail to reach a full agreement in mediation, they commonly reach a partial agreement, thus narrowing the issues in dispute (Walker, 2010). Moreover, an overemphasis on settlement can make mediation less family friendly, as mediators can be pressured (and, in turn, pressure parents) to focus on getting agreements rather than on promoting successful coparenting.

A more effective way of achieving the extremely important goal of keeping more families out of court would be to make mediation manda-tory,[3] because only a minority of parents pick mediation when given the option of doing so (Walker, 2010). This makes complete sense, because as I have said repeatedly, mediation is an emotionally *unnatural* choice in the midst of the hurt, pain, and anger of divorce. We therefore need to create a system that requires parents to at least experience mediation before proceeding with litigation, because mediation is an alternative that, on average, is demonstrably better for both their children and for them in the long run. I present a broad outline of such a dispute resolu-tion system at the end of this chapter.

Content of Agreements

Are there differences in the specifics of the settlements reached by media-tors, lawyers, or judges? In my studies, the content of the agreements were quite similar following mediation or adversary settlement. We found no statistically significant differences in primary residence (physi-cal custody), the number of days with the nonresidential parent, or the amount of child support. On the other hand, joint *legal* custody was significantly more common following mediation, although sole maternal custody (legal and physical) was the norm for both groups (Emery et al., 1991).[4]

Details, Details, Details

The content of the mediated and adversary agreements differed in one respect other than legal custody. Parenting plans were more detailed in the mediated agreements than in the adversary ones (Emery et al., 1991). Mediated agreements specified days and times for exchanging the children, and included agreements about other aspects of parenting such as childrearing goals. Adversary settlements were much more gen-eral, including such imprecise arrangements as "physical custody to the mother, liberal rights of visitation to the father."

Joan Kelly's (1990) important study of comprehensive mediation also found that mediated agreements were more specific than adversary settlements. Mediated agreements included many details about the sched-

---

[3] "Mandatory" only means that parents in dispute must attend at least one educational session, even if they do so separately. Reaching a settlement is *not* mandatory in mandatory mediation.

[4] The traditional agreements in my studies likely reflect a number of influences, including the lower income sample, local legal and social preferences, and the absence of any mention of the term "joint custody" in Virginia statutes during the time of the study.

ule and decision making. Kelly's "all issues" agreements also included more details about children's health insurance and about continuing child support beyond the age of 18.

In contrast to my research, however, Kelly found much higher rates of joint custody, a reflection of different state norms (California vs. Virginia). Joint legal custody was agreed upon in 100% of her mediation cases and 90% of her adversary settlement cases. Interestingly, primary father residence and limited father visitation *both* were more common among parents in her adversary group. Kelly (1990) termed this last result an "either/or" outcome, a reflection of the win–lose orientation of the adversary approach and the win–win goal of mediation.

Joint Custody Bias?

Are mediators biased in favor of particular settlement options? Various commentators have leveled accusations of bias, but the number of arguments far outstrips the number of studies, as is far too common in this field. The old (Fineman, 1988; Grillo, 1991) but still vehement debate about mediators' supposed embrace of joint custody offers a useful illustration of such debate—and of the value of data. Empirical evidence shows that in contested cases, in fact, mediated agreements contain *fewer* provisions specifying joint physical custody than either attorney settlements or judicial orders. Joint *legal* custody, in contrast, is more common in mediated agreements (Reynolds et al., 2007; see Chapter 6).

Overall, the findings suggest that, in comparison to adversary settlements, mediated agreements are more flexible, often anticipating future changes in the law. Less constrained by existing law and more focused on parenting, mediators negotiated specific parenting plans and embraced the symbolism of joint legal custody decades ago. These ideas were innovative at the time of my studies; today, they are standard practice. Now, many mediators address key financial matters outside of the realm of current law, for example, the cost of a college education. It seems that mediators also are more likely to point to the hazards of joint physical custody in high-conflict cases. I expect these foci also will become a part of standard practice for everyone in the not-too-distant future.

Time, Cost, and Compliance

Advocates have argued that mediation not only promotes settlement, but it also helps parents reach agreements more quickly, costs less, and leads to more compliance than settlements reached through adversary procedures. Is there evidence to support these claims? In my studies, we found that parents settled their disputes in about half the time when randomly assigned to mediation versus adversary settlement (Emery et al., 1991). We did not measure cost, but two years after settlement, we did find a trend for greater compliance with child support orders among nonresidential parents who mediated. However, noncompliance was quite high in both groups (51% vs. 71%) (Emery et al., 1994).

Some other investigators have found that mediation is faster (Peeples, Reynolds, & Harris, 2008; Thoennes, 2002), less expensive (Kelly, 1990; Pearson & Thoennes, 1989), and leads to higher rates of compliance agreements (Irving & Benjamin, 1992; Irving, Benjamin, Bohm, & MacDonald, 1981; Jones & Bodtker, 1999; Kelly, 1990; Pearson & Thoennes, 1989; Peeples et al., 2008). While most research to date is consistent with these conclusions, not all studies are (Beck & Sales, 2001; Kelly, 2004; Walker, 2010).

In considering these various efficiency topics, one issue that is critical to note is that, in my view, returning to mediation is *not* a failure. It is a *positive* outcome, reflecting the continued use of a cooperative forum for negotiating changes. At my 12-year follow-up, we found that parents who mediated had made *more* changes in their parenting plan in comparison to parents in the adversary settlement group (Emery et al., 2001). However, the average number of changes was only 1.4 over a 12-year period for the mediation group compared to rare changes (0.3 on average) in the adversary settlement group. Moreover, mediation parents made most of the changes informally.

Apparently, parents who mediated flexibly accommodated important changes in their own and their children's lives. This should not be surprising, since we encouraged them to view their parenting plan as a *living agreement* (Chapter 8). Thus, evidence that parents who mediate may use court services more often (Jones & Bodtker, 1999) may reflect a solution more than a problem. In fact, I often encourage recently separated parents to return to mediation once at the beginning of every "semester" in their children's lives, before school in the fall, after the first of the year, and before summer vacations.

PARENTS' SATISFACTION

A question we studied extensively was whether parents preferred mediation over adversary settlement. We consistently found that, on average, parents were more satisfied with mediation on items assessing both the presumed strengths of mediation (e.g., "Your feelings were understood") and the presumed strengths of the adversary system (e.g., "Your rights were protected"). Moreover, parents were happier with mediation than adversary settlement 6 weeks after dispute resolution (Emery & Wyer,

1987b; Emery et al., 1991), a year and a half later (Emery et al., 1994), and 12 years after the initial settlement (Emery et al., 2001). Other researchers also have found that parents report greater satisfaction following mediation than adversary settlement, and, in general, parents report a high level of satisfaction with mediation (Beck & Sales, 2001; Jones & Bodtker, 1998, 1999; Kelly, 1990, 2004; Tyda et al., 2010; Walker, 2010). Thus, a well-established finding is that parents report high levels of satisfaction with mediation, greater than they report following adversary settlement.

Differences for Mothers and Fathers?

A more controversial question is whether mediation benefits fathers more than mothers. In my studies, we consistently found that, in comparison to mothers, fathers reported more satisfaction with mediation than adversary settlement. In fact, we found that mothers in the *adversary* group reported more satisfaction on two items assessing whether they won or lost what they wanted (Emery & Wyer, 1987a). But we need to review these findings in some detail here, as I have elsewhere (Emery et al., 1991; Emery, 1994), because some commentators have wrongly suggested that these results support the claim that mediation harms women (e.g., Grillo, 1991).

Upon closer inspection, several aspects of my results counter the claim that mediation is bad for women. For one, mothers in the mediation group could not have been more satisfied than mothers in the adversary settlement group, because the adversary mothers were extremely happy. In fact, we encountered a "ceiling effect." Mothers in the adversary group were already at the top of our scales, so there was no way for the mothers in the mediation group to score higher than them.

Not only that, but a careful inspection of virtually every satisfaction item shows that mothers were very satisfied whether they mediated or continued with adversary settlement—as were fathers who mediated (Emery et al., 1991). Consistently, the outlying and unhappy group was fathers who continued with adversary settlement. Figure 9.2 portrays this pattern for four items reflecting different aspects of dispute resolution, "Concern was shown for your children," "Concern was shown for you," "Your rights were protected," and "Helped settle problems."

The results for fathers who litigated are explained by the predominant views of fathers and parenting in Virginia during the time of my study: Mothers almost always won full legal and physical custody in the adversary settlement group. Mediation gave fathers more of a "voice" in the process (Kitzmann & Emery, 1993) and more joint legal but not physical custody (Emery et al., 1991). Against a different legal and social

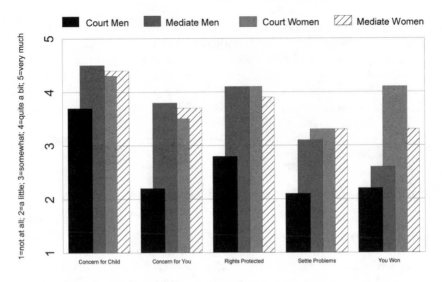

FIGURE 9.2. Mothers and fathers ratings of satisfaction with mediation and adversary settlement. Court fathers were consistently unhappy, while others were consistently happy—except for the "You Won" item. For this item, mediation produced "win–win" results; litigation caused "win–lose" outcomes.

backdrop in California during roughly the same time, Kelly and her colleagues found that *both* mothers and fathers were more satisfied with mediation than with adversary settlement (Kelly & Gigy, 1989; Kelly & Duryee, 1992).

Another aspect of my data also causes me to conclude that my findings do *not* suggest that mediation is bad for women. A familiar slogan is mediation promotes a "win–win" mentality, while adversary settlement takes a "win–lose" approach. The results for the two items that favored women in the adversary group are consistent with this characterization. In the adversary group, women reported high levels of winning what they wanted; men reported winning little. In contrast, women and men were closer to the middle in the mediation group. They both reported winning some—perhaps indicating greater compromise in this group (see Figure 9.2).

In fact, we found strong evidence for this interpretation. In the adversary group, mothers' and fathers' scores were negatively correlated: The more mothers felt they won, the *less* fathers felt they won, a win–lose outcome. In the mediation group, mothers' and fathers' scores were positively correlated: The more mothers felt they won, the *more* fathers felt they won, too (Emery et al., 1991). In my study, "win–win" was more than a slogan for mediation.

FAMILY RELATIONSHIPS
AND PSYCHOLOGICAL ADJUSTMENT

Advocates (including me) hoped that mediation and other more cooperative forms of dispute resolution would prove to be more "family
friendly." I specifically hypothesized that, in comparison with adversary
settlement, mediation would have more positive (or less negative)[5] effects
on divorced family relationships. I also hypothesized that reduced conflict and other improvements in family functioning would lead to better
psychological well-being, especially for children. For both philosophical
and empirical reasons, I was therefore disappointed when we found no
differences in relationship quality or psychological well-being when comparing the mediation and adversary settlement groups either immediately
after dispute resolution (Emery et al., 1991) or 1 year later (Emery et al.,
1994).

Things changed dramatically when we began to analyze the results
of the 12-year follow-up study. In initiating the long-term evaluation, I
hypothesized that the benefits of mediation might not be visible until a
period of time had passed, particularly until families moved through the
crisis phase of divorce. Although the hypothesis seemed reasonable—and
in conducting mediation I always told myself I was "planting a seed"
that would grow later—honestly, I was a bit skeptical. After all, very few
interventions have psychological benefits that last more than a few years,
let alone for more than a decade. Instead, the usual pattern for evidence-
based treatments like cognitive behavior therapy or interpersonal therapy
is for short-term benefits to diminish greatly or disappear within a couple
of years (see, e.g., Elkin at al., 1989).

Nonresidential Parent–Child Contact

I therefore was surprised and pleased when our research showed a very
different pattern for the long-term effects of mediation. We found that,
12 years later, an average of only about 6 hours of mediation caused
substantial long-term benefits for parents and children, particularly for
the relationships between children and their nonresidential parents and
between the parents themselves. Rather than diminishing over time, the
benefits of mediation apparently grew larger over the years.

One notable and very important benefit of mediation was increased
contact between the nonresidential parent (mostly fathers) and their chil-

---

[5] We found evidence for both of these possibilities. Parents who mediated reported that
conflict *decreased* 1 year later, while parents who litigated reported that conflict *increased*
over that time (Sbarra & Emery, 2008).

dren. Divorced fathers often see their children infrequently, distressingly so in my view, and contact typically decreases as time passes (Amato et al., 2009; Seltzer, 1991). I believe that one very important reason for this is that many adults manage the grief, hurt, and pain of a divorce in precisely the same way as most people deal with lost love: They exclaim, "I never want to see you again!" and eventually follow through with their threat (Emery, 2006; Chapter 3). The problem, however, is that partners who are also parents can end up divorcing their children as well as their former spouse. If mediation really is a forum for renegotiating relationships as well as negotiating agreements, it should help former partners to end their spousal relationship but not their relationship as parents (Chapter 4).

The data in Figure 9.3 show that being randomly assigned to mediation versus adversary settlement did indeed make a substantial difference in nonresidential parent–child contact. Thirty percent of nonresidential parents who mediated saw their children once a week or more 12 years later in comparison to only 9% of parents in the adversary group. At the opposite extreme, 39% of nonresidential parents in the adversary group had seen their children only once or not at all in the

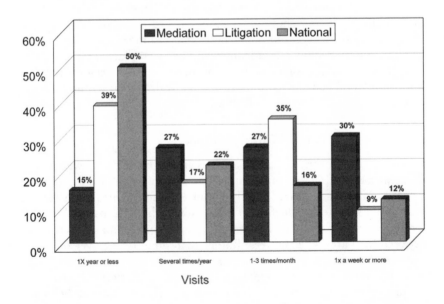

FIGURE 9.3. Direct nonresidential parent–child contact 12 years after random assignment to mediation or litigation. "National" is nonresidential father–child contact 11 or more years after divorce in a national sample (Seltzer, 1991), and is included only as a comparison.

last year compared to 15% in the mediation group. These differences are both statistically significant and substantively important (Emery et al., 2001).

We found even larger differences for telephone contact, which was probably a better measure of contact at long-term follow-up. After all, many parents moved during the course of 12 years, as is typical, particularly following a divorce. Many children moved too, including moving away from home. After all, the "children" ranged in age from adolescents to young adults at the time of the 12-year follow-up.

In fact, fully 54% of nonresidential parents who mediated spoke to their children on the telephone once a week or more. In contrast, 13% of nonresidential parents in the adversary group spoke to their children weekly. At the opposite extreme, 54% of nonresidential parents in the adversary settlement group had *not* spoken with their children on the telephone in the past year, or had done so only once, in comparison to 12% in the mediation group (see Figure 9.4). These differences are statistically significant (Emery et al., 2001), and in many ways, they are amazing. An average of less than 6 hours of mediation *caused* these huge differences in contact 12 years later.

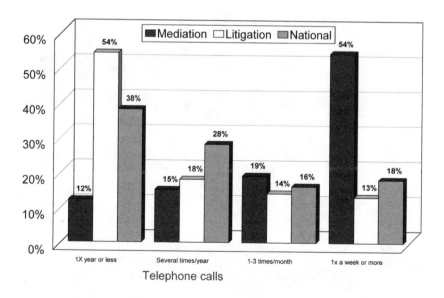

FIGURE 9.4. Nonresidential parent–child telephone contact 12 years after random assignment to mediation or litigation. "National" is nonresidential father–child contact 11 or more years after divorce in a national sample (Seltzer, 1991), and is included only as a comparison.

Parent–Child Relationship Quality

As is well known, the quality of parent–child relationships is more important to children than the quantity of contact (Amato & Gilbreth, 1999).[6] We found benefits owing to mediation in regard to parenting quality, too. Twelve years after being assigned at random to mediation, *residential* parents reported that the *nonresidential* parent was significantly more likely to discuss parenting problems with them and to have had a greater influence on childrearing decisions. Residential parents also said that, in comparison to those in the adversary group, nonresidential parents who mediated were significantly more involved in the children's discipline, grooming, moral training, errands, holidays, significant events, school or church functions, recreational activities, and vacations (Emery et al., 2001). In fact, nonresidential parents who mediated got significantly better "grades" in every area of parenting that we measured (see Figure 9.5).

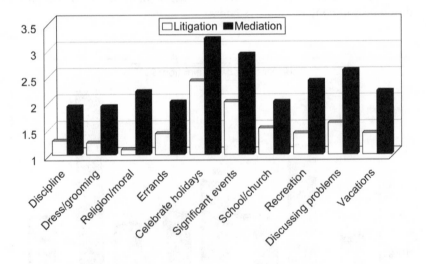

FIGURE 9.5. Residential parent's report of nonresidential parent's involvement in various areas of parenting 12 years after random assignment to mediation or litigation. Response alternatives ranged from 1 = never to 5 = always (Ahrons, 1981).

---

[6] Quantity still matters. Parents and children need some level of contact to maintain a quality relationship, and, more philosophically, spending time with your children or with a parent is important in its own right.

Coparenting Conflict

Of critical importance, conflict between parents did not increase as a result of the fact that both parents who mediated saw their children often and both were involved in parenting. In fact, in a methodologically sophisticated reanalysis of the data, we found that parents who mediated reported significantly *less* conflict when compared with parents who litigated (Sbarra & Emery, 2008). This is a particularly positive outcome, since parents who mediated must have had more opportunities to fight than parents who litigated. Parents who mediated were more likely to *both* remain more involved in their children's lives, which means that they were more involved with each other, too. Yet, these parents fought less, not more, about their children.

Despite the many benefits of mediation for parental conflict and involvement, on average, I should call attention to an important caveat. For a small subset of parents, *litigation* reduced conflict more substantially than mediation (Sbarra & Emery, 2008). As I discuss briefly toward the end of this chapter, I believe law and policy should strongly direct more divorcing parents to mediate. But we cannot expect all parents to mediate everything. We need a range of dispute resolution alternatives to deal with the range of divorcing families and their conflicts. Some troubled families can only resolve their disputes in the traditional manner: They use the courts and, in the end, ultimately end their conflict when one parent drops out of both the ex's and the children's lives.

Psychological Well-Being

Relative to adversary settlement, mediation caused many positive outcomes for family relationships, including more nonresidential parent–child contact, better parent–child relationship quality, and less coparenting conflict. Researchers repeatedly have found that these more positive aspects of postdivorce family life predict better psychological adjustment among parents and especially children (Emery, 1999; Hetherington & Kelly, 2002). At the long-term follow-up, however, we found no differences in the mental health of parents or children based on whether they mediated or proceeded with adversary settlement.

I do not have a definite explanation for this null result, but instead can offer three alternatives. The first is that a few hours of mediation simply may not cause improved mental health outcomes 12 years later. I could argue, in fact, that it would be ridiculous to expect so much. Isn't it enough that less than 6 hours of mediation kept a majority of high-conflict families out of court, saved them and the courts time and perhaps money, made parents notably happier with a great many different aspects of their experience with dispute resolution, and dramatically improved family relationships for years to come?!

A second possibility is that the null results are attributable to the study's limited statistical power to detect significant effects. Consider these observations. With one exception,[7] all of the results at 12-year follow-up were in the right direction, but the group differences fell short of statistical significance. That is, parents and especially children who mediated were better adjusted on a variety of measures in comparison to families who litigated, but the differences were not statistically reliable. Moreover, unpublished evidence shows that children whose parents mediated *were* significantly better adjusted on measures of depression and behavior problems—when we removed the handful of children from the mediation sample who moved back and forth repeatedly between their parents' homes. Methodologically, we cannot do this, of course, but the finding suggests that mediation might benefit children's mental health as long as parents are not *too* flexible in making changes in their basic parenting plan.

We also found that reduced parental conflict in *either* the mediation or the litigation group predicted better psychological adjustment among children a year and a half after dispute settlement (Kitzmann & Emery, 1994). Again, these findings suggest that mediation *may* have led to some mental health benefits, but the study did not have enough statistical power to detect them. As I write this, graduate students and I are exploring new, sophisticated data analytical techniques as a way to test this possibility further.

A third alternative is that some forms of mediation may have mental health benefits for children and/or parents, even though my emotionally informed approach does not. With few exceptions (Walton, Oliver, & Griffin, 1999), researchers have found no evidence of improved psychological well-being owing to mediation (Kelly, 1990). Still, it is possible, for example, that longer, therapeutic or "transformative" mediation has mental health benefits. Similarly, short-term mediation might aid mental health when paired with other evidence-based interventions in divorce such as parent groups (Wolchik et al., 2002) or children's groups (Pedro-Carroll & Alpert-Gillis, 1997).

---

[7] The one exception is that fathers who mediated reported significantly *less* acceptance of the end of their marriage (Sbarra & Emery, 2005b), an outcome that may reflect that not expressing their anger in mediation interfered with their grief—or that coparenting relatively cooperatively for 12 years made them think their ex wife was not such a jerk after all.

Children Beyond Dispute

In the *Children Beyond Dispute* studies, Australian researcher and clinical psychologist Jenn McIntosh and colleagues found that *child-inclusive* mediation led to reduced conduct problems among children 4 years later in comparison to *child-focused* mediation (McIntosh, Long, & Wells, 2009).[8] In the child-focused approach, the mediators focused on children's needs during the mediation process, which averaged 5 to 6 hours after intake. Child-inclusive mediation was similar with one key exception. A child specialist interviewed the children, and in a subsequent mediation session, gave feedback to parents about the child's experiences, concerns, and desires. This procedure added about an hour and a half to the mediation. Importantly, the child specialist's goal decidedly was *not* to turn children into decision makers. Rather, their feedback was intended to ensure that the children's agenda became central to the parents' agenda (McIntosh et al., 2009).

Although families were not randomly assigned, the study did employ a quasi-experimental design. Using the same sites and recruitment procedures, all child-inclusive cases were enrolled in the study after all child-focused cases were completed. A total of 169 families participated in the intervention, and 133 remained in the study at 4-year follow-up. Because of the child-inclusive procedure, only families with a child ages 5 to 16 were included in the study (McIntosh et al., 2009).

In addition to fewer conduct problems among children, child-inclusive mediation was linked with a number of benefits at 4-year follow-up, including less legal action over the children, fewer returns to mediation, more stability in parenting plans, more satisfaction with living arrangement reported by fathers and children, less acrimony, better management of parenting disputes, and children feeling less caught in the middle (McIntosh et al., 2009). Child-inclusive mediation also resulted in higher rates of overnights with fathers, but of critical importance, contact increased gradually over time rather than suddenly following mediation.

These are impressive findings, but they should not be misinterpreted. Child-inclusive mediation was *not* a "children's rights" intervention designed to give children a "voice" in the legal process. The child specialists were very sensitive in eliciting and communicating the child's perspective—and very firm in keeping the burden of decision making on parents, not children.[9] In fact, McIntosh and colleagues (2009) attribute

---

[8] I discuss this study at some length both because of its importance and because it is a model of the kind of research needed in the future.

[9] Among the many strengths of this research are the videos the investigators created to illustrate the different approaches.

the success of child-inclusive mediation to "the domino effects of the initial but profound change in parents' awareness about their children's needs" (p. 91). "At the head of the domino effect is the reduction of parent conflict and acrimony, and improved awareness and responsiveness, particularly for fathers ... " (p. 91). Simply put, the child-inclusive approach proved to be a more effective way to mediate.

I think there are two, big "take-home" messages from this important research by McIntosh and colleagues (2009). First, mediators need to constantly strive to keep children's needs in the forefront. Doing so almost certainly requires breaking the strict neutrality of facilitative mediation, and sometimes offering direct, evaluative feedback. Such feedback may be best delivered through an independent child specialist or evaluator, as long as the process maintains a clear emphasis on the parents', not the child's, responsibility for making decisions. Second, we need more research like the *Children Beyond Dispute* study. We need randomized trials of alternative approaches to mediation designed to identify what makes mediation work more or less effectively. Toward this end, let me share some speculations about the "active ingredients" in my emotionally informed mediation in the hope that these ideas may stimulate better future research and practice.

WHAT WORKED?

My research proved that mediation caused important and often sizeable improvements from the perspectives of the administration of justice, raising parents' satisfaction, and especially improving postdivorce family relationships. What my research did not and cannot prove is what elements of mediation (or of adversary settlement) were most important to producing these results, especially effects found 12 years later. Still, experience has helped me to hone hypotheses about what worked. Let me summarize five possibilities.

Taking the Long View

Many advocates suggest that cooperation is *the* active ingredient in ADR. The core idea here is that mediation teaches a model of resolving conflicts that parents will use, on their own, into the future.

While I certainly agree that the cooperative approach is important to mediation's success, I am not so optimistic about the "learning to resolve conflict" scenario. Why? My naïve hopes about how easily mediation might promote cooperation were crushed early in the enterprise. The families in my studies *were* high conflict, and our mediation sessions often were riddled with tension, anger, and outright hostility. Parents had failed to reach an agreement on their own, were requesting judicial intervention, and were assigned to mediation at random. We found them; they did not find us. Experience tells me that mediation did not turn these warring parents into pacifists.

So what did mediation do to promote cooperation over the long run? I believe mediation helped these parents to recognize the need for cooperation regarding their children in the long run, even if, in the midst of their divorce crisis, cooperating seemed impossible. I suspect that parents who mediated admitted, if only privately, that they *would* have to deal with each other for a very long time, and as a result, they resolved to find a way to do so—eventually.

In my estimation, mediation did not teach these parents to cooperate. Mediation helped them to take the long view of their relationship. They were divorcing each other, but they would be parents forever. It may have taken years before they could actually do what they knew they should do, but as my research shows, ultimately many did it. As I have often said to parents, to myself, and in print, the hard part for divorcing parents is *not* knowing what to do. The hard part is actually doing it.

Education about Emotions

Mediation also gave us an opportunity to educate parents about emotions, their children's and especially their own, and I believe this was another important element in its success. I train young, graduate student therapists to make therapy "an experience, not just an education." Parents' education about emotions decidedly was not a detached lesson in mediation, as it might be in a divorce education seminar. Mediation was and is a very real and intense emotional experience.

Consider the emotional experience, for example, when a parent's furious outburst in a joint session quickly dissolves into tears of desperation during caucus. Many parents in this circumstance will admit that they are hurt, grieving, and hoping to reconcile—or to punish their ex. In that moment, they recognize or admit that these feelings fuel much of their anger.

Of course, these same parents may "forget" the emotional lesson later, when they are forced to deal with an angry ex, or simply are all alone and lonely. In plumbing parents' emotions in mediation, I do not expect to be therapeutic. I do not think parents can resolve their grief in a few hours, while simultaneously working out a parenting plan! However, I do believe that parents eventually remember the potent and powerful emotional lessons that they learned in mediation.

Business-Like Boundaries

I suspect that a third, key component to the success of mediation was encouraging former partners to develop business-like boundaries around their coparenting relationship. As noted in Chapter 1, most of the couples in my study had one-sided breakups, as I suspect is true in most acrimonious divorces. My solution to the central dilemma faced by the leaver and the left party is to encourage a type of relationship that *neither* of them wants. They cannot be lovers. They cannot be friends. But they can become partners in a more formal, business-like parenting partnership (see Chapter 4). I believe strongly in this emotional and practical compromise, so much so that I made it a central part of the advice I offer in my book for parents (Emery, 2006).

Avoiding Becoming Adversaries

Another possibility is that mediation leads to relatively little direct benefit to divorcing families. Instead, the advantage of mediation may be keeping parents in conflict from going all the way through with the adversary route. Feeling hurt, angry, and mistreated are understandable emotions in divorce, and powerful motivations for wanting to tell your former partner (literally or metaphorically), "I'll see you in court!" However, the gulf created by these divisive feelings typically grows wider in the adversary system. Hardball negotiations and custody trials can cause severely strained relationships to deteriorate further, perhaps irreparably. While I do not believe that preventing the wound of divorce from festering in the adversary system is the only benefit of mediation, I do believe it is an important contribution to the dispute resolution alternative's success.

Enthusiasm and Commitment

Finally, it is only fair to acknowledge that a big part of the success of mediation in my studies probably is attributable to our enthusiasm and commitment—my own, the mediators', the judges', and everyone involved in the work. We believed that mediation could make a difference, and we were willing to go the extra mile to try to make that happen. I think that was true in my study, and I think that has been true for the practice of divorce mediation since it was created a few decades ago.

Much of what makes any new intervention successful *is* high hopes, dedication, and wanting to help. Sadly, many members of the first generation of mediators are passing by. I wonder if the next generation will carry the flag of this now not-so-new intervention with similar enthusiasm and commitment. I certainly believe that someone needs to get into the middle of parents' custody disputes in order to get the children out of the middle. But it takes strength, energy, perseverance, enthusiasm, and commitment to enter the fray. We did. I hope others will.

TREATING DIVORCED PARENTS LIKE MARRIED PARENTS

I sometimes think that we, as professionals and as a society, do not go far enough in promoting parental self-determination in custody disputes. I sometimes think that we should treat separated, divorced, and never married parents exactly like we treat married parents. How is that? Courts throughout the United States have *refused* to hear parenting disputes between husbands and wives, ruling that allowing married parents to litigate their childrearing disputes would be contrary to the broad, public interest (Emery & Emery, 2008). For example, in 1936 the New York Court of Appeals ruled:

> Dispute between parents when it does not involve anything immoral or harmful to the welfare of the child is beyond the reach of the law. The vast majority of matters concerning the upbringing of children must be left to the conscience, patience, and self restraint of father and mother. No end of difficulties would arise should judges try to tell parents how to bring up their children.[10]

This quotation very well could be a call for mediation in divorce custody disputes. But instead it is an endorsement of family privacy and autonomy—for married parents. The parents in this case could not agree about their child's education, and they turned to the courts for a resolution. The New York Court of Appeals said: Work this out yourselves.

I believe it is an interesting thought experiment to ask why, philosophically, courts take this wise position with regard to married parents, yet we expect our legal system to resolve childrearing disputes, big and small, when they occur between separated, divorced, or never-married parents. This is a particularly pressing thought experiment today, when 40–50% of first marriages end in divorce, and 40% of children are born *outside* of marriage (Emery et al., in press). For some philosophical reason that I cannot articulate, courts do *not* think that disputes between the huge number of separated, divorced, or never-married parents are "beyond the reach of the law."

---

[10] *People v. Sisson,* 2 N.E.2d 660 (1936)

A System of Dispute Resolution Alternatives

Of course, I do not realistically expect our legal system to get out of the custody dispute resolution business altogether. Yes, I do believe that we need to strongly encourage parents to use less adversarial methods of dispute resolution. For example, I believe that laws should mandate an effort at mediation. Still, I recognize that courts (and parents) need a range of dispute resolution mechanisms. Figure 9.6 portrays many of the current range of alternatives.

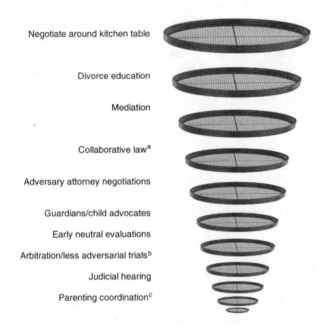

Negotiate around kitchen table

Divorce education

Mediation

Collaborative law[a]

Adversary attorney negotiations

Guardians/child advocates

Early neutral evaluations

Arbitration/less adversarial trials[b]

Judicial hearing

Parenting coordination[c]

FIGURE 9.6. A hierarchy—"funnel"—of commonly used dispute resolution methods for divorce custody conflicts. More cooperative, less intrusive alternatives appear nearer the top, and have bigger "screens" reflecting that most cases should be and are settled using these methods. The successive screens suggest that families should move through the procedures from top to bottom, leaving few cases for the filters at the bottom.

[a]In collaborative law, attorneys contract to negotiate in a principled manner, and will not represent their clients in court if they fail to settle the case.

[b]The less adversarial trial is a new, less formal judicial proceeding used in Australia.

[c]Parenting coordination is a med-arb procedure used with repeat litigators, where the mental health or lawyer mediator has limited decision-making (quasi-judicial) authority.

Dispute resolution efforts that involve greater parental self-determination and more parental cooperation appear nearer to the top of the figure. Those that involve increasingly adversarial procedures and third-party decision making are placed nearer to the bottom. The figure has a funnel shape, reflecting that most cases should be resolved using dispute resolution procedures nearer to the top, which, in practice, they are (Maccoby & Mnookin, 1992). However, there is considerable variation across courts in how wide the funnel is at the top and how narrow it is at the bottom. A goal for administrators, courts, and judges is to push more and more cases upward, so that the wide end of the funnel grows wider and the narrow end grows narrower (Edwards, 2007).

The figure also portrays each successively more intrusive form of dispute resolution as a screen. The concept this is intended to illustrate is processing divorce custody disputes through a series of dispute resolution filters, from top to bottom, like sifting sand through increasingly fine screens. Sorting cases through such a series of dispute resolution screens should leave very few families to be sifted through the bottom filters.

An Agenda

In addition to suggesting how a well-thought-out dispute resolution system might be constructed, one that includes mediation as just one part, albeit a prominent one (Edwards, 2007), Figure 9.1 also lays out a research agenda. As I look at the funnel, some of the many questions that occur to me include: How are all those families at the wide end of the funnel faring, especially the large number of *pro se* (unrepresented) cases? Is the much-discussed collaborative law alternative attracting clients, settling cases, and being viewed more positively by divorcing parents than traditional adversary alternatives? Are custody evaluations *really* a form of *de facto* arbitration, as I believe they are, especially given the recent invention of "early neutral evaluations" designed specifically to promote settlement? How do custody evaluations affect the dispute resolution process more generally (Kelly & Ramsey, 2009)? What *really* happens in attorney negotiations and in custody hearings?[11] How well does parenting coordination work in terms of keeping repeat litigators out of court and perhaps even beginning to settle contentious disputes? We had some initial, innovative research in this area (Johnston & Campbell, 1988), but there has been little follow-up.

---

[11] Even basic statistics describing the process (e.g., time, cost) and outcome (e.g., custody arrangements) of traditional legal procedures in divorce are abysmal. Our best studies of legal practices are the control groups from mediation studies!

These are not mere academic questions. These are issues that affect hundreds of thousands of families every year. These are issues that pertain to the single biggest reason for court intervention in the United States today. Mediation is probably the *best* studied legal intervention in divorce custody disputes. We know far less about the effects and effectiveness of litigation, collaborative law, custody evaluations, parenting coordination, and other old and new procedures aimed at helping families to resolve divorce and custody conflicts.

As with divorcing parents, the hard part for courts, judges, lawyers, mental health professionals, and academic research is not knowing what to do with custody disputes. The hard part is doing it. We have made a beginning. We are far from the end.

REFERENCES

Ahrons, C. R. (1981). The continuing coparental relationship between divorced spouses. *American Journal of Orthopsychiatary, 51,* 415–428.

Ahrons, C. R. (1995). *The good divorce: Keeping your family together when your marriage comes apart.* New York: HarperCollins.

Amato, P. R., & Gilbreth, J. (1999). Nonresident fathers and children's well-being: A meta-analysis. *Journal of Marriage and the Family, 61,* 557–573.

Amato, P. R., Meyers, C., & Emery, R. E. (2009). Changes in nonresident father visitation over four decades. *Family Relations, 58,* 41–53.

American Law Institute. (2002). *Principles of the law of family dissolution: Analysis and recommendations.* Newark, NJ: Bender.

Archer, J. (2001). Grief from an evolutionary perspective. In M. S. Stroebe, R. O. Hansson, W. Stroebe, & H. Schut (Eds.), *Handbook of bereavement research: Consequences, coping, and care* (pp. 263–283). Washington, DC: American Psychological Association.

Atwood, B. A. (2007). Comment on Warshak: The approximation rule as a work in progress. *Child Development Perspectives, 1,* 126–128.

Baumrind, D. (1971). Current patterns of parental authority. *Developmental Psychology Monograph, 4*(1, Pt. 2).

Bauserman, R. (2002). Child adjustment in joint-custody versus sole-custody arrangements: A meta-analytic review. *Journal of Family Psychology, 16,* 91–102.

Beck, C. J. A., & Sales, B. D. (2001). *Family mediation: Facts, myths, and future prospects.* Washington, DC: American Psychological Association.

Beck, C. J. A., Walsh, M. E., Mechanic, M. B., & Taylor, C. S. (2010). Intimate partner violence screening and accommodations provided for safety in mandatory divorce mediation. *Law and Human Behavior, 34,* 227–240.

Benjamin, L. S. (2002). *Interpersonal diagnosis and treatment of personality disorders* (2nd ed.). New York: Guilford Press.

Berger, L. M., Brown, P. R., Joung, E., Melli, M. S., & Wimer, L. (2007). *The stability of shared child physical placements following divorce: Evidence from Wisconsin.* Unpublished manuscript, Institute for Research on Poverty, University of Wisconsin–Madison.

Berger, L. M., Brown, P. R., Joung, E., Melli, M. S., & Wimer, L. (2008). The stability of child physical placements following divorce: Descriptive evidence from Wisconsin. *Journal of Marriage and the Family, 70,* 273–283.

Berkowitz, L. (1993). Pain and aggression: Some findings and implications. *Motivation and Emotion, 17,* 277–293.

Bernard, J. (1972). *The future of marriage.* New York: World.

Bianchi, S. M. (2000). Maternal employment and time with children: Dramatic change or surprising continuity? *Demography, 37,* 401–414.

Bickerdike, A. J., & Littlefield, L. (2000). Divorce adjustment and mediation: Theoretically grounded process research. *Mediation Quarterly, 18,* 181–201.

Bienenfeld, F. (1983). *Child custody mediation: Techniques for counselors, attorneys and parents.* Palo Alto, CA: Science & Behavior Books.

Bonanno, G. A. (2004). Loss, trauma, and human resilience: Have we underestimated the human capacity to thrive after extremely aversive events? *American Psychologist, 59,* 20–28.

Boss, P. (1999). *Ambiguous loss: Learning to live with unresolved grief.* Cambridge, MA: Harvard University Press.

Bowlby, J. (1969). *Attachment and loss: Vol. 1. Attachment.* London: Hogarth Press.

Bowlby, J. (1973). *Attachment and loss: Vol. 2. Separation.* London: Hogarth Press.

Bowlby, J. (1979). *The making and breaking of affectional bonds.* London: Tavistock.

Bowlby, J. (1980). *Attachment and loss: Vol. 3. Loss.* London: Hogarth Press.

Bracha, H. S., Ralston, T. C., Matsukawa, J. M., Williams, A. E., & Bracha, A. S. (2004). Does "fight or flight" need updating? *Psychosomatics, 45,* 448–449.

Braver, S. L., Shapiro, J. R., & Goodman, M. R. (2006). Consequences of divorce for parents. In M. A. Fine & J. H. Harvey (Eds.), *Handbook of divorce and relationship dissolution* (pp. 313–337). Mahwah, NJ: Erlbaum.

Brown, P., & Brito, T. (2007). *Characteristics of shared placement child support formulas used in the fifty states.* Unpublished manuscript, Institute for Research on Poverty, University of Wisconsin–Madison.

Brown, P., Joung, E. H., & Berger, L. M. (2006). *Divorced Wisconsin families with shared placement.* Unpublished manuscript, Institute for Research on Poverty, University of Wisconsin–Madison.

Buchanan, C. M., & Jahromi, P. L. (2008). A psychological perspective on shared custody arrangements. *Wake Forest University Law Review, 2,* 419–439.

Buchanan, C. M., Maccoby, E. E., & Dornbusch, S. M. (1991). Caught between parents: Adolescents' experience in divorced homes. *Child Development, 62,* 1008–1029.

Buchanan, C. M., Maccoby, E. E., & Dornbusch, S. M. (1996). *Adolescents after divorce.* Cambridge, MA: Harvard University Press.

Bush, R. A. B., & Pope, S. G. (2004). Transformative mediation: Changing the quality of family conflict interaction. In J. Folberg, A. L. Milne, & P. Salem (Eds.), *Divorce and family mediation: Models, techniques, and applications* (pp. 53–71). New York: Guilford Press.

Cameron, N., & Rychlak, J. F. (1985). *Personality development and psychopathology: A dynamic approach.* Boston: Houghton Mifflin.

Cannon, W. B. (1935). Stress and strains of homeostasis. *American Journal of Medical Science, 189,* 1–14.

Caputo, R. K. (2000). Second-generation parenthood: A panel study of grandmother and grandchild coresidency among low-income families, 1967–1992. *Journal of Sociology and Social Welfare, 27,* 3–20.

Cassidy, J., & Shaver, P. R. (Eds.). (2008). *Handbook of attachment: Theory, research, and clinical applications* (2nd ed.). New York: Guilford Press.

Child-Centered Residential Schedules. (1996). Available from the Spokane County Bar Association, 1116 West Broadway, Room 404, Spokane, WA 99260-0030; (509) 623-2665.

Chung, Y., & Emery, R. E. (2010). Early adolescents and divorce in South Korea: Risk, resilience, and pain. *Journal of Comparative Family Studies, 51,* 855–870.

Coan, J. A. (2008). Toward a neuroscience of attachment. In J. Cassidy & P. R. Shaver (Eds.), *Handbook of attachment: Theory, research, and clinical applications* (2nd ed., pp. 241–265). New York: Guilford Press.

Coates, C. A., Deutsch, R., Starnes, H., Sullivan, M. J., & Sydlik, B. (2004). Parenting coordination for high-conflict families. *Family Court Review, 42,* 246–262.

Coogler, O. J. (1978). *Structured mediation in divorce settlement.* Lexington, MA: Heath.

Cowan, P., & Cowan, P. A. (1999). *When partners become parents.* Hillsdale, NJ: Erlbaum.

Cummings, E. M. (1987). Coping with background anger in early childhood. *Child Development, 58,* 976–984.

Cummings, E. M., & Davies, P. T. (2010). *Marital conflict and children: An emotional security perspective.* New York: Guilford Press.

Davis, G., Bevan, G., Clisby, S., Cumming, Z., Dingwall, R., Fenn, P., et al. (2000). *Monitoring publicly funded mediation.* Report to the Legal Services Commission. London: Legal Services Commission.

de Waal, F. B. M., & Tyack, P. L. (2003). *Animal social complexity.* Cambridge, MA: Harvard University Press.

Depner, C. E., Cannata, K. V., & Simon, M. B. (1992). Building a uniform statistical reporting system: A snapshot of California Family Court services. *Family and Conciliation Courts Review, 30,* 185–206.

D'Zurilla, T., & Goldfried, M. (1971). Problem solving and behavior modification. *Journal of Abnormal Psychology, 78,* 107–126.

Edwards, L. (2007). Comments on the Miller Commission Report: A California perspective. *Pace Law Review, 27,* 1–59.

Eekelaar, J. (1991). *Regulating divorce*. New York: Oxford University Press.

Eldridge, K. A., & Christensen, A. (2002). Demand-withdraw communication during couple conflict: A review and analysis. In P. Noller & J. A. Feeney (Eds.), *Understanding marriage: Developments in the study of couple interaction* (pp. 289–322). New York: Cambridge University Press.

Elkin, I., Shea, M. T., Watkins, J. T., Imber, S. D., Sotsky, S. M., Collins, J. F., et al. (1989). National Institute of Mental Health Treatment of Depression Collaborative Research Program: General effectiveness of treatments. *Archives of General Psychiatry, 46*, 971–983.

Ellis, D., & Stuckless, N. (2006). Domestic violence, DOVE, and divorce mediation. *Family Court Review, 44*, 658–671.

Ellis, J. W. (1990). Plans, protections, and professional intervention: Innovations in divorce custody reform and the role of legal professionals. *University of Michigan Journal of Law Reform, 24*, 65–188.

Emery, R. E. (1982). Interparental conflict and the children of discord and divorce. *Psychological Bulletin, 92*, 310–330.

Emery, R. E. (1988). *Marriage, divorce, and children's adjustment*. Beverly Hills, CA: Sage.

Emery, R. E. (1992). Family conflict and its developmental implications: A conceptual analysis of deep meanings and systemic processes. In C. U. Shantz & W. W. Hartup (Eds.), *Conflict in child and adolescent development* (pp. 270–298). London: Cambridge University Press.

Emery, R. E. (1994). *Renegotiating family relationships: Divorce, child custody, and mediation*. New York: Guilford Press.

Emery, R. E. (1999). *Marriage, divorce, and children's adjustment* (2nd ed.). Thousand Oaks, CA: Sage.

Emery, R. E. (2003). Children's voices: Listening—and deciding—is an adult responsibility. *Arizona Law Review, 45*, 621–627.

Emery, R. E. (2004). *The truth about children and divorce: Dealing with the emotions so you and your children can thrive*. New York: Viking/Penguin.

Emery, R. E. (2006). *The truth about children and divorce: Dealing with the emotions so you and your children can thrive*. New York: Plume.

Emery, R. E. (2007). Rule or Rorschach? Approximating children's best interests. *Child Development Perspectives, 1*, 132–134.

Emery, R. E., Beam, C., & Rowen, J. (in press). Adolescents' experience of parental divorce. In B. Brown & M. Prinstein (Eds.), *Encyclopedia of adolescence*. New York: Academic Press.

Emery, R. E., & Emery, K. C. (2008). Should courts or parents make child-rearing decisions? Married parents as a paradigm for parents who live apart. *Wake Forest Law Review, 43*, 365–390.

Emery, R. E., Joyce, S. A., & Fincham, F. D. (1987). The assessment of marital and child problems. In K. D. O'Leary (Ed.), *Assessment of marital discord* (pp. 223–262). Hillsdale, NJ: Erlbaum.

Emery, R. E., Laumann-Billings, L., Waldron, M., Sbarra, D. A., & Dillon, P. (2001). Child custody mediation and litigation: Custody, contact, and co-parenting 12 years after initial dispute resolution. *Journal of Consulting and Clinical Psychology, 69*, 323–332.

Emery, R. E., Matthews, S., & Kitzmann, K. M. (1994). Child custody mediation and litigation: Parents' satisfaction and functioning a year after settlement. *Journal of Consulting and Clinical Psychology, 62,* 124–129.

Emery, R. E., Matthews, S., & Wyer, M. M. (1991). Child custody mediation and litigation: Further evidence on the differing views of mothers and fathers. *Journal of Consulting and Clinical Psychology, 59,* 410–418.

Emery, R. E., Otto, R. K., & O'Donohue, W. (2005). A critical assessment of child custody evaluations: Limited science and a flawed system. *Psychological Science in the Public Interest, 6,* 1–29.

Emery, R. E., & Sbarra, D. A. (2002). What couples therapists need to know about divorce. In A. S. Gurman & N. S. Jacobson (Eds.), *Clinical handbook of couple therapy* (3rd ed., pp. 508–532). New York: Guilford Press.

Emery, R. E., Sbarra, D. A., & Grover, T. (2005). Divorce mediation: Research and reflections. *Family Court Review, 43,* 22–37.

Emery, R. E., Shaw, D. S., & Jackson, J. A. (1987). A clinical description of a model of child custody mediation. In J. P. Vincent (Ed.), *Advances in family intervention, assessment, and theory* (Vol. 4, pp. 309–333). Greenwich, CT: JAI.

Emery, R. E., & Tuer, M. (1993). Parenting and the marital relationship. In T. Luster & L. Okagaki (Eds.), *Parenting: An ecological perspective* (pp. 121–148). Hillsdale, NJ: Erlbaum.

Emery, R. E., & Wyer, M. M. (1987a). Child custody mediation and litigation: An experimental evaluation of the experience of parents. *Journal of Consulting and Clinical Psychology, 55,* 179–186.

Emery, R. E., & Wyer, M. M. (1987b). Divorce mediation. *American Psychologist, 42,* 472–480.

English, P., & Neilson, L. (2004). Certifying mediators. In J. Folberg, A. L. Milne, & P. Salem (Eds.), *Divorce and family mediation: Models, techniques, and applications* (pp. 483–515). New York: Guilford Press.

Erikson, E. H. (1959, 1980). *Identity and the life cycle.* New York: Norton.

Fabricius, W. V., & Luecken, L. J. (2007). Post-divorce living arrangements, parent conflict, and long-term physical health correlates for children of divorce. *Journal of Family Psychology, 21,* 195–205.

Fineman, M. (1988). Dominant discourse, professional language, and legal change in child custody decision making. *Harvard Law Review, 101,* 727–774.

Fisher, R., & Ury, W. (1981). *Getting to yes.* New York: Houghton Mifflin.

Fleming, S., & Robinson, P. (2001). Grief and cognitive-behavioral therapy: The reconstruction of meaning. In M. S. Stroebe, R. O. Hansson, W. Stroebe, & H. Schut (Eds.), *Handbook of bereavement research: Consequences, coping, and care* (pp. 647–669). Washington, DC: American Psychological Association.

Folberg, J. (1988). Confidentiality and privilege in divorce mediation. In J. Folberg & A. Milne (Eds.), *Divorce mediation: Theory and practice* (pp. 319–340). New York: Guilford Press.

Folberg, J., Milne, A. L., & Salem, P. (Eds.) (2004). *Divorce and family mediation: Models, techniques, and applications.* New York: Guilford Press.

Furstenberg, F. F., Peterson, J. L., Nord, C. W., & Zill, N. (1983). The life course of children of divorce: Marital disruption and parental contact. *American Sociological Review, 48,* 656–668.

Gilmore, S. (2006). Contact/shared residence and child well-being: Research evidence and its implications for legal decision-making. *International Journal of Law, Policy, and the Family, 20,* 344–365.

Goodman, C. C. (2007). Intergenerational triads in skipped-generation grandfamilies. *Intergenerational Journal of Aging and Human Development, 65,* 231–258.

Grall, T. S. (2007). Custodial mothers and fathers and their child support: 2005. *Current Population Reports, P60-234.* Washington, DC: U.S. Census Bureau.

Grillo, T. (1991). The mediation alternative: Process dangers for women. *Yale Law Journal, 100,* 1545–1610.

Grossberg, M. (1985). *Governing the hearth.* Chapel Hill: University of North Carolina Press.

Grych, J. H., & Fincham, F. D. (1990). Marital conflict and children's adjustment: A cognitive-contextual framework. *Psychological Bulletin, 108,* 267–290.

Haidt, J. (2001). The emotional dog and its rational tail: A social intuitionist approach to moral judgment. *Psychological Review, 108,* 814–834.

Harlow, Harry F. (1959). Love in infant monkeys. *Scientific American, 200*(6), 68–74.

Haynes, J. M. (1981). *Divorce mediation: A practical guide for therapists and counselors.* New York: Springer.

Healy, J. M., Malley, J. E., & Stewart, A. J. (1990). Children and their fathers after separation. *American Journal of Orthopsychiatry, 60,* 531–543.

Hetherington, E. M., & Kelly, J. (2002). *For better or for worse: Divorce reconsidered.* New York: Norton.

Holtzworth-Munroe, A., Beck, C. J. A., & Applegate, A. G. (2010). The Mediator's Assessment of Safety Issues and Concerns (MASIC): A screening interview for intimate partner violence and abuse available in the public domain. *Family Court Review, 48,* 646–662.

Horney, K. (1939). *New ways in psychoanalysis.* New York: International Universities Press.

Huang, C., Han, W., & Garfinkel, I. (2003). Child support enforcement, joint legal custody, and parental involvement. *Social Service Review, 77,* 255–278.

Irving, H. H. (1980). *Divorce mediation: A rational alternative to the adversary system.* New York: Universe Books.

Irving, H. H., & Benjamin, M. (1992). An evaluation of process and outcome in a private family mediation service. *Mediation Quarterly, 10,* 35–55.

Janoff-Bulman, R. (1992). *Shattered assumptions: Towards a new psychology of trauma.* New York: Free Press.

Jansen, M., Mortelmans, D., & Snoeckx, L. (2009). Repartnering and (re)employment: Strategies to cope with the economic consequences of partnership dissolution. *Journal of Marriage and Family, 71,* 1271–1293.

Johnston, J. R., & Campbell, L. E. G. (1988). *Impasses of divorce: The dynamics of and resolution of family conflict.* New York: Free Press.

Johnston, J. R., Kline, M., & Tschann, J. M. (1989). Ongoing post-divorce conflict in families contesting custody: Effects on children of joint custody and frequent access. *American Journal of Orthopsychiatry, 59,* 576–592.

Johnston, J. R., Lee, S., Olesen, N. W., & Walters, M. G. (2005). Allegations and substantiations of abuse in custody-disputing families. *Family Court Review, 43,* 283–294.

Jones, T. S., & Bodtker, A. (1998). Satisfaction with custody mediation: Results from the York County custody mediation program. *Mediation Quarterly, 16,* 185–200.

Jones, T. S., & Bodtker, A. (1999). Agreement, maintenance, satisfaction and relitigation in mediated and non-mediated custody cases: A research note. *Journal of Divorce and Remarriage, 32,* 17–30.

Kelly, J. B. (1983). Mediation and psychotherapy: Distinguishing the differences. *Mediation Quarterly, 1,* 33–44.

Kelly, J. B. (1989). Mediated and adversarial divorce: Respondents' perceptions of their processes and outcomes. *Mediation Quarterly, 24,* 71–88.

Kelly, J. B. (1990). *Final report. Mediated and adversarial divorce resolution processes: An analysis of post-divorce outcomes.* Available from the author, Northern California Mediation Center, P.O. Box 7063, Corte Madera, CA, 94976.

Kelly, J. B. (2004). Family mediation research: Is there empirical support for the field? *Conflict Resolution Quarterly, 22,* 3–35.

Kelly, J. B. (2006). Children's living arrangements following separation and divorce: Insights from empirical and clinical research. *Family Process, 46,* 35–52.

Kelly, J. B., & Duryee, M. A. (1992). Women's and men's views of mediation in voluntary and mandatory mediation settings. *Family and Conciliation Courts Review, 30,* 34–49.

Kelly, J. B., & Gigy, L. (1989). Divorce mediation: Characteristics of clients and outcomes. In K. Kressel & D. G. Pruitt (Eds.), *Mediation research* (pp. 263–283). San Francisco: Jossey-Bass.

Kelly, J. B., & Johnson, M. P. (2008). Differentiation among types of intimate partner violence: Research update and implications for interventions. *Family Court Review, 46,* 476–499.

Kelly, J. B., & Lamb, M. E. (2000). Using child development research to make appropriate custody and access decisions for young children. *Family and Conciliation Courts Review, 38,* 297–311.

Kelly, R. F., & Ramsey, S. H. (2009). Child custody evaluations: The need for systems-level outcome assessments. *Family Court Review, 47,* 286–303.

Kisthardt, M. K. (2008). Re-thinking alimony: The AAML's considerations for calculating alimony, spousal support or maintenance. *Journal of the American Academy of Matrimonial Lawyers, 21,* 61–85.

Kitzmann, K. M., & Emery, R. E. (1993). Procedural justice and parents' satisfaction in a field study of child custody dispute resolution. *Law and Human Behavior, 17,* 553–567.

Kitzmann, K. M., & Emery, R. E. (1994). Child and family coping one year following mediated and litigated child custody disputes. *Journal of Family Psychology, 8,* 150–159.

Krecker, M. L., Brown, P., Melli, M. S., & Wimer, L. (2003). *Children's liv-*

ing arrangements in divorced Wisconsin families with shared placement. Unpublished manuscript, Institute for Research on Poverty, University of Wisconsin–Madison.

Kruk, E. (2005). Shared parental responsibility: A harm reduction-based approach to divorce law reform. *Journal of Divorce and Remarriage, 43,* 119–141.

Kübler-Ross, E. (1969). *On death and dying.* New York: Macmillan.

Kurdek, L. A., & Berg, B. (1987). Children's beliefs about parental divorce scale: Psychometric characteristics and concurrent validity. *Journal of Consulting and Clincal Psychology, 55,* 712–718.

Lamborn, S., Mounts, N., & Steinberg, L. (1991). Patterns of competence and adjustment among adolescents from authoritative, authoritarian, indulgent, and neglectful families. *Child Development, 62,* 1049–1065.

Laumann-Billings, L., & Emery, R. E. (2000). Distress among young adults from divorced families. *Journal of Family Psychology, 14,* 671–687.

Leary, T. (1957). *Interpersonal diagnosis of personality.* New York: Ronald Press.

Lee, M. (2002). A model of children's postdivorce behavioral adjustment in maternal- and dual-residence arrangements. *Journal of Family Issues, 23,* 672–697.

Lee, R. D., Ensminger, M. E., & Laveist, T. A. (2005). The responsibility continuum: Never primary, coresident and caregiver-heterogeneity in the African-American grandmother experience. *International Journal of Aging and Human Development, 60,* 295–304.

Lind, G. (2008). *Common law marriage: A legal institution for cohabitation.* New York: Oxford University Press.

Lowry, L. R. (2004). Evaluative mediation. In J. Folberg, A. L. Milne, and P. Salem (Eds.), *Divorce and family mediation: Models, techniques, and applications* (pp. 72–91). New York: Guilford Press.

Maccoby, E. E., & Martin, J. A. (1983). Socialization in the context of the family: Parent–child interaction. In E. M. Hetherington (Ed.), *Handbook of child psychology* (4th ed., Vol. 4, pp. 1–101). New York: Wiley.

Maccoby, E. E., & Mnookin, R. H. (1992). *Dividing the child: Social and legal dilemmas of custody.* Cambridge, MA: Harvard University Press.

MacDonald, G., & Leary, M. R. (2005). Why does social exclusion hurt? The relationship between social and physical pain. *Psychological Bulletin, 131,* 202–223.

Mayer, B. (2004). Facilitative mediation. In J. Folberg, A. L. Milne, and P. Salem (Eds.), *Divorce and family mediation: Models, techniques, and applications* (pp. 29–52). New York: Guilford Press.

McIntosh, J., & Chisholm, R. (2008). Cautionary notes on the shared care of children in conflicted parental separation. *Journal of Family Studies, 14,* 37–52.

McIntosh, J., Smyth, B., Kelaher, M., Wells, Y., & Long, C. (2010). Post-separation parenting arrangements: Patterns and developmental outcomes for infants and children: Synopsis of two studies. *Australian Government Report.* Victoria, Australia: Family Transitions.

McIntosh, J. E., Long, C. M., & Wells, Y. D. (2009). Children beyond dispute:

A four year follow up study of outcomes from Child Focused and Child Inclusive post-separation family dispute resolution. *Australian Government Report*. Victoria, Australia: Family Transitions.

McIsaac, H. (2010). A response to Peter Salem's article: "The emergence of triage in family court services: Beginning of the end for mandatory mediation." *Family Court Review, 48*, 190–194.

McKeever, M., & Wolfinger, N. H. (2001). Reexamining the economic costs of marital disruption for women. *Social Science Quarterly, 82*, 202–217.

Melli, M., & Brown, P. R. (2008). Exploring a new family form—The shared time family. *International Journal of Law, Policy and the Family, 22*, 231–269.

Minuchin, P. (1985). Families and individual development: Provocations from the field of family therapy. *Child Development, 56*, 289–302.

Minuchin, S. (1974). *Families and family therapy*. Cambridge, MA: Harvard University Press.

Mnookin, R. H. (1975). Child-custody adjudication: Judicial functions in the face of indeterminacy. *Law and Contemporary Problems, 39*, 226–292.

Moloney, L., Smyth, B., Weston, R., & Hall, E. (2008). Different types of intimate partner violence: Reply to Wangmann's comments in the AIFS report. *Australian Journal of Family Law, 22*, 279–295.

Moore, C. W. (1986). *The mediation process: Practical strategies for resolving conflicts*. San Francisco: Jossey-Bass.

Moss, C. (2000). *Elephant memories: Thirteen years in the life of an elephant family*. Chicago: University of Chicago Press.

Mussen, P., & Eisenberg, N. (2001). Prosocial development in context. In A. C. Bohart & D. J. Stipek (Eds.), *Constructive and destructive behavior: Implications for family, school, and society* (pp. 103–126). Washington, DC: American Psychological Association.

O'Connell, M. E. (2007). When noble aspirations fail: Why we need the approximation rule. *Child Development Perspectives, 1*, 129–131.

Oldham, J. T. (2008). Changes in the economic consequences of divorces. 1958–2008. *Family Law Quarterly, 42*, 419–447.

Oltmanns, T. F., & Emery, R. E. (2010). *Abnormal psychology* (6th ed.). Upper Saddle River, NJ: Prentice Hall.

Panksepp, J. (1998). *Affective neuroscience: The foundations of human and animal emotions*. London: Oxford University Press.

Panksepp, J. (2005). Why does separation distress hurt? Comment on MacDonald and Leary. *Psychological Bulletin, 131*, 224–230.

Parke, R. D., & Buriel, R. (1998). Socialization in the family: Ethnic and ecological perspectives. In W. Damon (Series Ed.) & N. Eisenberg (Vol. Ed.), *Handbook of child psychology: Social, emotional, and personality development* (Vol. 3, 473–501). New York: Wiley.

Pasupathi, M. (2001). The social construction of the personal past and its implications for adult development. *Psychological Bulletin, 127*, 651–672.

Patterson, G. R. (1982). *Coercive family processes*. Eugene, OR: Castalia.

Peacey, V., & Hunt, J. (2008). Problematic contact after separation and divorce? A national survey of parents. London: One Parent Families/Gingerbread.

Pearson, J., & Thoennes, N. (1989). Divorce mediation: Reflections on a decade of research. In K. Kressel & D. Pruitt (Eds.), *Mediation research* (pp. 9–30). San Francisco: Jossey-Bass.

Pedro-Carroll, J., & Alpert-Gillis, L. (1997). Preventative interventions for children of divorce: A developmental model for 5 and 6 year old children. *Journal of Primary Prevention, 18,* 5–23.

Peeples, R. A., Reynolds, S., & Harris, C. T. (2008). It's the conflict, stupid: An empirical study of factors that inhibit successful mediation in high-conflict custody cases. *Wake Forest Law Review, 43,* 505–531.

Peris, T., & Emery, R. E. (2005). Redefining the parent-child relationship following divorce: Examining the risk for boundary dissolution. *Journal of Emotional Abuse, 5,* 169–189.

Peris, T. S., Goeke-Morey, M. C., Cummings, E. M., & Emery, R. E. (2008). Marital conflict and support-seeking by parents in adolescence: Empirical support for the parentification construct. *Journal of Family Psychology, 22,* 633–642.

Peterson, J. L., & Zill, N. (1986). Marital disruption, parent–child relationships, and behavior problems in children. *Journal of Marriage and the Family, 48,* 295–307.

Peterson, R. R. (1996). A re-evaluation of the economic consequences of divorce. *American Sociological Review, 61,* 528–536.

Plateris, A. (1974). 100 years of marriage and divorce statistics, 1867–1967. *Vital and Health Statistics* (Series 21, No. 24). (DHEW Publication No. [HRA] 74–1902. Health Resources Administration.) Washington, DC: U.S. Government Printing Office.

Plutchik, R., & Conte, H. R. (Eds.). (1997). *Circumplex models of personality and emotions.* Washington, DC: American Psychological Association.

Pruett, M. K., Ebling, R., & Insabella, G. (2004). Critical aspects of parenting plans for young children: Interjecting data into the debate about overnights. *Family Court Review, 42,* 39–59.

Pryor, J. (2008). *The international handbook of stepfamilies: Policy and practice in legal, research, and clinical environments.* Hoboken, NJ: Wiley.

Reynolds, S., Harris, C. T., & Peeples, R. A. (2007). Back to the future: An empirical study of child custody outcomes. *North Carolina Law Review, 85,* 1629–1686.

Ricci, I. (2004). Court-based mandatory mediation: Special considerations. In J. Folberg, A. L. Milne, & P. Salem (Eds.), *Divorce and family mediation: Models, techniques, and applications* (pp. 397–419). New York: Guilford Press.

Riskin, L. L. (1996). Understanding mediators' orientations, strategies, and techniques: A grid for the perplexed. *Harvard Negotiation Law Review, 1,* 7–51.

Salem, P., & Dunford-Jackson, B. L. (2008). Beyond politics and positions: A call for collaboration between family court and domestic violence professionals. *Family Court Review, 46,* 437–453.

Saposnek, D. T. (1983). *Mediating child custody disputes.* San Francisco: Jossey-Bass.

Sbarra, D. A. (2006). Predicting the onset of emotional recovery following nonmarital relationship dissolution: Survival analyses of sadness and anger. *Personality and Social Psychology Bulletin, 32,* 298–312.

Sbarra, D. A., & Emery, R. E. (2005a). The emotional sequelae of non-marital relationship dissolution: Descriptive evidence from a 28-day prospective study. *Personal Relationships, 12,* 213–232.

Sbarra, D. A., & Emery, R. E. (2005b). Coparenting conflict, nonacceptance, and depression among divorced adults: Results from a 12-year follow-up study of child custody mediation using multiple imputation. *American Journal of Orthopsychiatry, 75,* 63–75.

Sbarra, D. A., & Emery, R. E. (2006). In the presence of grief: The role of cognitive-emotional adaptation in contemporary divorce mediation. In M. A. Fine & J. H. Harvey (Eds.), *Handbook of divorce and relationship dissolution* (pp. 553–574). Mahwah, NJ: Erlbaum.

Sbarra, D. A., & Emery, R. E. (2008). Deeper into divorce: Using actor–partner analyses to explore systemic differences in coparenting following mediation and litigation of custody disputes. *Journal of Family Psychology, 22,* 144–152.

Sbarra, D. A., & Ferrer, E. (2006). The structure and process of emotional experience following nonmarital relationship dissolution: Dynamic factor analyses of love, anger, and sadness. *Emotion, 6,* 224–238.

Schepard, A. (2004). The model standards of practice for family and divorce mediation. In J. Folberg, A. L. Milne, & P. Salem (Eds.), *Divorce and family mediation: Models, techniques, and applications* (pp. 516–543). New York: Guilford Press.

Scott, E. S. (1992). Pluralism, parental preference, and child custody. *California Law Review, 80,* 615–672.

Seltzer, J. A. (1991). Relationships between fathers and children who live apart: The father's role after separation. *Journal of Marriage and the Family, 53,* 79–101.

Seltzer, J. A. (1998). Father by law: Effects of joint legal custody on nonresident fathers' involvement with children. *Demography, 35,* 135–146.

Sloman, L., Gardner, R., & Price, J. (1989). Biology of family systems and mood disorders. *Family Process, 28,* 387–398.

Smyth, B. (2004). Parent–child contact schedules after divorce. *Family Matters, 69,* 32–34.

Smyth, B. (2009). A 5-year retrospective of post-separation shared care research in Australia. *Journal of Family Studies, 15,* 36–59.

Smyth, B., & Moloney, L. (2008). Changes in patterns of post-separation parenting over time: A brief review. *Journal of Family Studies, 14,* 7–22.

Soloman, J., & Biringen, Z. (2001). Another look at the developmental research: Commentary on Kelly and Lamb's "Using child development research to make appropriate custody and access decisions for young children." *Family Court Review, 39,* 355–364.

Soloman, J., & George, C. (1999a). The development of attachment in separated and divorced families: Effects of overnight visitation, parent, and couple variables. *Attachment and Human Development, 1,* 2–33.

Soloman, J., & George, C. (1999b). The effects of overnight visitation in divorced and separated families: A longitudinal follow-up. In J. Soloman & C. George (Eds.), *Attachment disorganization* (pp. 243–264). New York: Guilford Press.

Standards of practice for family mediators. (1984). *Family Law Quarterly, 17,* 455–460.

Steinberg, L., Dornbusch, S. M., & Brown, B. B. (1992). Ethnic differences in adolescent achievement: An ecological perspective. *American Psychologist, 47,* 723–729.

Stroebe, M. S., Hansson, R. O., Schut, H., & Stroebe, W. (Eds.). (2008). *Handbook of bereavement research and practice: Advances in theory and intervention.* Washington, DC: American Psychological Association.

Sullivan, H. S. (1953). *The interpersonal theory of psychiatry.* New York: Norton.

Superior Court Guardian Ad Litem Committee. (1996). *Child-centered residential schedules.* Spokane, WA: Spokane County Bar Association.

Teachman, J. (2008). Complex life course patterns and the risk of divorce in second marriages. *Journal of Marriage and Family, 70,* 294–305.

Tesler, P. H., & Thompson, P. (2007). *Collaborative divorce: The revolutionary new way to restructure your family, resolve legal issues, and move on with your life.* New York: HarperCollins.

Thoennes, N. (2002). *Mediating disputes including parenting time and responsibilities in Colorado's Tenth Judicial District: Assessing the benefits to courts.* Denver, CO: Center for Policy Research.

Trinder, L. (in press). Shared care: A review of recent research evidence. *Child and Family Law Quarterly.*

Trinder, L., & Kellett, J. (2007). Fairness, efficiency and effectiveness in court-based dispute resolution schemes in England. *International Journal of Law, Policy and the Family, 21,* 322–340.

Tyda, K., Chang, C., & Piazza, D. (2010). Snapshot study 2008: Summary findings. Judicial Council of California. Available at *www.courts.ca.gov/programs.htm.*

Uniform Marriage and Divorce Act, 9A Uniform Laws Annotated, Sec. 316 (1979).

Uunk, W. (2004). The economic consequences of divorce for women in the European Union: The impact of welfare state arrangements. *European Journal of Population, 20,* 251–285.

Ver Steegh, N. (2003). Yes, no, and maybe: Informed decision making about divorce mediation in the presence of domestic violence. *William and Mary Journal of Women and the Law, 9,* 145–206.

Ver Steegh, N. (2005). Differentiating types of domestic violence: Implications for child study. *Louisiana Law Review, 65,* 1379–1431.

Vuchinich, S., Emery, R. E., & Cassidy, J. (1988). Family members as third parties in dyadic family conflict: Strategies, alliances, and outcomes. *Child Development, 59,* 1293–1302.

Walker, J. A. (2010). *Assessment of family mediation service in Ireland: International Benchmarking.* Available from the author, Institute of Health and Society, Newcastle University, Newcastle, England.

Walker, J., McCarthy, P., & Timms, N. (1994). *Mediation: The making and remaking of cooperative relationships: An evaluation of the effectiveness of comprehensive mediation.* Newcastle, UK: Relate Centre for Family Studies, Newcastle University.

Wallerstein, J., & Kelly, J. B. (1980). *Surviving the breakup: How children actually cope with divorce.* New York: Basic Books.

Walton, L., Oliver, C., & Griffin, C. (1999). Divorce mediation: The impact of mediation on the psychological well-being of children and parents. *Journal of Community and Applied Social Psychology, 9,* 35–36.

Warshak, R. A. (2007). The approximation rule, child development research, and children's best interests after divorce. *Child Development Perspectives, 1,* 119–125.

Weiss, R. S. (1979b). Issues in the adjudication of custody when parents separate. In G. Levinger & O. C. Moles (Eds.), *Divorce and separation* (pp. 324–336). New York: Basic Books.

Weitzman, L. J. (1985). *The divorce revolution.* New York: Free Press.

Welsh, N. A. (2004). Reconciling self-determination, coercion, and settlement in court-connected mediation. In J. Folberg, A. L. Milne, and P. Salem (Eds.), *Divorce and family mediation: Models, techniques, and applications* (pp. 420–446). New York: Guilford Press.

Wiggins, J. S. (1982). Circumplex models of interpersonal behavior in clinical psychology. In P. C. Kendall & J. N. Butcher (Eds.), *Handbook of research methods in clinical psychology* (pp. 183–221). New York: Wiley.

Wilson, M. (1989). Child development in the context of the Black extended family. *American Psychologist, 44,* 380–385.

Wolchik, S. A., Sandler, I. N., Millsap, R. E., Plummer, B. A., Greene, S. M., Anderson, E. R., et al. (2002). Six-year follow-up of preventive interventions for children of divorce. A randomized controlled trial. *Journal of the American Medical Association, 288,* 1874–1881.

Wortman, C. B., & Silver, R. C. (1989). The myths of coping with loss. *Journal of Consulting and Clinical Psychology, 57,* 349–357.

Wortman, C. B., & Silver, R. C. (2001). The myths of coping with loss revisited. In M. S. Stroebe, R. O. Hansson, W. Stroebe, and H. Schut (Eds.) *Handbook of bereavement research: Consequences, coping, and care* (pp. 405–429). Washington, DC: American Psychological Association.

Zuberbuhler, J. (2001). Early intervention mediation: The use of court-ordered mediation in the initial stages of divorce litigation to resolve parenting issues. *Family Court Review, 39,* 203–206.

INDEX

236

238